INDIAN PRAIRIE PUBLIC LIBRARY DISTRICT

3 1946 00334 5318

JAN 4 2005

7-11 (15)
1-13 (2)
8-13 (23)

W9-AQG-656

Noted Minor Damage in Book
Page Markings: _____ Water: X
Date: 4-1-19 Int.: my

INDIAN PRAIRIE PUBLIC LIBRARY
401 Plainfield Road
Darien, IL 60561

One Giant Leap

One Giant Leap

Neil Armstrong's Stellar American Journey

Leon Wagener

A Tom Doherty Associates Book
New York

INDIAN PRAIRIE PUBLIC LIBRARY
401 Plainfield Road
Darien, IL 60561

ONE GIANT LEAP: NEIL ARMSTRONG'S STELLAR AMERICAN JOURNEY

Copyright © 2004 by Leon Wagener

Introduction copyright © 2004 by Bill Pogue

All rights reserved, including the right to reproduce this book, or portions thereof, in any form.

This book is printed on acid-free paper.

Book design by Michael Collica

A Forge Book
Published by Tom Doherty Associates, LLC
175 Fifth Avenue
New York, NY 10010

www.tor.com

Forge® is a registered trademark of Tom Doherty Associates, LLC.

ISBN 0-312-87343-3
EAN 978-0312-87343-1

Printed in the United States of America

0 9 8 7 6 5 4 3 2

Dedication

This book is dedicated to the brave men of the United States Navy Fighter Squadron VF-51 for their service to our country during the Korean War and as thanks for their invaluable help in researching this book.

Ernest Beauchamp
John Moore
Bill Bowers
Ken Danneberg
Herschel Gott
Thomas Hayward
Francis Jones
Robert Kaps
Kenneth Kramer
W. A. Mackey
Daniel Marshall
Harold Schwan

Acknowledgments

Many thanks to my agent, Denise Marcil, for her dedication above and beyond the call of duty to making this book happen; my editor, Bob Gleason, for his patience, advice, and encouragement; and astronaut Bill Pogue for his invaluable help keeping technical and historical details correct.

The other moon pioneer, Buzz Aldrin, was very generous with his insight and memories of the epic journey, for which I am very appreciative. NASA's Washington, D.C., library opened its doors and files to me, for which I am very grateful.

I conducted over one hundred taped interviews over a period of two years, which wouldn't have been possible without my being pointed in the right direction by Dill Hunley at Dryden, Hill Goodspeed at the National Museum of Aviation, VF-51 historian Ernest Thabet, Gregory Zawisza, and Cindy Robertson of Purdue University.

In addition, I am grateful for the recollections of Purdue alumni Marvin Schlenberg, Carl Blechschmidt, Russell Hopf, Ted Dunn, Edward Jordan, Ronald Pierce, John Rich, Lyle Genens, Sally Lugar, Gilbert Sievers, and Ronald Snyder.

I am in debt to many who served at Edwards Air Force Base, including Betty Love, Dick Day, Bill Dana, Stan Butchard, Roy Bryant, Daniel Marshall, and NASA's Rocco Petrone.

Dr. Henry Heimlich contributed to this effort greatly with his patient explanations of the complex medical research he conducted with Neil Armstrong and their team at the University of Cincinnati.

Former White House advisor Clay Whitehead was a great help

with his explanations of the intricate political aspects of the space program.

And I would like to thank Zeke O'Connor of the Edmund Hillary Foundation, the Naval Historical Center in Washington, D.C., Wapakoneta, Ohio's public library, the *Wapakoneta Daily News*, the Neil Armstrong Air and Space Museum and its director, John Zwez, and Richard Schwer, Mike Trude, Ned Keiber, and Elizabeth Stewart.

Finally, my love to my wife, Rochelle, and daughter, Madison, for their patience and support while I struggled with this effort, and my gratitude for the wise counsel of my mother, Shirley Chamberlain.

Introduction

One Giant Leap is an intriguing account of an individual with a seemingly impossible dream but one that is realized with a string of achievements any one of which would be a centerpiece of life memories for the rest of us. I believe the author has made a contribution to the aviation and space history of the twentieth century by researching details of Neil's life and weaving them into a story of achievement and the defeat of overwhelming odds. To say that I have respect and admiration for Neil would be a gross understatement. His tolerance for overbearing imposition on his personal life was and is a testimony to his forbearance and essential good nature. Enough words from me—read this life story of a great person.

—Bill Pogue

The world is a better place to live in because it contains human beings who will give up ease and security and stake their own lives in order to do what they themselves think worth doing. It is somehow reassuring to think that there are also men and women who take the risks themselves, who pit themselves not against their fellow beings but against the immensity and the violence of the natural world, who are brave enough without cruelty to others and impassioned with an idea that dignifies all who contemplate it. They are the things that are undertaken not for some definite, measurable result, but because someone, not counting the costs or calculating the consequences, is moved by curiosity, the love of excellence, a point of honor, the compulsion to invent or to make or to understand. In such persons mankind overcomes the inertia which would keep it earthbound forever in its habitual ways. And what they prove to themselves and to others is that man is no mere creature of his habits, no mere cog in the collective machine, but that in the dust of which he is made there is also fire, lighted now and then by great winds from the sky.

Walter Lippmann— "A Requiem for Amelia Earhart"
July 8, 1937

Armstrong was apparently in communion with some string in the universe others did not think to play.

—Norman Mailer, in *Of a Fire on the Moon*

The dream was so exquisite and so vibrantly real that six-year-old Neil Armstrong was afraid to tell anyone of it lest the magic tarnish and fade. Some nights when he fell into the grip of deep sleep, when consciousness was but a shimmering, faraway pinpoint of light, he would float. Free from earth's mean bonds, he would soar effortlessly, silently, above the white church steeples of Wapakoneta, Ohio, which seemed cocooned in green, miles past the orderly, tidy, checkerboard farm fields, whirling, pirouetting, following the muddy eddies and lazy curves of the Ohio River. Needing only force of will, his untrammeled spirit reached higher and higher until finally, with just that extra bit of effort, the apogee of imagination was reached and the modest, blue Midwestern sky yielded to a darker, purple realm and all that lay beyond could be imagined and grasped.

Chapter One

To see the earth as it truly is, small and blue and beautiful in that eternal silence where it floats is to see ourselves as riders on the earth together, as brothers who know they are truly brothers.
—Archibald MacLeish

For one crowning moment we were creatures of the cosmic ocean, a moment that a thousand years hence may be seen as the signature of our century. . . .
—Buzz Aldrin

During that one bright shining instant in July 1969, humankind enjoyed a collective jolt that transcended the quotidian anxieties of life. Earthmen had succeeded where Icarus failed, flying toward the sun without melting their wings, setting foot in the heavens, on the shore of another world. Suddenly, as two of our number walked on an alien orb a quarter-million miles in space and stared with awe and longing back at our blue-green world, we realized where we were; that man was alone, precariously clinging to a spinning ball in the vastness of space. Through their eyes and the black-and-white flickering television images of them, and the images of ourselves they sent back, we finally had a fledgling "you are here" map of the universe in our collective mind.

Even if the cynical view of the launch of Apollo 11, which said it was just spectacle to take our minds off the Vietnam War and the other troubles of the day, was true, it was nevertheless pageant on the grandest of scales, and the whole world reacted in kind.

More than a million people were drawn to northern Florida's eastern coast to bask in proximity to the capes where the phenomenal voyage was to begin.

Cape Kennedy—as it was called for a decade until it was quietly decided the nation had gone overboard naming things after the slain president—was the space center, a hive of frenetic activity, where thousands labored to fulfill John Kennedy's promise to send a man to the moon and bring him safely back before the end of the seventh decade of the twentieth century.

In the days and weeks before blastoff a ragtag army assembled, ranging from drug-addled nomadic hippies to families on vacation to retirees in campers. Vehicles of all sorts sported American flag stickers—generally taken to mean to send a message that the occupants were against the people who were against the war in Vietnam. The flag stickers were fairly ubiquitous that summer; sixty-eight million of them had been distributed via copies of the *Reader's Digest* the previous winter.

Pilgrims descended on the area, erecting tent cities, drawing their recreational vehicles, jalopies, high-finned Cadillacs, and VW minibuses in circles, camping around the sulphurous estuaries, mangroves, and sand dunes surrounding the cape. Lotus-like, they emptied grocery store shelves, culled 7-Elevens of beer and soda, depleted the region's McDonalds of their last all-beef patties, and finally, like any voracious army, turned to the land for succour, harvesting grapefruit trees and orange bushes and provoking outraged local farmers to brandish shotguns. Bars were sold out of liquor, and drugstores out of suntan oil.

Motel rooms had been spoken for many months earlier. Even the nineteen state governors who attended were forced to stay sixty-five miles away in Daytona Beach. Service stations posted NO GAS signs—an eerie foreshadowing of oil shortages that would roil America in the seventies. The city of Cocoa Beach parked a gasoline tanker and posted an armed guard behind city hall to supply police cars.

Making matters more desperate, the incredible tangle of traffic that clogged the highways for miles around made timely resupply difficult. A blazing sun, eighty-five-degree heat, and 75 percent humidity begat frayed tempers, uncountable fender benders, and endless lines of crippled cars and campers, hoods raised, spouting geysers of steam. Curses, fistfights, and worse punctuated the mad tableau.

Some who came were blissfully ignorant of the years of preparation and publicity that had preceded the launch, but were inexplicably
drawn to the scene. One vacationing family sleeping in their overheated car told a reporter: "We were somewhere in the Midwest when
we heard about it. We thought it was going to be last Wednesday, so
we've been here a week."

Bill Emerton, then forty-nine years old and a very serious runner,
covered the 1,034 miles from Houston to Cape Kennedy on foot.

Visitors who had planned ahead parked in the Celestial Trailer
Court, or checked into the Polaris, Sea Missile, or Satellite motels.
They dined at the Astro-Diner Outer Space Eat In, and used restrooms
marked ASTRONAUTS and ASTRONETTES. Pan American Airlines had a
stewardess dressed in a head-to-knee plastic bubble taking reservations for the first charter flight to the moon.

Distinguished guests included Jack Benny, Johnny Carson, Charles
Lindbergh, 205 congressmen, 69 ambassadors, and thousands of the
celebrated, well-connected, or merely rich. The privileged were feted
at lavish parties thrown by contractors, many of whom had gotten
very rich off the $24 billion spent to put men on the moon.

President Richard Nixon had wanted to attend, but demurred
when he concluded his presence would be dwarfed by the event. His
chief aide, the fearsomely loyal H. R. "Bob" Haldeman, known for
his henchman-like mien and deliberately unfashionable brush haircut, laid out the president's reservations in a memo: "He definitely
wants to go ahead with plans to visit the Cape for the shoot and was
interested in using the boat for his Presidential reception. He wants
to be sure, however, that this would clearly be the President's affair—
not NASA's—and he is afraid that if the boat belongs to NASA, and
the VIP's are housed on it, that it will become their function rather
than his."

Instead of taking a chance on being upstaged at the launch,
Nixon canceled the trip, making plans to talk to the astronauts while
they walked on the moon, pictured next to them on a split-screen
television—in effect, putting him on the moon with them, doubtless
one of the most brilliant public-relations coups in history.

The Banana and Indian rivers, which offered good views of the
launchpad, likewise were jammed bow to transom; police estimates
were three thousand craft of every description. The skies around the
cape were peppered with hundreds of small planes buzzing back and

forth, often precariously close to colliding, which led worried NASA officials to ask the Federal Aviation Agency to intervene and avert a disaster.

News coverage of the event, particularly television coverage, was unprecedented, precisely because there was no precedent. Never had the twenty-year-old medium covered a history-making news event that would "break" continuously for a week and be watched by a half-billion people around the world.

CBS, NBC, and ABC, America's three networks, canceled their regular programming and broadcast thirty-one continuous hours of coverage and analysis. At the crucial moment of Armstrong and Aldrin's walk on the moon, Walter Cronkite, the paterfamilias news grandee, of whom it was said, only half-jokingly, that "he'll get them back safely," was struck dumb. "Wow, oh, boy," seemed the only sound he could make. Desperately, drowning in his elation, Cronkite croaked to his co-host, astronaut Wally Schirra, "say something, Wally." The press corps on July 16, 1969, numbered an amazing 3,100 and ranged in seriousness from distinguished historians to a French magazine that passed out "gay" straw hats, a fact that William Greider, the *Washington Post* writer who reported it, fretted would be lost to history.

The million citizens, six thousand VIPs invited by the government, and throng of journalists representing fifty-four countries had come to see the Saturn V rocket, which stood amid all the hubris and carnival, alone, silent, and dignified on its concrete pad. Brilliantly bathed in xenon spotlights, shimmering a pale indigo, skirted by a diaphanous mist of venting liquid hydrogen, Saturn rose thirty-seven stories tall, sixty feet higher than the Statue of Liberty and fifteen times heavier; it was the most powerful machine ever built by man.

Saturn's passengers, commander Neil Armstrong, Edwin "Buzz" Aldrin, Jr., and Michael Collins slept less than four fitful hours the night of July 15.

The three had much in common. They were all born in 1930, were engineers and jet fighter pilots, and each possessed the suprahuman ability to face the maw of death with steely calm. But beneath the surface their personalities were divergent and occasionally even rancorous. The great voyage that lay ahead was reason enough for fitfulness, but the astronauts had numerous other vexations that had long been seething.

Buzz Aldrin was described by a writer as "powerful as a small bull . . . all meat and stone." He had graduated third in his West Point class and was a decorated Korean War fighter pilot. Aldrin earned a doctorate in astronautics from the Massachusetts Institute of Technology, and was the son of a general with an M.I.T. doctorate. The astronautics specialty that appealed to him was spacecraft rendezvous, a rather arcane subject in 1961, before John Glenn had achieved three tentative orbits of the earth—even before there was any certainty there would be a space program.

"I wish I could play the tapes back of those days and find out what I was thinking," he muses now. As with most of the happenstances that eventually winnowed the pool of potential space explorers to twelve stout-hearted Americans, Aldrin's choice of postgraduate study would be one significant step that in retrospect seems like predestination, because it made him the one man in tens of millions just right for the exacting job of navigating the new interplanetary ocean.

In the weeks leading up to the launch of Apollo 11, Aldrin was deeply troubled over NASA's indecision about precisely what he and Armstrong were going to do once they landed on the moon. Aldrin felt strongly that his duty was pointing out the safety concerns involved, and he refused to ignore an issue that could have put the mission in jeopardy.

"I could have just shut up, behaved like a normal person, and did what I was told, or I could speak my thoughts," he laughs. "Let's face it. It was a group of people in which most spoke their thoughts."

Aldrin felt that, due to the "critical nature of emergencies that could occur on the lunar surface," they might have to lift off in a do-or-die rush. If Commander Armstrong was at that moment bouncing along on the moon's surface, the escape window—the short period of time when rendezvous with the orbiting mother ship was possible—might be shut, dooming the mission and both astronauts.

In addition, the precedent during space walks was for commanders to stay with the ship while junior crew members did what NASA dubbed "extra vehicular activity," or EVA.

"The commander could oversee what was going on by remaining in the spacecraft and communicating with ground control," argued Aldrin. "There was also an extremely heavy training load on the commander and a lighter load on junior crew members. So it was logical to put the additional burden of spacewalking on the crew."

What came to be the more-or-less official version of the decision to have Armstrong first on the moon was that the landing module was so small, and the men's spacesuits so large and cumbersome, that it would be difficult for Buzz to get around Neil and out the narrow hatch.

At the time, he felt Armstrong was going to make the first steps on the moon simply because he was a civilian, and NASA felt it was the politically correct thing to do in the highly charged atmosphere of the Vietnam War protest era. "It would have been an insult to the service. There was no difference between us. We both learned to fly in Korea. When I was satisfied that wasn't the issue, I dropped the matter completely, and we got on with the mission."

Aldrin's safety concerns were addressed by planning to immediately prepare for liftoff upon landing, and by waiting until all systems were sound and ready for ascent before either man began the moonwalk.

Unfortunately for Aldrin, in the macho-gotcha world of the astronaut corps his queries led to smirking accusations that he was campaigning to be number one on the moon. "That gave fuel to others to say, 'Buzz was running around the office trying to get support for his being first on the moon,'" Aldrin says. "Well, bullshit. That was the interpretation of people who loved to pick apart what other people did."

Aldrin felt then and still feels he was something of an outcast in the tight-knit world of the astronauts, despite being as qualified, or more qualified, than the rest of the men. "I was not what you would call an insider. I was not a carrier-based Navy flier. I was an egghead academician. They were competitive in pursuing their career agendas. I can't think of a single Navy test pilot who didn't do everything he could to enhance his career.

"When I first got into the astronaut program, there was a fun-poking where if you caught another guy doing something, you pointed it out and everybody had their chuckles. I didn't mind being called Dr. Rendezvous. But sometimes it was more than just fun-poking. It bordered on ridiculing the egghead. At least there was an undercurrent of that."

To add to the pressure, Aldrin's influential dad, General Edwin, Sr., threatened to fire an outraged broadside across NASA's bow demanding his son be first off the lander.

In frustration, Buzz decided to take up the issue of "the order of exiting" the moon landing vehicle with mission commander Armstrong directly, hoping to end a controversy that was embarrassing and was beginning to "hamper our training."

"I went into Neil's office and said I thought we needed a decision on this regardless of anyone's feelings or point of view."

Five years later, in his autobiography, *Return to Earth,* Aldrin wrote that Armstrong reacted "with a coldness I had not known he possessed. He said the decision was quite historical and he didn't want to rule out the possibility of going first."

Looking back through the lens of twenty-two years of sobriety, Aldrin says, his life was in turmoil when he okayed the final revisions to the book, and suggests he was harsh in his interpretation of Neil's remarks.

"I was going through the beginnings of personal problems that were significant—alcoholism misdiagnosed as depression."

Michael Collins was destined to become famous as the man who did not walk on the moon. But instead he would be "Carrying the Fire"—the title of his 1974 autobiography. That is, he would orbit the moon alone in the command module *Columbia* while Neil and Buzz descended to the lunar surface in the landing craft *Eagle.* The daunting nature of Collins's job was that he was in control of the only ticket home. The astronauts wouldn't travel to the moon in a powered ship; rather, once blasted free of earth's gravity, they would rely on their forward momentum to coast toward the pull of the moon's gravity. Then, like a slingshot, the five-thousand-pound ship would be captured by the lunar gravity; when Apollo 11 fired its engine for about six minutes, it would slow from 5,600 miles per hour to 3,600 and insert itself into a sixty-mile-high orbit.

After circling a dozen times, *Eagle* would separate from the mother ship while on the far side of the moon and begin an hourlong descent to the surface. Collins had to keep *Colombia* on a perfectly steady course for the 21 hours and 36 minutes *Eagle* spent on the moon. Then he had to be at the appointed position in lunar orbit in preparation for the tricky rendezvous and docking procedures for the return home.

The nightmare that haunted him was that if something happened to Neil and Buzz—if *Eagle* crashed or if its ascent engine refused to fire—there would be no way to reach them. Collins would have no choice but to leave his crewmates to die and make an unspeakably lonely return to earth.

Though Collins's role in the Apollo 11 mission was fraught with both tension and frustration, it resonated with the experiences of another pioneer airman, Charles Lindbergh, who a scant forty-two years earlier had made history by flying solo across the Atlantic Ocean. "From Armstrong and Aldrin's spectacular movements, my mind shifted to Collins's lunar orbiting. He had time for contemplation, time to study both the nearby surface of the moon and the distant moonlike world. Only once before had I felt such a connection as when I thought of astronaut Collins. That was over the Atlantic in the *Spirit of St. Louis*."

Unlike his driven, near-obsessive crewmates, Collins, who was born in Rome, had been an indifferent student, having barely made the grade at West Point, and was a test pilot at Edwards Air Force Base with a laid-back attitude, and, tellingly, was known to occasionally sport a mustache, a daring fashion statement for a 1950s-era test pilot.

New York Times science writer John Noble Wilford, who covered the astronauts and the space program for a number of years, wrote: "Collins's existence was drifting and unfocused until fairly late in life, leading some of his colleagues to expect that he would never do anything special."

But the space program finally fired his ambition and imagination. The first six months of 1969, with nearly every waking second devoted to training for the trip to the moon, were the most grueling of the astronauts' lives. Collins remembers particularly loathing the centrifuge, which whirled its victims around faster and faster until it imitated the crushing effect of reentering earth's atmosphere at 36,000 feet per second, subjecting the astronauts to ten times normal earth gravity. "My chest caved in and my vision narrowed, and when I finally reeled out of the torture chamber, I dared not turn my head left or right lest I fall over in an undignified heap."

The flight simulators were frustrating and worrying. Sometimes Collins was able to solve the dozens of vexing combinations of technical malfunctions that controllers threw at him as he tried to steer past earth's unforgiving atmosphere, but most often the flight would end in a virtual disaster, plunging into the sea, killing Buzz, Neil, and himself. Nonetheless, the simulators, which cost millions and required hundreds of engineers to program and maintain, were considered essential to the mission. Neil's wife, Jan, was at times concerned for his health: "Neil used to come home with his face drawn white. I was worried about him. I was worried about all of them. They were worried about whether there was time enough to learn all the things they had to learn if this mission was to work."

The three men trained for eighteen hours a day during the early summer, desperately trying to meet an arbitrary deadline that had to do with the Cold War and a world that, aside from our closest allies, believed years of highly adept KGB propaganda and placed the Soviets far ahead of the U.S. in space science. And, of course, the quagmire in Vietnam was damaging American prestige even amongst our closest friends in the world.

A *Los Angeles Times* front-page headline on July 13 said it succinctly: PRESTIGE OF U.S. RIDES ON APOLLO. Calling Apollo 11 a "$24 billion gamble," the *Times* said that the United States was committing its "national pride . . . to showing the world it can still fulfill a dream." And the paper was far from sanguine as to the chances of success. "It will send three young men on a human adventure of mythological proportions with the whole of the civilized world invited to watch— for better or worse. . . . The journey is fraught with perils understood by few except the three astronauts who must face and overcome them." The *Times* quoted a Harvard professor who suggested that "sophisticates" of the 1960s no longer trusted science in any event. "Science is DDT, germ warfare and Thalidomide."

The astronauts knew all too well the perils they faced. Despite a supporting cast of 400,000, it would come down to their pushing all the right buttons at the right times. Collins called the mission "an extremely long, fragile daisy chain of events." Failure anywhere could mean disaster. In the long run, U.S. "prestige" would survive, but the astronauts might not, in which case the space program likely would die with them.

The final month before blastoff was spent in isolated crew quarters where maids sewed names in their underwear and a former tugboat cook served meals consisting almost solely of various meats, potatoes, and pastries. It was like a football training table and the three men quickly tired of eating the monotonous fare.

President Richard Nixon was forbidden by NASA medical director Dr. Chuck Berry from joining them for dinner out of fear he would contaminate them with germs. Apollo 8 astronaut Frank Borman promptly called a press conference blasting Berry, saying the doctor should keep his mouth shut. But the White House, wary of doing anything that could be interpreted as jeopardizing the mission, bowed out anyway.

The life of an astronaut had changed drastically from the heady days of the Mercury missions, when Wally Schirra, Alan Shephard, and their mates tooled around Houston in gratis Corvettes. The windowless quarantine quarters with three small sterile bedrooms and perforated walls that filtered the air were testament to that.

During one of the final examinations, the Apollo 11 crew were puzzled when doctors photographed and took biopsies of their skin. The explanation was that each would be photographed and sampled when they returned from the moon to make sure they hadn't brought back any predatory moon organisms. That was a sobering thought.

As July 16 drew near, pressure mounted during the long days and was increasingly assuaged with drink. Collins noted in *Carrying the Fire* that "Neil was clicking along like a well-oiled machine, his manner nonchalant. . . . Generally quiet and incapable of small talk, Buzz could get wound up on any number of technical pet projects far into the night, with or without a bottle of Scotch for lubrication." Just weeks before the sixteenth, Neil crashed in the lunar module simulator after refusing Aldrin's, and eventually Houston's, insistence that he abort. Buzz felt it had made them look incompetent and worse in front of the mission-control engineers, and was furious. Neil was intent upon testing the outer parameters of the landing module's (LM) capabilities and didn't care what anybody thought. Wasn't that the purpose of a simulator? The argument was bandied back and forth over dinner and into the evening. After a nightcap, Neil gave up and went to bed just as Buzz was getting wound up. As his Scotch kicked in, Buzz became louder and ever more slashing in his critique of Neil's aeronautic skills. Suddenly, Armstrong burst through the door in a cold rage, obviously having heard more than enough. After the two had at one another, Collins recalls "creeping off to bed."

Collins made no secret of being somewhat intimidated by Armstrong and Aldrin, modestly writing, "both of them [are] far better engineers than I." He very much wished his crewmates were more capable of indulging in some small talk to ease the tension they were under. The three were going to spend a month in quarantine before the journey, travel 826,300 miles in a tiny spacecraft together, then be forced into three weeks of biological isolation to avert the possibility of contaminating the earth with moon germs; a total of two solid months together. Tensions and potential for conflict ran deep among the three. Thirty years later, Aldrin admits he was very uncomfortable being the junior member of a team Armstrong was commanding, and throughout the journey suffered "twinges of intimidation."

Neil was less than thrilled as well, and defied the quarantine order that had canceled a dinner with the U.S. President to drink a few beers and have dinner with old Navy buddies John Moore, who had been manager of Apollo Test Operations, and Ken Danneberg. Moore was Armstrong's instructor at Pensacola Naval Air Station, and in Korea Neil became Moore's wingman. Neil showed up with fellow astronaut Alan Shephard. The four men relaxed on Moore's porch at his home in Cocoa Beach before dinner to talk about the upcoming mission, but most importantly to spend some hours with their own kind, speaking in the shorthand of their engineer/test-pilot patois. Despite the crew friction, Armstrong was completely confident and refused to accept that Apollo 11 was different from any other test mission. He was merely going to put the equipment through the paces and would probably get to walk on the moon. The success of the mission was 100 percent in his mind; getting to walk on the moon was questionable, maybe fifty-fifty.

In 1963, when Neil Armstrong moved to Houston with his wife, Jan, and their sons, six-year-old Rick and baby Mark, his reputation as a flyer was well established. He was a decorated Korean War air hero, having flown seventy-eight missions, had soared 207,000 feet high to the edge of space at four thousand miles per hour in the "hypersonic glider" dubbed X-15, and was a survivor of numerous brushes with death, which were blandly referred to by test pilots as "coping with the unexpected."

The Armstrong family had moved into a ranch-style house in the El Lago development near Mission Control that was favored by the majority of the astronauts. The modest house had bright red doors, a small rock garden in front, and a good-sized swimming pool protected from prying eyes—of which there would soon be many—by a six-foot-high wooden fence.

Jan Armstrong had a lifelong passion for swimming. She had been on the swim team in college and taught swimming and lifesaving while the couple lived in the California desert. But this was the first time they had their own pool; a real plus as far as she was concerned.

Soon after settling in at El Lago, Jan had organized both a synchronized swimming and a racing team. Both Jan and Neil were big baseball fans, and supporters of the Little League, for which Jan organized fund-raising suppers and Neil coached—when not on a seven-day-a-week training schedule at NASA.

Their next-door neighbors were Ed and Pat White. Ed, who would die in the 1967 Apollo 1 fire disaster, had encouraged Buzz Aldrin to apply for selection as an astronaut with the third group, which was forming in late 1963. Buzz and Ed had a long history together, having been one class apart at West Point and members of the track team. In 1955 and '56 they represented their squadron in NATO, flying state-of-the-art Air Force F-100 Super Sabres based in Germany. While Buzz was on temporary assignment with the Air Force in Houston, charged with exploring the proper role of the air arm in space, White invited him to a barbecue to meet some members of the astronauts corps he hoped to soon join.

Neil Armstrong's reputation as a taciturn, steely-eyed test pilot preceded him to Houston, so it was with wonder that turned into glee that Buzz reacted to his first glimpse at the man with whom he would make history. Followed by a gaggle of kids, Neil was gracefully roller-skating around Ed White's pool deck. "He was quite adept at roller-skating," Aldrin laughs. "It wasn't exactly what men in their early thirties were doing."

But Armstrong's nephew Mike Trude recalls that that was typical. "Uncle Neil always joined in with the kids' games. When his family visited us in Chicago, or we visited them in Houston, he always had time for the kids, whether to take us to the Astrodome for a baseball game, or to play Wiffle ball in the backyard, skating, or any kind of sports. He played with us all the time."

In the final days before launch, Jan Armstrong's informal support group gathered at the house in El Lago, quietly helping out with the day-to-day running of the house and the care of her boys, knowing that the pressure on her would be immense. Jan's sister Carolyn Trude and her husband, Alfred, flew down from Barrington, Illinois. Neil's Navy friend Ken Danneberg came down from Colorado. And the astronauts and their wives, the only people alive who could truly understand the roller coaster of anxieties and joys Jan was experiencing, because they had been there, too, gathered around the family.

Neil had asked Jan not to come to see the launch, but he had said the same about his first space mission Gemini 8, and she had regretted missing it. This time she was going to be there, as were the boys. So they flew down to Florida and watched the blastoff, with the other two Apollo 11 wives, Joan Aldrin and Patricia Collins, from one of the best possible vantage points, a boat moored in the Banana River. A boat had the additional advantage of being out of shouting distance of the throngs of reporters. Mark, then six, was well aware that Daddy was perched at the top of the gleaming candle everyone was watching with awe. He knew his father's trip to the moon would take three days and hoped one day to join him on a return trip. He and Rick, who was twelve, caught up in the giddy, carnival atmosphere, squealed and cheered. When their husbands were safely en route to the moon, the wives returned to Houston to sweat out every minute of the following week.

The neighborhood buzzed with friends and relatives. The Armstrongs' bedroom was littered with maps of the moon's surface so they could follow Neil's travels as though he was on a road trip to another state. A speaker set up by NASA in the living room monitored all conversations between the astronauts and mission control.

Dave Scott, who had survived the nearly disastrous Gemini 8 mission with Armstrong, Jim Lovell, who would later live to tell the tale of the harrowing Apollo 13, and Ken Danneberg started a pool to guess where on the moon Neil would land the LM. Scott won by figuring he would go long, knowing Neil as a perfectionist who would not be easily satisfied with the first landing site he saw, but never imagining he would be forced to search so long that the LM would come within seconds of running out of fuel.

With the entire world's attention centered on his dad's daring deeds, six-year-old Mark tried to wring a bit of attention out of the swarm of adults surrounding his mom. While his dad was about to tread on the moon, his little feet were bouncing on the house's tile roof, debatably a more dangerous pursuit than traveling to the moon. Danneberg recalls: "Mark was the wildest kid I ever saw. He was on the roof, stuck up in trees, up to every kind of mischief, and his mother was trying in vain to get him to do his chores." No only was Mark not the center of attention, but Dad had, of necessity, been absent for what must have seemed most of his life, training for space missions.

As the astronauts tossed and turned during their last night on earth, Saturn was being filled with six million pounds of volatile liquid oxygen, liquid hydrogen, and kerosene.

They were awakened from their restless slumber by Deke Slayton, one of the original seven astronauts, who had been grounded with a heart ailment, and, though tough and crusty, became the esteemed and loved head of the astronaut corps. Deke gently rapped on the three doors and led the groggy, bathrobe-and-slipper-clad astronauts to Nurse Dee O'Hara's examination room, where they were weighed and given one last medical exam. All three men also handed their personal belongings—clothes, wallets—over to O'Hara to forward to their homes in Houston. It was an odd feeling for all concerned, but necessary because no matter what happened they weren't coming back to the cape. The important thing was not to say good-bye. It was part of the astronaut etiquette that one never did on launch day.

Countdown resumed at 11:00 P.M. on July 15. Crews led by Rocco Petrone, the launch director, began chilling down the rocket's systems so they would accept the ultracold propellants, liquid hydrogen and liquid oxygen, otherwise known as "cryogenics." They would be followed by highly volatile kerosene.

Once the tanks were filled, everything seemed to be running so smoothly that Petrone decided to get a bite to eat in the cafeteria. Halfway through his break came potentially catastrophic news. "A guy came down and said, 'Hey, we've got the same leak we had last week.'" Petrone fought off a sense of dread. The astronauts were aboard, and nobody could forget Apollo 1 and the flash fire that incinerated its crew eighteen months before.

Scrambling back to the firing control room, Petrone saw on television monitors highly flammable hydrogen hemorrhaging from the fully loaded bird—which had the potential of exploding with the force of a million pounds of TNT. "Leaking hydrogen isn't something you fool around with. There was a danger of fire." The exact same leak, at the same time in the countdown, had occurred a week prior during a practice loading, without the crew aboard. "It turned out one bolt was a little too long—about a quarter inch. It only showed itself when the cryogenics were flowing through. It shrank and gave you a leak. Because it had happened a week before, we knew that as soon as we finished loading hydrogen the leak would stop because it would warm up and expand." An emergency crew determined that the leak had indeed sealed itself. They cleaned up and the countdown continued. "If the leak hadn't stopped we would have had to divert the flow and probably abort the mission."

On the other side of the world, a similarly simple design flaw led to a cataclysmic disaster that all but ended the Soviets' race to the moon. Thirteen days earlier, on July 3, a Soviet N-1 rocket lifted off its pad at a secret location in the desolate steppes of Central Asia. Less than one minute into flight, one of the rockets' forty-three engines inhaled tiny scraps of loose metal and exploded. With the force of a nuclear explosion, the booster rocket slammed to the earth and destroyed all life for miles around. At that moment the space race was effectively over, though few people, save for U.S. intelligence, which had been closely monitoring the Soviet space program, knew about it. Two similar first-stage crashes later, in 1971 and '72, led furious, humiliated Soviet leaders to order the whole moon landing program scrapped. The remaining rockets were dismantled and recycled; one was ignominiously turned into a pigpen. All that were left were the unmanned Luna sample-return missions, which would, ironically, suffer yet another disaster on the very day of America's, and Neil Armstrong's, greatest triumph.

Cosmonaut Alexei Leonor, who endured and eventually commanded a Soyuz flight that linked with an American capsule, was devastated. "When Apollo 8 went around the moon, I was very proud for mankind, and I wished the astronauts every success. But it was very, very sad for us. We'd held everything in our hands—after spending huge amounts of money and years of our lives—we let it slip away from us. It was a pity." The moon silently awaited the victors.

The flight of Apollo 11 was a television event, and television's flickering images would be seared in the world's collective consciousness, but it would not come close to capturing the majesty—and the danger—of Saturn. From the viewing stands three and a half miles away, the initial flame first appeared as a bright yellow-orange star, then, as the other four engines fired, a clattering noise like a tearing of the fabric of the sky rose louder and louder until the sound felt to viewers like a thumping against the solar plexus and blew over them in hot waves. Huge iron talons held the rocket in place for 8.9 seconds, as two-hundred-foot-long plumes of fire licked the tarmac. Miles from Cape Kennedy, the earth trembled. When full power was reached, a din that seemed to rend the universe caused the crowd of a million awestruck witnesses to muffle their ears and silently exclaim. Suddenly unfettered, Saturn was a ball of fire, slowly reaching for the sky, finally clearing the scaffolding and blazing like a second sun. Gradually winning the bout with gravity, it raced for the clouds, gracefully rolling over, controls set for the unfathomable 24,667 miles per hour necessary to escape Mother Earth and reach the moon. Two and a half minutes after ignition, Saturn had expended five million pounds of fuel. In three minutes it was traveling at 6,340 miles per hour.

A journalist at the launch asked renowned orator William F. Buckley for a comment seconds after the launch.

"You're an eloquent man, Mr. Buckley," said the interviewer. "How would you describe what you have just seen?"

"With silence," was his answer.

Chapter TWO

Neil Armstrong's sixteenth-century ancestors in Scotland were a mixed lot at best. One infamously roguish relation was highwayman Johnnie Armstrong who led missions of plunder across the English border for cattle and sheep, and eventually met his fate at the end of a hangman's rope. Fortunately, members of the clan who emigrated to America were cut of more virtuous cloth. Great, great, great-grandfather Captain John Armstrong (1768–1833) was a soldier, merchant, and land speculator who literally hacked his way through the dense forests of western Ohio to make a home for his family. He was succeeded by generations of Armstrongs who played a large part in settling and developing the Auglaize Valley of northwestern Ohio. Tales of Captain Armstrong's heroics are abundant in historical accounts of the Indian battles that accompanied settlement of the region and help illustrate the strength and intrepidity inherited by his astronaut descendant.

According to one contemporaneous report, typically replete with the ethnocentrism of the time, "Captain Armstrong broke through the pursuing Indians, receiving severe wounds, and plunged into one of the deepest morasses, where he remained to his chin all night in water, his head concealed by a tussock of grass. Here he was compelled to listen to the nocturnal orgies of the Indians, dancing and yelling around the dead bodies of his brave soldiers. As day approached they retired for rest, and Armstrong, chilled to the last degree, extricated himself from the swamp. By aid of a fire he recovered his feelings, and use of his limbs, and at length reached the safety of the camp."

Equally remarkable were Armstrong's maternal family, the Koenigs. Frederick Koenig, Neil's great-grandfather, was spirited away from his Bavarian village in the mid-nineteenth century by his father, who desperately wanted to save his youngest son from dying in the Prussian Wars, which had been the fate of his two elder sons. Thus he began a perilous, picaresque journey through Europe, across the ocean, and eventually to the American frontier in Ohio, where he was promptly drafted to fight in the one of the great Indian uprisings of the century. Barely surviving wounds sustained in what was then the Indian settlement of Wapakoneta, Frederick was rewarded for his bravery in battle with a Union Army commission. For the following four years he fought in the Civil War. His abundant progeny, like the Armstrongs, helped shape the territory in numerous ways. They were judges, congressmen, educators, and businessmen who always seemed to have time, at some point in their lives, to till the earth and farm.

When Neil Armstrong returned from the moon and was feted in his hometown, he looked out over the adoring crowd and acknowledged: "I guess I'm related to most of you." It was hardly an exaggeration.

Neil Armstrong's junior high school math and chemistry teacher, John Crites, vividly remembered a warm moonlit fall night when the teenaged future astronaut sauntered up to his porch and joined him on the swing. Neil was one of his brightest and best-behaved students, serious about his studies and well advanced beyond any boy or girl in the class. Serious reading occupied a great deal of his time. Just fourteen, he had read over a hundred books, including most of the works of Shakespeare, and he knew the Bible front and back. In fact, Crites reflected, Armstrong was advanced well beyond any student he had ever had. More than once, a particularly keen question from the slender, shy, freckle-faced blond boy had sent him to the library for an answer.

Listening to Armstrong discuss flying and even the phantasmagoric tales of space travel he regularly read in *Air Trails* magazine, his blue eyes gleaming with possibility, Crites knew a career in aviation was inevitable. Fortunately, Neil, only ten years old in 1940, would be too young to fight in the coming war that had Europe in flames and was already roiling most of the rest of the world. (It surely would have appalled the soft-spoken Ohio school teacher had he known that the United States would be engaged in shooting wars in almost twenty of the succeeding thirty-four years.) But, knowing the modest government wages earned by Neil's father, Stephen, a financial auditor, the teacher was sure the Army Air Corps would be the only route to pilot an aircraft more advanced than the crop dusters that droned over the farms during planting time. But Neil was certainly bright enough, and God knew he had a single-minded dedication to be a fighter pilot or commander of one of the newly pressurized commercial planes like the Boeing 314 Clipper that was transporting people across the oceans while pretty stewardesses waited on them.

Half-listening to young Armstrong's dreams and thinking about the practicality of what the boy's future would likely be, Crites was startled when the lad admitted his real goal. Between bites of a big green apple, Neil had been staring at the great harvest moon that looked close enough to reach out and touch. He turned, looked straight at the older man, and announced: "Some day I want to go to that moon."

After Neil Alden Armstrong had not only gone to "that moon" but had placed his footprint in dust never touched in a billion years and spent nearly twenty-four hours on its craggy, dusty wasteland, John Crites recalled: "I knew Neil was a dreamer and there wasn't any way to answer him. So I just smiled and said nothing."

Even when Neil could hold the secret of his nocturnal soaring no longer, the dreams continued. Stephen Armstrong, as imperturbable, sound, and reliable as Neil would grow up to be, listened in silence to his son. When the rhapsodic dreams of "hovering" over the earth were spilled out with all the urgency of fact, Stephen took the boy by the hand and silently led him off the shady porch to the nearly new, neat-as-a-pin black Ford with the Buckeye State seal emblazoned on the driver's side door.

Stephen Armstrong felt duty-bound to drive his son to the airport outside Warren, in northeastern Ohio, where he was then working and his family temporarily living, for a first plane ride.

"I was supposed to be taking Neil to Sunday school," the senior Armstrong recalled. "My wife, Viola, had the younger children, Dean and June, at home. On our way to the church Neil and I passed by a field where The Tin Goose, a Ford Trimotor plane, was taking people up for rides. The earlier in the day that you flew the cheaper it was, so we didn't get to Sunday school that day. We took a plane ride."

When his father pulled up to the airfield, the plane immediately caught Neil's eye. He ran pell-mell toward the great beast, took a breath, and caressed it reverently.

It slightly resembled a fat, clumsy goose, and in many ways it was a harbinger of the world's tumultuous transition from the Great Depression to total war. The Ford Trimotor was capable of carrying military ordnance and as many as thirty troops at a then-impressive 150 miles per hour. It was based on a design perfected by the brilliant German, Hugo Junkers, during World War I. It was the first plane made entirely of corrugated sheet metal, with cantilevered wings that greatly cut wind resistance by eliminating the need for external wing braces. In short, it was the first proper flying man-of-war.

The German war machine in the thirties was supposedly still incapacitated by the terms of the loathed Versailles Treaty that Germany was forced by the World War I allies to accept as the price of defeat. But the Junker company was spawning generation after generation of warplanes. Hugo Junker, who died in 1935, had thrust aviation ahead by an awesome leap. His designs paved the way for the Luftwaffe's fearsome Stuka (*Sturzkampflugzeug*) dive bomber, a key to the Blitzkrieg offense. And during the war Junker's acolytes turned out the first turbojet, called the "Jumo" engine.

Years later, as a professor at the University of Cincinnati, Armstrong lectured his students about the work of Hugo Junkers with some of the rapture he felt in his youth when touching the gleaming, muscular warplane that had visited Ohio.

Neil and his father took their places at the end of a long line consisting largely of men with their sons waiting nervously to fly for the first time in their lives. Bristling with anticipation, hardly able to keep from jumping up and down despite amused pleas from Stephen to keep still, the youth watched as load after load of passengers climbed aboard the airship. Many stopped shy of stepping inside the door, hesitating as though having second thoughts about walking into the maw of the beast. Once inside and fumbling with the unfamiliar seatbelts, the looks on the pioneers' faces seen through the plane's portholes were akin to terror.

Stephen shared the common anxiety when his and Neil's turn came. He struggled not to let on to Neil just how terrified he was and how fearful he was that his impetuous decision to please his son would leave Viola a widow with two children. But the boy was oblivious. He helped Dad with the seatbelt, which he had read about in *Air Trails* magazine, and strained to look out the window as the propellers took their first tenuous turns. The mighty engine choked as if clearing its throat, then screamed a high-pitched banshee cry, making the propeller bite the air and fade into a hell wind. A few seconds after the second engine was similarly ignited, the passengers lurched as one and clutched at one another for comfort. Eyes were shut tight and lips trembled with silent prayer, but when the bone-jarring race down the runway ended, a diorama of their farms, village, and lakes slowly spread out beneath them. Silent o's formed on every mouth as they saw the world as if for the first time. In fact, it would never look the same to them again. Neil wished the short flight around the airfield would never end (despite the hateful, creeping motion-sickness monster in his stomach, which he was desperately trying to ignore). Stephen could not make himself look over his son's head and out the window, though he knew he must because people would be asking him for years to come what he had seen. When finally he stole a glimpse, his reaction was terror. Suddenly the plane banked hard to the left and rapidly lost altitude, lining up for landing after barely fifteen minutes aloft. One passenger choked out a shrill wail, most faces went white, fathers clutched at their sons as if for the final time, and the sickening, sulphurous stench of vomit filled the air.

Once returned to terra firma, Stephen led his son away on wobbly legs without looking back once. But, despite himself, there was a feeling of having accomplished something that he would talk about for the rest of his life. "It was one hell of a ride," Stephen remembered, awe in his voice at the memory a half-century later. Whatever the elder Armstrong's intent in arranging Neil's first flight, the effect was instant and irreversible. The boy's bedroom was soon filled with increasingly detailed and complex model airplanes—built not from kits, but from scratch. With Mom's tacit, amused consent they eventually spread throughout the house, giving the spacious old Victorian home the feeling of being anchored in two centuries at once.

Soaring over heat streams of potbelly stoves were Fokker Trimotors. Vying for space with paintings of Armstrong kin was an Italian Marchetti SM73. A huge, twelve-motored German Dornier WAL flying boat roared past Viola's treadle-powered Domestic brand sewing machine.

The hobbies and interests of Neil's baby brother Dean and younger sister June were likewise encouraged and given the run of the house on many occasions as they grew. It was just that Neil's interests in space, astronomy, and flight seemed to become palpable, living entities. They weren't the usual passing fancies of youth that came and went in a matter of days, but consuming interests that spanned in different directions, growing more complex and serious. Neil Armstrong was a child of destiny and everybody seemed to know it—and to treat him that way—from a very early age.

Typically laconic, Stephen didn't say at the time whether he took his son for a plane ride hoping to cure him of his obsession with flying or to inspire further interest. The latter would have been somewhat surprising. Neil Armstrong would remember his father as a man who tenaciously clung to the values of the past as well as the old ways of getting things done.

"My father believed that the tractor would never replace the horse, but things change," he said ten years after walking on the moon. And Stephen Armstrong personally hated flying. He disliked his first ride with his enthralled six-year-old son and was edgy and uncomfortable on every subsequent journey, leading him to refuse the offer of a NASA flight to his son's Florida blastoff on the Gemini 8 orbital mission in 1966. Instead, Stephen and Viola "leisurely motored" the thousand miles from Ohio to Cape Canaveral. "I was kind of old hat about things like that; I liked flying with one foot on the ground," laughed Stephen. In fact, over the course of Neil's long career as a fighter pilot, test pilot, and astronaut, Stephen Armstrong accepted it with a Calvinist sense of inevitability. But seared in his memory was every sleepless night, every sweat-soaked nightmare of his son's hideous death in a blazing, supersonic inferno or in some godforsaken black hole in a distant cosmos. Years after the last glorious adventure, sitting holding hands with his Viola on a florid couch at the Dorothy Love Retirement Community in Sydney, Ohio, a few miles from where they were both born, Stephen's voice cracked with palpable pain, his aged eyes teared, and he glanced heavenward. "We have learned to live with danger," he said with simple dignity.

Back in 1936, Stephen was conflicted as to whether the plane ride had been the right thing to do, and by his remarks over the years seems to have remained so. Viola knew some seminal event had occurred the instant father and son walked through the door. "Dad especially looked so guilty, but Neil clearly loved it. He was really impressed, and I think his love for flying started that day."

A year or so earlier, Stephen had taken Neil to the National Air Races in Cleveland, which fanned the fire in the boy's soul. The deafening whine of the powerful engines, the acrid pungency of the smell of high-octane fuel cascading from the sky like a celestial perfume mesmerized and hypnotized him. Stephen saw the powerful narcotic of flying flowing through his son's veins and, unaccountably, liked seeing the passion it produced. Unlike the giddy, unfocused, destructive hunger he so mistrusted and disliked in men, Neil's yearning to fly seemed to be an orderly, disciplined thing. He thirsted for not just the thrill, but for the knowledge required to master aviation.

Flying was a perilous activity in the 1930s. Daring young men flew the first airmail runs, allowing something approaching prompt cross-country delivery for the first time, finally linking the vast country. They probably suffered as many or more losses than their Pony Express forebears had braving hostile, unforgiving deserts, mountains, and wilderness. Crashes were a daily occurrence. The public viewed flight as a glamorous but inordinately foolhardy pursuit.

Despite their misgivings, something in Neil's character convinced his parents to let him pursue his dream. "He was so faithful about things, so steady and dependable, we felt he would be all right," Viola said.

"We used to park at the Cleveland Airport and watch the planes come and go. The stunts and exhibitions they did then were called barnstorming. Neil didn't want to leave. He kept saying, 'One more, one more.'"

Stephen Armstrong was an auditor for the state of Ohio. He saw himself as a fiscal lawman and took his job dead seriously. In fact, throughout the state of Ohio's bureaucracy, the senior Armstrong was called "serious as a heart attack." More than one miscreant was sent to prison as a result of his audits. Stephen was a man who was true to his stern Highland Scots roots. In some ways, he acted as though each day was a crucible to be endured. His jet-black hair was parted with a razor-sharp crease, slicked to the side in a no-nonsense way and crowned by a gray fedora. The three-piece suits he wore nearly every waking hour were always immaculate and the Windsor-knotted tie and button-on starched shirt collars impeccable. His sharpened pencils he occasionally licked to provide emphasis on a particularly telling spreadsheet tally. The tall, elder Armstrong was a Herbert Hoover Republican who thought it almost onerous that the government should have any of the peoples' money and his mission was to make damn sure every penny was accounted for. And yet he was a man, like Neil, with a sharp bark of a laugh that charmed women and put men at ease.

Like his pioneer ancestors, the future astronaut had a high tolerance for danger, but no love of it for its own sake. His love was of understanding and mastering unknown frontiers through the power of reason and diligent study.

"Neil was the most motivated kid in our school," said classmate Joe Carter. "His interest was in anything and everything that related to aviation. Radio was an early obsession because it was so important to flying. The family radio was probed and poked, taken very nearly apart and reassembled. And he borrowed a towering pile of books on the subject. Mathematics, weather, chemistry, and, of course, astronomy were also subjects he mastered as well as conceivable for a schoolboy.

"At age nine he was given a telescope he gazed into for endless hours. I imagine he was thinking about the day he would fly into space himself. A few years later we heard that a local fellow named Jacob Zint, an engineer who lived over on Pearl Street, just a few blocks from the Armstrongs, had built a small observatory with a dome and an eight-inch telescope. Neil couldn't believe it—a real observatory in Wapak. I'd never seen him so excited; his eyes were on fire. He said, 'Do you think he'll let us look through it? He just has to. We have to make friends with him.' I was the older kid so I volunteered to ask Mr. Zint if we could come by the next time I saw him in town. He was thrilled we were interested, so the next day Neil, another boy, and I stopped by after school. It turned out he was every bit as fascinated with aviation and astronomy as Neil. He had ground the glass for the telescope himself and used simple roller-skate wheels to rotate it. That first night, the distant sky lit up with a full-blown meteor shower that I know to Neil seemed an omen he had found his destiny.

"Neil spent much of his free time with Mr. Zint that winter, learning everything he possibly could from him about the constellations, celestial navigation, and the million-mile-wide clouds of sparkling gas called nebula. When Neil was staring through that telescope he was no longer on this planet; he was already out there."

The relationship between Armstrong and Wapakoneta's eccentric astronomer continued and grew stronger over the years as both men learned more about the science of space. In the early fifties, when Armstrong joined the National Advisory Committee on Aeronautics, the forerunner of NASA, Jacob Zint came aboard, too, designing rocket engines.

After Armstrong became a full-fledged astronaut, Zint told the *Wapakoneta Daily News,* "Neil liked to talk about the heavens and the moon. He would get a very intent look whenever he looked through the scope. He was always asking if there was life out there. I would say Mars had the best possibility. He always dwelled on possible habitation of space. But I do believe the moon was Neil's point of interest right from the start."

Neil was exceptional by all accounts in terms of his intensity, his vision, and willingness to give his all, qualities that won him veneration from friends and enmity from some who felt they couldn't keep up with him. Even hard taskmaster Stephen marveled, "The boy had a wonderful capacity for doing hard work." It was a useful trait in a family where idleness was considered a scourge and industry akin to godliness. But those who couldn't or wouldn't keep up the pace groused. An anonymous NASA engineer was quoted as saying: "Neil's all scrubbed up on the outside, but inside he has nothing but contempt for the rest of mankind that isn't willing to work as hard as he does."

But lifelong friends still see Armstrong as a shy country boy who wanted desperately to please, and to have the greatest adventure of any Midwestern farm boy—ever.

"By the time we were in high school, he had read more books than the rest of the class combined. He could quote from most of Shakespeare's works and knew the Bible inside out," said classmate Richard Schwere.

Neil's goal at school was to read 101 books before turning four-teen. They included several primer aviation books, such as *Principles of Flight* by Burt Shields, *Modern Flight* by Cloyd Clevenger, *Science of Pre-Flight Aeronautics for High School, The Young American's Aviation Annual,* and anything he could find about his heroes Orville and Wilbur Wright, who practically invented modern aviation in their bicycle shop in nearby Dayton. ("He read everything about them," said Viola. "He thought they were the greatest of men.") Each book title was logged into a notebook Neil carried around. The magic num-ber was passed well ahead of the goal. He was skipped ahead a year and graduated two months before his seventeenth birthday.

"Neil was never a social guy by any stretch of the imagination," continued Schwere. "In fact, he was quiet to the point where some people thought him rude, and too smart by half, though that was cer-tainly not the case. It was more that he didn't care to speak unless he had something important to say and then he would say it and fall silent. He was always introspective, thoughtful, and deliberate, and unlike the rest of us he knew exactly where he was going."

Neil's younger brother Dean says, "Neil liked school. Once he asked a teacher to instruct him in trigonometry and calculus in prepa-ration for college. He had already taken all the math the school offered. Math and science were his favorite subjects. He read every-thing, he devoured books. But he wasn't what you would call a book-worm because he had too many other interests."

Neil Armstrong's sensibility was shaped by the crucible of the Depression and World War II. His dreams of flying and burning ambition to soar above the dusty farmland of northwestern Ohio surely were reactions to the deprivations he saw all around him and the relatively minor want the Armstrongs experienced. But given the desperate state of the American republic and the appalling circum-stances a great number, perhaps a plurality, of Armstrong's country-men were enduring, it's a tribute to the human spirit that he and others could envision a project beyond the scope of any previous endeavor attempted by mankind.

Neil Alden Armstrong was born on Tuesday, August 5, 1930, in a two-story St. Mary's, Ohio, farmhouse, the fourth generation of his family born there. At the time the U.S. population was 124,848,664, approximately half what it is as of this writing. Prime beef was a fraction of its present cost; in Wapakoneta, Ohio, which would become Neil's hometown, it fetched just twenty cents, that is if fresh meat could be found at all.

In addition to economic collapse, the limestone prairie of southwestern Ohio was suffering from drought and a heat wave so severe at least 40 percent of dairy farms had no cattle at all. So many hungry families roamed the countryside in desperate search of nourishment that farmers spent nights sleeping in their ripening fields, clutching a shotgun, determined to prevent hungry thieves from stripping their harvest.

The *Wapakoneta Daily News* reported "waves of children" stealing chickens from area farms. Lester Coy of St. Mary's vowed not to take it anymore. He spent a sleepless night in his potato patch the night Neil was born. Morning after morning he had awakened to find whole sections of his weather-decimated crops stolen: Enough was enough. When the twenty-three-year-old farmer heard rustling and the sound of potatoes being uprooted, he sprang to his feet and fired a blinding sheet of double-aught buckshot in the direction of the noise. Hot lead tore into the faces and chests of Elmer Tilton and his seventeen-year-old boy, Louis.

Coy had successfully defended his potato patch and made six children fatherless. When news of the slayings filtered out in Auglaize County, an angry mob gathered and strode through the scorched fields, intent on exacting vengeance. Fortunately for Coy, they only staged what amounted to a demonstration: smashing a few windows, shaking fists, and uttering oaths. Coy would simply have to spend the rest of a long life thinking about the relative value of spuds.

A few counties away in Marion, Indiana, far north of the Mason-Dixon Line, two black men accused of beating a white man and molesting his girlfriend weren't so lucky. A throng, as angry with the gods as Farmer Coy, needed someone to blame for their plight and decided the accused blacks would do nicely. They overpowered the guards, forced entry into the prison, and lynched them. Nineteen-thirty was a big year for lynching.

Oddly, as though day-to-day life wasn't enough to abide, endurance contests of all kinds were going on. Pole sitters, porch sitters, and roof sitters vied for attention trying to set records. In nearby

Russell's Point on Indian Lake, soul- and bone-weary dancers propped one another up hoping to win eating money by outlasting other luckless wretches. The winners (?) stood on their feet a mind-numbing 1,034 hours, more than forty days.

Down south at Lambert's Field in St. Louis, a different type of record was being set, one with a practical point that Neil Armstrong might have approved of; one that could be seen, taking place as it did during his nativity, as a herald of the world's first interplanetary wayfarer. Two daring young pilots, Forest O'Brine and Dale Jackson, were flying an orange-and-yellow monoplane called the *Greater St. Louis* in great circles, hoping to spend a thousand hours aloft with only the briefest pit stops. The pair managed to keep their craft airborne for 647 hours, 28 minutes, a footnote in aviation history that was soon surpassed and forgotten, but proved naysayers wrong and launched a score of other, increasingly ambitious flights, expanding the range of the possible in a score of ways.

Almost six decades later, the hardships of the Great Depression still pain Armstrong's now-grizzling classmates like fresh paper cuts.

"Nobody was eating high on the hog," recalls Richard Schwere. "You didn't go to the dentist unless it hurt really bad. I mean, you had to be in agony. I remember stepping on a rusty nail and really hurting. That was serious enough to call for action. There were no antibiotics, so the doctor taped raw bacon at the point of entry on my foot. That drew out the poison. Paying the doctor meant sacrificing something else. Maybe you couldn't get that new pair of shoes you needed, or maybe it meant Mom had to cut back on meals for a while.

"In those days, if you missed a single payment on your farm, they foreclosed, threw your furniture out front, and you with it. They talk about homelessness now, but during the Depression there was an army of homeless, mostly people who had known nothing but hard work and bad luck most of their lives.

"Neil's granddaddy, Willie Korspeter, had a farm in Washington Township that had been in his wife's family for over a hundred years. They built the house Neil was born in with their own hands. Fortunately they didn't have a mortgage on it or they probably would have lost it like most of their neighbors. Neil's grandfather and father had

both been reluctantly driven out of farming years before. It was getting all but impossible to support a family by farming this area, no
matter how hard you worked. Grandpa Willie, who came from a long
line of German farmers, like most of the people in the area, worked for
the county government. Neil's daddy had worked for the state of Ohio
since 1930. Granddad Willie was heartbroken he couldn't make a living as a farmer, working with his hands, which he believed was about
the only legitimate way. Years later, when the town gave Neil a big
parade to welcome him back from his first space journey, I saw Willie
standing alone by himself wearing his bib coveralls, which was his
'business suit.' He was kinda hiding round a corner hoping not to be
recognized and fussed over by anybody."

On the day Neil was born, his father was out driving around the
state, auditing books. There was no way to get in touch; the nearest
telephone was miles away from the farm. It fell to Grandma Caroline
Korspeter to act as her daughter's midwife, a job she had done many
times for other women. The front room of the old farmhouse was prepared, water was boiled, the usual procedure. Stephen finally arrived
breathlessly at the door and was presented with his first son. Grandma
Korspeter was humming the new hit song they had heard on the radio,
Cole Porter's "Where Have You Been," and smiling from ear to ear.

The first years of Neil's life were blissful, living in the warm
embrace of the old farmhouse and his doting grandparents, as well as
an extended family that numbered well over a hundred. It seemed as
though everybody in the town of St. Mary's and the surrounding
farmland was kin.

Practically before Neil could walk, Grandpa Will Korspeter had
him riding bareback on a pony called Maggie. Cold early mornings,
pitching hay for the cattle, slopping hogs, and hard farm work were no
problem for the boy. But he drew the line at the ritual of picking
a plump chicken from the roost, sequestering the bird in a special fat-
tening house, then wringing its neck for Sunday dinner with a special
visitor like the town preacher.

"He was never really interested in farming," said Grandma
Korspeter. Ironically, though, after his adventures in space were
behind him, Armstrong would return to a farm, which would probably have surprised and pleased his grandparents.

In summer he swam in the deep, crystalline waters of Lake St.
Mary with his cousins. When was not on the road, his dad taught Neil

the fine points of fishing in the freshwater of Auglaize County streams and lakes, a sport he would enjoy all his life. Blue-and-yellow catfish were plentiful, as were perch and rock bass. In the springtime hickory shad, heavy with roe, could be reeled in for Grandma Korspeter to bake.

Viola Armstrong added to her son's education, teaching him to share her love of music. She remembered her son getting interested in listening to radio programs at age six, the same year he fell in love with flying. "When we lived in Warren, many mornings we would hear Neil tiptoeing downstairs at 6:00 A.M. to turn the radio on. He was crazy about a program called *Hank Keene's Gang,* which featured songs and funny patter. He played the set very quietly because he was afraid he would be made to go back to bed if we discovered him."

Everything from Franz Lizst to Broadway show tunes to jazz was played on the family Victrola. And Neil learned to read music, play the piano, and what proved to be his favorite, the baritone horn, which he was introduced to by a junior high band teacher. Mother and son spent happy hours playing piano duets from recent musicals like *Oklahoma!* to the current Hoagy Carmichael hit "Ivy."

Later, when the family settled in Wapakoneta for good in 1942, he formed a jazz combo simply called "The German Band" in honor of its members' roots. The band was forever known after their first paid performance at the Uniopolis Fireman's Jamboree, as loud "with a capital L." The boys wailed away at the firemen with happy feet with songs like "Two Hearts in Three Quarter Time" (or the German version, "Zwei Herzen im Dreivierteltakt"), which was a hit when Neil was born in 1930. The following year the band's name was discreetly changed to the more politically appealing "Mississippi Moonshiners Band."

Stephen enjoyed music as well and reveled in seeing his children learn from their mother. He was frustrated at the fact he was forced to be on the road so often, missing his children's impromptu recitals and gradual musical progress, though he was typically stoic. But often he insisted they accompany him on his grueling trips, a chore none relished but all endured with grace.

From the time Neil was two or three he was a traveler, albeit a reluctant and less than happy one. Stephen's work required him to drive over Ohio's torturous, bumpy back roads from town hall to town hall. Many of the highways were, in the thirties, little better than wagon trails, not much improved over the ones traversed by Armstrong pioneers who came to Ohio by way of Virginia in the early eighteenth century. The one advantage was that little towns like St. Mary's could live in "splendid isolation" from encroachments and depredations of the outside world.

During car or train trips, Neil often would "go a bit green in the gills," as his mother later remembered. At first they assumed it was something he had eaten or just his tender age. But soon it became obvious that when bouncing over the semipaved and unpaved roads, Neil became violently ill almost every time. Travel became an excruciating ordeal for the family. All manner of Korspeter home remedies were tested on the boy, doctors were consulted, and prayers fervently offered. But the severe case of motion sickness persisted. Stephen could drive for fifteen or twenty minutes at a time, then would have to stop until the nausea and dizziness subsided. It was an inauspicious start to a career as an aviator. The discomfort persisted for years, up until he was enrolled in naval flight school in Pensacola, Florida. Remedies never helped at all, but through sheer force of will he was finally able to slay the monster that had lurked in his stomach as long as he could remember.

Despite suffering a sometimes debilitating malaise, Neil was never coddled by his parents nor was he ever frail or sickly, save for occasional episodes from which he quickly recovered. "Neil never participated in sports, though he enjoyed them," recalled Viola. "But he was a hard worker. When we lived in Upper Sandusky [Ohio], he got his first job. He was in about the seventh grade and decided he wanted to buy his own baritone horn and take lessons. It was a large task he had set for himself because the horn cost nearly seventy-five dollars and we really couldn't help much."

"In our family," Dean said, "if you wanted something, you'd better work. Everybody started working when he was eight or nine years old—and you just never stopped. You always had a job. Neil's first job was cutting grass in a cemetery for twenty-five cents an hour. Then in winter he went to the bakery, cleaning out the ovens at Neumeister's Bakery. Because he was small but strong, he was able to crawl into the bread-mixer machine and clean it every night. It made him invaluable to them and I think he earned a bit more money," he said laughingly.

During the summer of 1944, Neil filled his spare time with odd jobs, to earn money for space magazines and models, and later to take flying lessons. He was a substitute paper boy for the *Wapakoneta Daily News* and worked in Clara Wahrer's grocery store. The longest stretch of employment was as a stockboy at Rhine and Brading's Drug Store on Main Street in Wapakoneta, where he stocked the shelves and swept the floor for forty cents an hour.

Owner Richard Brading remembered Neil as an excellent employee. "He was conscientious and hardworking, never wasted his time reading comic books. But he would jump at the flying magazines when they came in."

Brading's son Charles, who was five years younger than Armstrong, tried to befriend him, but found him too "inward," though Neil wasn't above teasing the younger boy. "I was a Cincinnati Reds fan and he would call them the 'Cincy Bloomer Girls' just to make me mad."

By that time the world war was raging, Allied troops in Europe were marching toward the Rhine and battling island-to-island in the Pacific. The country's factories hummed around the clock to produce war matériel, and despite a tangible sense of national anguish, people had money to spend for the first time in a long while. There was little to spend it on with most everything rationed, so Neil didn't have to help support the family. Instead, the money went to save up for nine-dollar-an-hour flying lessons, or for the science experiments he was always working on.

One of the inventive lad's more daring experiments was a wind tunnel that he built in the basement of the Armstrong house on West Benton Street. Started as a miniature wind tunnel for a senior physics class, the project grew a bit outsized for the family cellar to contain. It is a subject still talked about in Wapakoneta. He had read that wind tunnels were vital to aeronautical engineers designing planes, so he felt he had to have one.

Dean Armstrong recalled, "We got parts, like old stovepipes, from a junkyard and bought other parts, like an electric motor, a rheostat, and an old airplane propeller. The thing developed tremendous force, and we kept blowing fuses. After we got it rigged up pretty well, Neil sent me upstairs to invite Mom down to see it. Dad was away at the time. The opening of the wind tunnel was aimed at the basement stairway. I didn't know what Neil had in mind, but when Mom reached the bottom step, Neil turned on the switch and the blast blew her housecoat off and blew out the basement window. He thought that was the funniest thing he'd ever done—but Mother didn't."

Shortly afterward, Neil timidly told his parents he had been working on a project he hadn't mentioned to them. Exchanging concerned glances, Viola put her hand on Stephen's shoulder bracing for what was coming from their son, who always turned slightly pixie-faced when called to the carpet about his experiments.

Teacher John Crites said: "Neil had bought a wrecked Navy plane that was war surplus and put it together from the original specs. He did a remarkable job. By the time he told his parents, the thing was about ready to fly."

Even the unflappable Armstrongs grew agitated over the thought of their boy actually flying the remnants of some detritus he had salvaged from a wartime crash and jury-rigged. Stephen put his foot down and forbade any attempt to restore the plane's engine to working order.

Other less extravagant experiments included a tiny working steam turbine, crystal radios, and even a photo-electric cell that converted light into electricity.

"The flying lessons were most important to us," recalled Schwere. "Both Neil and I saved every penny we could for those lessons. It wasn't just Neil who was crazy about flying; most of the boys in town were. A local company called Aeronco started manufacturing a light little plane they called the Champion with a sixty-five-horsepower engine, which sold for $2,200.00. Neil was about fifteen years old and too young to drive, so he pedaled his bike out the Old Brewery Road to Port Koneta airport, which had two Champions available for lessons. The Aeronco company and old Aubrey Knudegard, who ran the flying school, gambled that many of the men coming home from the war who had learned to fly would be dying to get in the cockpit of an affordable plane like the Champion. But 'dying' turned out to be the key word. So many of them had come close to dying in the war they wanted no part of it. Aeronco lost the gamble on the returning vets, so they worked to convince us younger guys we should fly.

"Port Koneta hardly merited the word 'airport.' It was a complete podunk of a place. They planted rye seed all over the area to break up the hard ground, so when you taxied down the so-called runway the prop would chop up grass and send it flying back onto the windshield. It was also a challenging place to fly into. You had to land from southwest to northeast into some very hard winds in the wintertime. And, unfortunately, Champions were designed in a way that forced the pilot to cut power almost completely on approach. It was a controlled stall, like landing a glider. Once you mastered landing at Port Koneta, you could land anyplace."

Neil was a natural from the start, quickly mastering the difficult little plane and the unforgiving airfield, soon soloing with ease. He was getting the early training that would prepare him for aircraft-carrier landings and other, greater challenges only he and a handful of other visionaries dared imagine in 1945. But another nascent young aviator was not as skillful or lucky.

Schwere recalled: "Neil was an avid Boy Scout, loved camping out and hiking, in part because his dad was a scout leader and had encouraged it from the time he was a small boy. On one hike near Port Koneta, we saw one of the two instructional planes coming in fast and low for a landing. Everybody looked up in horror, knowing the plane was far too low for safety. The landing gear caught an electric wire, causing the plane to pitch forward and head at a steep angle for the ground. The pilot made a last desperate effort to pull the nose up, but couldn't get the power up for a climb in the few seconds that remained. The little Champion plane slammed into the hard earth with a sickening crunch. Everyone but Neil stood dumbstruck and immobile; he sprinted toward the crash and struggled to free the canopy.

"I remember wondering at that moment if the plane was going to explode in flames, as always seems to happen in movies, and kill Neil. But he managed to get the instructor, who had been in the rear seat, out and on his feet. Incredibly, he appeared to be unharmed. But the instructor had pitched forward into the student sitting in the front seat, who was mortally injured. Neil gently eased him out; we recognized to our horror he was Chuck Finkenbine, one of our classmates. He held the boy's shattered body in his arms, where he died a few minutes later."

It was a defining moment for Neil. He saw the terribly serious side of flying: the reason for all the safety precautions, the instruments, all the preparations, and the silent prayers many pilots muttered before climbing into the cockpit. And he must have had an awful premonition that death would be an almost daily part of life for an aviation pioneer—which was the career he desperately wanted. For the next few days he went into semiseclusion, avoiding conversation at school and going straight home to his room afterward. It was a time of deep reflection. His faith in the magic of air travel had been jarred, but in the end was strengthened. His reaction was to study twice as hard and to vow to be the best and safest flyer he possibly could be.

The seriousness with which Neil took his scouting studies left a lasting impression on his fellows. "No ordinary kid of that tender age could have consciously possessed the super-maturity to stick to his regimen and ignore the games we played in Troop 25 meeting room, but Neil often did," recalled Richard Widman, who became a staff writer for the *Cleveland Plain Dealer*. "While we were Indian arm-and-leg wrestling, working a dingbat game, and horsing around, Neil was buckling down to learning things like flag semaphore code and first aid."

According to Dean, years spent in Boy Scout Troop 25 taught Neil that he could measure up and compete. "Several times Neil and I have discussed the important part scouting played in his growing up. He was quiet and smaller than most of his classmates in high school. Scouting helped him gain confidence in himself."

It also gave the future astronaut a chance to exercise his sense of right and wrong, with a touch of humor. Former Scoutmaster Stanley Maxson recalled how Neil as senior patrol leader was inspecting troop sites at summer camp. One was immaculate—the clear winner. But just as they were about to receive their award Neil discovered they had tossed all their trash over an embankment, litering the park with trash and garbage. The award ceremony went on as scheduled, only Neil substituted a dirty dish towel for the trophy.

On the morning of August 5, 1946, Neil rose at first light, wolfed down a quick breakfast, and bid his parents and siblings good-bye. As he was running for his bike, Stephen yelled: "You know sooner or later they'll be turning that airfield back into a cornfield."

Neil smiled and pedaled his bike furiously to the Auglaize Flying Field to take the Ohio state test for his flying license. The instructors had fully expected him to be there when they arrived, and he was, giving the rule book one last quick perusal. Grading the test and putting him through the motions of showing he knew how to handle the plane were totally perfunctory. He was awarded his aviator's license and could fly before he could drive a car.

The crash and the boy's death sent shock waves reverberating through Wapakoneta. The war was over and young men were not supposed to be falling out of the sky to their deaths anymore. Several parents canceled their sons' flying lessons and forbade them to go near Port Koneta again. Some of the older residents even harkened back to a simpler prewar world where one could get away with sentiments along the lines of "if man were meant to fly . . ." But the genie was out of the bottle. The village, like the United States, would never be safe from the outside world again. Televisions had begun to rear their ugly screens. The Armstrongs had watched one in a department store in Dayton. The drone of airplane engines rent the air regularly and plans were being laid to build an interstate highway system, which would roar right by the outskirts of Wapakoneta.

Stephen and Viola, being the parents of the town's number-one flying teenager, felt the pain of Chuck Finkenbine's death keenly. They attended St. Paul's United Church of Christ with his family. Viola had served him cookies in her kitchen. But it was their ardent faith that allowed them to continue to encourage Neil's flying. In future years they would spend a great deal of time at their rather rigidly orthodox spiritual home, St. Paul's. Throughout Neil's childhood, the church had been in many ways the center of the extended Armstrong family life. Each Sunday was something of a reunion. Cousins, aunts, and uncles from all over the Auglaize Valley came to worship as well as to share gossip and news. Certainly, growing up in a large family that for many generations subscribed wholly to a stern theology emphasizing self-reliance, demureness, hard work, and total faith in the Lord's grand design was a decisive influence on young Neil, which helps to explain his inordinate tranquillity when staring into the face of death. He was probably completely honest protesting that he was neither an adventurer or a daredevil. He was simply playing the role God had assigned him. And it was beyond the pale to consider crassly cashing in on it by embracing fame or fortune.

Neil's faith in technology, in addition to his faith in God, gave him the strength and will to conquer space. With his parents it was pure, unadulterated trust in the Lord. In a sense, it was the same kind of faith that had brought their ancestral families across the sea and into a wilderness inhabited by often hostile aboriginal peoples with whom they would inevitably clash, beasts of the forests and fields unlike any they had previously known, and all manner of other challenges.

Manifest destiny played a role in his ancestors' restless searching, and in his as well. It was that unique American faith that made Viola and Stephen allow, and even encourage, their first-born to pursue the next frontier and to begin the quest at such a tender age.

In spring of 1947, at the age of sixteen, Armstrong was poised to graduate from Blume High School in Wapakoneta. If the teachers had had their way, he would have graduated at fifteen. But Stephen Armstrong, who had been uncomfortable with his boy being pushed so far, so fast, put his foot down. By some accounts the teachers were correct in assessing him too bright for the school. The fact was he constantly stumped them with his questions, an embarrassment they were only too pleased to end by passing him along to the next batch of teachers.

But in their zeal to push the obviously bright boy along, the teachers may have been doing him a disservice. Examining his report cards from the years 1943 through 1947, it's obvious he dazzled only when it came to the subjects he liked and thought germane to his goals. His algebra, plane geometry, and physics grades were consistently "E" for excellent, in the grading of the day. While in his first year of high school, however, his English achievement was rated only "Average" or "Good," and at drawing, which he studied for half the year, he earned a flat-out "F" for failure. Likewise, his Latin was only average through the first year, sinking into failing marks the next term. Perhaps his adding orchestra and glee club to band (and, of course, flying and astronomy) as extracurricular activities cut down on his time spent conjugating Latin verbs. During his very busy senior year, his English improved to "Excellent," but his lifelong refusal to be dragged into politics, like numerous fellow astronauts including John Glenn, or writing, the second career of many other astronauts, was presaged. In social studies he earned a straight "F," as he did in Typing I.

Some, like mathematics teacher Victor Blanke, were skeptical of the accolades that seemed daily heaped on the charismatic lad. "Neil was a nice boy and never caused anyone any trouble," he told the *St. Mary's News* in 1969. "He did what was expected of him, was president of his junior class, and held an office in the school band. But he was just an average student."

Yet even doubter Blanke was intrigued by the boy and sensed the cryptic quality that would inspire profilers to describe him as "astral" and "unearthly." "But I'll say for Neil that even though he didn't seem to be outstanding, he was a quiet person and no one ever knew what he was thinking."

Most were wholehearted cheerleaders, however. The 1947 Blume High School yearbook *Retrospect* paid a biblical-sounding tribute. Under Armstrong's senior class picture was the epithet: "He Thinks, He Acts, T'is Done." While no one seems to be able to remember the author, it seems unlikely to have been a student and almost certainly was the work of one of his mesmerized faculty admirers.

In addition to Armstrong's academic weaknesses, which they were somewhat painfully aware of, Stephen and Viola were uncomfortable with the baby-faced youth being in a class where all the students were a head taller and far more socially sophisticated. Neil knew more math and science than his fellows and "made us look like farmboys" according to one classmate, though he had yet to go on a date and probably knew next to nothing about sex.

Classmate Schwere recalled: "Neil wasn't a guy to run and play. While we were running around roughhousing he was usually up in the lab, doing experiments. He had a good, wry sense of humor that set him apart to begin with because high school boys don't generally traffic in subtlety and nuance when it comes to humor. But he simply wasn't a socially minded boy. To my knowledge he never dated any girls at all, first because he was too busy, second because all the girls in our class were older and taller. He was totally marching to his own music. Neil was a boy with his own agenda."

In addition to being slow to grow to his full five feet eleven inches, Neil was afflicted with the genetic anomaly of having a "baby" brother who sprouted and nearly grew taller than him. "Neil wasn't tall until he was about eighteen and went into the Navy," says Dean. "But I grew up fast." The two had a close, affectionate relationship, but Dean strained to get a rise out of his unflappable sibling with practical jokes that sometimes bordered on the coarse. One memorably gross hoax at Scout camp involved a package of chewing tobacco meant as a present for Neil's dad, Stephen. One of the boys filched a few plugs of the tobacco, hollowed out a chocolate bar, filled it with tobacco, and smoothed it over. Neil accepted the candy bar and ate it without a trace of a grimace. "Neil's like that," Dean says, "He's a guy that has great self-control. I delighted in playing jokes on him. I'm a bit more ornery than he is. But even when I'd 'get' him, he'd infuriate me because he wouldn't react."

Armstrong would never in his young life be mistaken for the life of the party. In fact, through his life he was seen as stiff and boring by people who couldn't or wouldn't penetrate his Midwestern reserve. Though during the NASA years when he was forced to socialize a great deal with fellow astronauts as well as outsiders, Neil and his first wife, Janet Elizabeth, would sometimes break the ice playing piano duets, much as he had learned to do with his mother. The one attempt in his life to wear a silly hat and allow himself to be laughed at was in his junior year in high school, when he played "Bunny Hatter" in *The Mad Hatters,* which concerned the loss of Grandma Hatter's false teeth when she makes a parachute jump.

"Everybody was surprised Neil signed on for such a silly show," said Don Frame, who co-starred. "Maybe it was all the pretty girls in the play. I don't think he realized how good-looking girls thought he was until doing that show. He had quite an effect on them. But he wasn't much as an actor. The director had to get on him all the time about learning his lines. At rehearsal he flubbed them all the time and made everybody laugh. On the day of the play he had them down, but that was the last time he did anything that silly."

But he was more than capable of tweaking pompous adults with pranks. Unaccountably, while marching in the high school band, the usually button-down Armstrong would turn his cap around and march backward, driving the band director to distraction. Pressed to get involved in some other extracurricular activity, and threatened with the concept that he wouldn't get into a good college and become a pilot without it, Neil joined the Junior Hi-Y, a Christian-service group affiliated with the YMCA and dedicated to "clean living, clean speech, clean scholarship and clean sportsmanship." With America and Ohio as prosperous as they had ever been, the natural place for charity was abroad. It didn't take many *You Are There* newsreels at the Wapa Theater to convince the Hi-Y boys and girls that European refugees were the issue. The term "refugee" had been invented just the year before to describe the forlorn masses, numbering well into the millions, who had fled advancing (and retreating) armies. Europe was a vast wasteland; the water was poisoned, raw sewage backed up into the streets, roads were impassable, electricity was nonexistent. The doelike eyes of starving children stared pleadingly from the big screen as Wapakoneta kids munched buttered popcorn and tentatively groped one another in the dark. Energized by their good cause, Neil and his schoolmates went door to door carrying sacks, begging old clothes, and looking a bit like cornfed refugees themselves.

As the year wore on, many of the Blume High Class of '47 worried more about what college they would be attending than the fate of Europe. Wapakoneta had been thrust into a new age by a combination of communications technology, the social turmoil caused by global war, and the decline of the small farm. Never again would a graduating class send the majority of its students back to the fields. There were places to go and things to do in the great world beyond the corn rows.

There never was a doubt in Neil's mind that he was going to go to a top-flight college with a good aeronautics department. His parents shared the sentiment, but were faced with a dilemma. With three children and a modest government salary, they had never been able to set any money aside. American universities in 1947 were filled to the brim with World War II veterans on the G.I. Bill. The very nature of American society was being transformed. Middle- and lower-class Americans who prior to the war wouldn't even have considered college a possibility were streaming through the ivy-covered gates by the thousand and tens of thousand. Of course elitists at the great universities were appalled; the University of Chicago's Robert Maynard Hutchins claimed the hallowed halls were being turned into "hobo jungles." The war had changed everything and there was simply no turning back.

For a boy turning seventeen in 1947, the new academic landscape posed a dilemma. Even a near-genius with a strong scientific bent would face daunting odds getting into a good technically oriented university program, needing nearly a full scholarship. Science and technology universities like Purdue and the Massachusetts Institute of Technology, the two at the top of Armstrong's list, were particularly inclined to accept veterans with experience rather than teenagers fresh out of high school. West Point and the Naval Academy were likely not a consideration given his less-than-stellar grades in subjects other than the sciences.

Neil bided his time over the summer of '47, working odd jobs at the Port Koneta Airfield; cleaning engines, honing his flying skills, taking advanced lessons when he could afford the nine dollars, occasionally doing work for the instructors in direct exchange for lessons. Though he didn't share it with his parents or friends, Neil had gotten information on the Navy's V-12 program, which would provide a student with a four-year college education in exchange for an obligation to serve four years of active duty. The only solution was to promise to become a veteran in exchange for an education. It was, in effect, a reverse G.I. Bill.

The decision was obvious as far as Neil was concerned. He was reading, with bated breath, accounts of Chuck Yeager's planned flight in an experimental X-1 rocket plane to break the sound barrier, a feat some serious scientists regarded as impossible or even having potentially cataclysmic consequences for humankind, somehow unlocking a door man was not meant to open. Neil, like the bombastic Yeager, wanted all the doors to aviation hurled open. He was thrilled that Yeager's bold flight would prove beyond a doubt the so-called sound "barrier," which would have made it impossible to fly much faster than six hundred miles per hour and rendered man a prisoner of planet earth, was in fact most likely a paper obstruction. "Breaking" it would simply cause a loud boom and have no other consequences. Supersonic speeds necessary to rend the gummy bonds of earth would indeed be possible. The following October, Yeager bet his life on it and proved the theory correct.

Energized with news of the planned breakthrough, which would probably be the most momentous since the first flight of Orville Wright (then living just sixty miles away in Dayton, in the last year of his life), Neil drove north to Lima and joined the U.S. Navy. Viola Armstrong had always been supportive of Neil's precocity, even tolerating the occasional temblors caused by his basement laboratory and accepting the fact he was going to be a flyer. But news that her eldest, fair-haired boy was going to be an airborne warrior, training to be fodder in the seemingly inevitable clash with Communism, would not go down at all well. Neil had come of age living through the horror of World War II. The *Wapakoneta News* almost daily listed the village's dead sons. He had seen the weeping mothers bearing the sorrow of loss. Several of his kith and kin were among the one million casualties the United States suffered. The men who weren't coming home were very real to him.

A few months after Neil's graduation from Blume High School, the grim harvest of war began to be sown. On the first two days during which American dead were returned home from Europe and the Pacific, a staggering total of 9,276 soldiers were handed over to bereaved loved ones for burial. And though America was the victor of the costliest war in the history of man and the colossus astride Europe and Asia, Communism was the new hydra menacing the battle-weary world. The Red Army, still advancing in lockstep despite the price it had paid for victory, was literally on the march in Eastern Europe in 1947, adding Romania to its list of imprisoned "satellites." In Berlin, just two years before the seat of the evil Nazi empire and scene of carnage unprecedented, Soviet and Allied tanks stood muzzle-to-muzzle across a narrow no-man's-land. Blazing with revolutionary fervor and imbued with precious little concern for human life, guerilla leader nonpareil Mao Tse-tung was poised to gain control of the hearts and minds of almost a billion Chinese. Westerners peppered their conversations with words like "yellow peril" with palpable fear and revulsion. Most famously and ominously, Winston Churchill, in a Fulton, Missouri, speech, had warned America the year before: "From Stettin in the Baltic to Trieste in the Adriatic an Iron Curtain has descended across the continent." In Hollywood the House Committee on Un-American Activities took over the ballroom of a downtown hotel and issued subpoenas to dozens of movie stars, directors, and writers, promising to expose "a hotbed of Communism." The dramatic hearings, later dubbed "witch-hunts" by some, were held to root out disloyal, pro-Soviet actors and writers. In the end, ten who refused to answer questions about their political activities were "blacklisted," becoming martyrs for the cause of free speech and political expression.

So pervasive was the sense of peril in the world's mightiest nation that President Truman abruptly announced any "return to normalcy" following the convulsions of World War II was impossible. Instead, he announced terms of the strongly anti-Communist "Truman Doctrine," which would define foreign policy for four decades leading to the Korean War, Vietnam, and a hundred minor skirmishes—but would ultimately help destroy the Soviet empire.

Almost simultaneously, the National Security Act was passed by Congress, creating the Central Intelligence Agency, empowered to carry out its own secret foreign policy, overthrowing or "destabilizing" regimes in the then-new language of bureaucratic spook-speak. The CIA would quickly become emblematic of means-justify-ends Cold War tactics, deposing or sometimes ineptly trying to oust regimes from Iran to Cuba to Vietnam. Though for every overtly imperialistic, ham-fisted act the American espionage community committed, their counterparts in the Soviet KGB could be said accurately to have carried out ten. After the fall of the Soviets, with the release to scholars of formerly top-secret documents, it could be seen that Soviet intentions were sufficiently wicked to make some of our worst national paranoia seem absolutely tepid and constrained. They lived up to the Boris-and-Nastasha cartoon image more often than not.

The Armstrong family had long been involved in politics in one fashion or another, and dinner conversation often revolved around the issues of the day. The danger of more war and even thermonuclear war was often discussed and fretted over by Stephen with visiting kin from his and his wife's very large clan in the Wapakoneta area. Indeed, the "duck and cover" days were just a few years off. There seemed no respite following the great conflagration. Two of the most popular and discussed books of the year were W. H. Auden's *The Age of Anxiety* and *The Cold War* by Walter Lippmann.

Certainly in the American heartland, in towns like Wapakoneta, which had offered more than their share of strapping farm boys to prosecute the war, there was no taste for more fighting in Europe or anywhere else in the world. Yet there was a certainty that a nuclear Pandora's box had been loosed by the country reluctantly taking up the mantle of the free world's leader.

One of the most heartfelt prayers in Wapakoneta and all over the country was that another generation of boys would not be killed, crippled, and mutilated in another insane orgy of violence. Yet the Russian Bear, despite suffering probably twenty-five million or more dead, seemed to have developed a singular taste for mass suffering. Already orchestrating the next movement was mad "Uncle Joe" Stalin.

In the fall of 1947, when Neil strolled into his mother's kitchen, where she was putting up fruit and cooking his favorite apple dumpling dessert, the world and its horrors seemed as distant as it had when he was a toddler pulling on her apron strings.

Seemingly overnight, as far as Viola was concerned, Neil had turned into a man. He had filled out with broad shoulders and grown as tall as his dad, just shy of six feet. But more than his physical good looks, which everyone noticed, was the way he carried himself. He walked like a man with a mission. His sparkling blue eyes seemed focused out in midfield, slightly beyond the subject at hand. Yet he was grounded very much in reality and was more than willing to take life one step at a time, the slow, difficult, old-fashioned way. He had learned a great deal from time spent on his grandfather Will's farm in St. Mary's. He had seen the exhausting work and long hours it took to run even a small farm intended to do little more than supply fresh food for the family. And he had learned the risks of farming—how easy it was to work all season and get wiped out by a fluke of the weather in a half-hour's time.

All in all she was confident they had raised their eldest boy right and felt sure he would make his way in the world, if only his love of flying didn't somehow get him into a fighting war with the Russians or the Chinese or any of the rest of those sword-rattlers. The minute Neil walked into the room, sat at the kitchen table, and eagerly dug into a plate of hot apple dumplings, she knew something was on his mind. Her mother's intuition told her so, but she couldn't quite read him. As a young boy, he had been able to put up a shield blocking anyone from peering into his soul. Stephen more than once laughed that he would have made a good poker player, though he was far too Christian and sensible to ever gamble for money. "I was never one to pester my children," said Viola. "I knew that he was agonizing over what to do about college and would get around to discussing it with us in good time.

"I was racing around the kitchen, working frantically because I didn't want to be late for a Women's Guild meeting, and had a lot of fruit to jar. Neil just sat there in silent thought. I assumed he was going to lay out the different options he had and we would discuss them.

"Instead, he stood up, looked me right in the eye, and said, 'Mom, I've joined the Navy, and I'm going to be a fighter pilot.'"

"Well, this was our worst fear. It wasn't that we didn't want him to serve our country. It was just that there had been so much sacrifice from our family in the last war. I was so startled I completely forgot about the large jar filled with peaches I had in my hands. It crashed to the floor, landing smack-dab on my big toe, and exploded all over the room. Oh, the pain was terrible. I screeched and I guess kind of did a little dance, it hurt so I didn't know what else to do. Neil was standing there with his mouth open. What a sight I must have been, hopping up and down in a pile of peach jam, covered from head to toe. He tried to comfort me and slid in the jam. When Dad came into the kitchen, he didn't know quite what to do. He was just standing there with his newspaper in hand, unable to believe what his eyes were seeing.

"My foot hurt like crazy, but the real pain was in my heart." The thought of Neil coming home in a flag-draped coffin, or missing a leg like so many of the boys from World War II, was more than she could bear. "Finally we got possession of ourselves, and Dad and Neil took me to the doctor."

The moment of the pivotal declaration, punctuated by Viola's broken toe, would be remembered forever by the Armstrong family.

Chapter Three

In 1947, as America grappled with its unfamiliar perch as leader of the free world, standing toe-to-toe with the Soviet Union in a cold war that would shortly turn hot in Korea, Neil Armstrong won a competitive Navy scholarship to attend Purdue University and study aeronautics.

M.I.T. had been at the top of his list, but he was convinced by his teachers and parents that Purdue, in relatively nearby Lafayette, Indiana, had an excellent reputation for aeronautics—indeed, it would one day boast of being the alma mater of astronauts, with sixteen graduate spacemen—more than any college save the U.S. Naval Academy. Plus, the Armstrongs weren't crazy about the idea of Neil going off to far-away New England to study.

In early September, Mom, Dad, June, and Dean drove Neil to Purdue, bouncing down country roads through western Ohio's endless cornfields and into northern Indiana's farm country, a 150-mile journey that took almost an entire day. Neil gamely struggled against the familiar nausea the rough ride caused. Most highways were barely paved macadam, loose gravel, or not paved at all. Car travel through the American heartland in those years was simply a wretched ordeal, a conclusion Dwight Eisenhower as a young captain before World War II made while commanding a cross-country convoy. Ike vowed to do something about it, and followed up as president, creating the biggest peacetime public-works project ever, the Interstate Highway System.

The Armstrongs found Layfayette and the Purdue campus bumper-to-bumper, the sidewalks bustling with students carrying their belongings like refugees, thousands of students all trying to find their way around. The school was so crammed with G.I. Bill students that Neil was unable to secure a dorm room, a source of consternation for Viola. Dean and dad Stephen helped move Neil's steamer trunk, books, a few model airplanes, and other essentials into a tiny apartment in West Layfayette that the university's housing office had apologetically lined up, which would be home for the following three semesters. Neil strutted off heady and triumphant at suddenly being so much and so suddenly on his own, while Viola tearfully said goodbye to her boy. She looked forlornly at the blond teenager, far from convinced he was old enough to be on his own far from home.

At first it was daunting, particularly to small-town boys like Neil, who had never before had to learn their way around a complex academic bureaucracy, with no familiar faces to turn to. But just when it seemed he was lost in a labyrinth, Neil happened upon an old friend from scouting and junior high days, when the Armstrongs lived in Upper Sandusky, north of Cincinnati.

A lifetime later, John Blackford recalled: "Purdue was a giant school and we were lost. It was a very confusing time for Neil and I. Three quarters of the students were returning veterans from World War II that we looked at in awe.

"Probably the only reason we found each other was the happenstance of the alphabet. We were placed in the same mechanical drawing and chemistry classes, and in one of those we spotted each other across the crowded room. I barely recognized him because we hadn't seen each other in several years, since ninth grade. But it was a great relief to see a familiar face. We promised each other we would renew our friendship and spend a great deal of time together. Unfortunately, with Neil's naval training and band, he didn't have a lot of free time."

Blackford was one of the "lucky" ones able to get dormitory space. "I spent my first semester in the attic of a dorm with about fifty other students."

The campus life Neil was about to experience was light years from the co-ed dorms, anything-goes environment future generations found. Dorm mothers supervised the comings and goings of their charges, enforcing lights-out, locking the doors after 10:00 at night, and writing letters to parents of miscreants.

When a boy pinned a girl, meaning they were going steady, the boy's fraternity brothers came to her sorority, serenaded her with songs of love, and gently ribbed the couple about their "almost" engaged status. Social life was to a large degree centered around the sororities and fraternities. Each fraternity had a sister sorority with which it regularly arranged dances, charity drives, and other sanctioned activities. The result was a great deal of dating, romance, and eventual marriage between members of the affiliated Greek societies. Decades later, Armstrong and his first wife, Jan, were still friends with numerous other couples who had met and married at those socials.

The transition from quiet, mannerly Wapakoneta to the bustling Purdue campus, which was bursting at the seams with war veterans, was a trauma. At least a year younger than his contemporaries, having skipped a grade, Neil was ages younger than the many World War II veterans. For the most part he kept focused on academics, at which he excelled, particularly math, science, and anything related to aeronautics. But conversations with friends a few years later paint a picture of a shy, sensitive boy fairly far out of his depth socially, and struggling to survive day-to-day.

Always an early riser, Neil happily took a job delivering the *Lafayette Courier Journal* newspaper around the still campus during the early mornings to earn extra money. Other than milkmen, who were still common in the late 1940s, few trod in his wake—an added bonus. He kept the job, for reasons even his best friends couldn't quite fathom, even after returning from Korea, a decorated war hero and a grown man. It was the fraction of the day when the bustling campus was almost as quiet as Grandpa Willis's farm on St. Mary's River after the working day was over.

In renewing his friendship with John Blackford, naturally the topic of scouting in which they had formed their initial bond back in Upper Sandusky came up. He was surprised, and jealous, that Bud had reached Eagle Scout, the highest rank, while Neil had attained only Star Scout level. The idea that his friend had set a goal, stuck with it, and attained the ultimate prize while he had not, stung. There was no question but that his failure would have to be remedied.

Despite suffering some teasing for continuing with scouting while a grown-up college man, and a naval officer trainee, he determined to finish the job he had started.

As busy as Armstrong was, learning to drill, keeping navy cadet shoes spit-shined, studying seamanship, and taking small-weapons instructions, plus all the regular academics, and band practice, he managed to make time to achieve Eagle Scout level. At the end of the year he had earned twenty-six merit badges, five more than required, including Scholarship, Aviation, Pathfinding, and Pioneering.

Bud Blackford and Neil played baritone horn in the varsity band and renewed their friendship, learning their way around the campus together and gathering a small circle of friends. Armstrong also marched with the Purdue Military Band on the football field, playing the sousaphone, a small tuba with a bell. During one halftime presentation, dressed in full military regalia with tasseled hats, the band formed in the shape of a woman, using long bands of paper stretched out to form a skirt. "The band portrays how women have engulfed Purdue," read a *Debris* yearbook caption; a post–World War II phenomenon then beginning to be reckoned with.

It took no time to conclude Purdue had been the right choice for a boy who wanted more than anything to be a flyer. The aeronautics school and its proud alumni list of distinguished pilots in both military and civilian life was convincing. The future astronaut signed on as a member of the American Rocket Society, one of a group of scholarly organizations that originally formed in Germany, Austria, the Soviet Union, Great Britain, and the United States between 1927 and '33 to provide a forum for scientists to share research, conduct experiments, and publish journals. But for eager undergraduates at Purdue, the society was a club where like-minded young men could gather and discuss the bright, shining future they envisioned, for themselves and their nation, in space.

Neil later boasted that the rocket society was the only organization that was making plans to go to the moon, which in 1947 struck a few as visionary, most as loony.

He also joined the Aero Club, a group of young men who shared his passion for flight, and, eventually, after returning from Korea, became club president. The group was interested in everything about aviation, and carried the airplane modeling he had loved since childhood to new dimensions.

During balmy weather there were great open areas around the campus to fly model airplanes, but on frosty winter mornings, sometimes as early as 3:00 A.M., Neil and his comrades would slip into the old fieldhouse and thrill as their latest creations soared across the immense, still auditorium.

As Armstrong completed his third college semester during the fall of 1948, the world was rapidly becoming a very dangerous place. For the first time in history, two enemies with the power to literally destroy the world were facing each other down at a dozen potential flashpoints. For over six months the Soviets had been blocking all supplies, including food, medicine, and even water from traveling through their sector of eastern Germany and reaching isolated West Berlin. Soviet and Allied tanks were facing one another muzzle-to-muzzle at the border, where the infamous Berlin Wall would soon be erected. Refusing to abandon the city, British and American planes made trips in and out every three minutes, twenty-four hours a day. When the siege was finally over after 318 days, one and a half million tons of supplies had been delivered. While the West chalked up a hard-won victory in Germany, democracy suffered a defeat in Czechoslovakia, where the duly elected government of President Eduard Beneš was brutally replaced by that of Klement Gottwald, a Stalinist puppet, completing the Communist consolidation of Eastern Europe.

But at home, Americans were settling into peace and prosperity, storing the tragedy and bitter taste of the dark war years in the attic with mothballed uniforms that would never again accommodate their flourishing bellies.

America was in the midst of the greatest economic boom in its history, and the social landscape was changing more rapidly than it ever had before. It was becoming a suburban nation, as Levittown-style developments sprouted everywhere. Milton Berle was the biggest star of the medium that would make him Mr. Television, and Alfred Kinsey fired the first shot of the sexual revolution with the publication of the first of his *Sexual Behavior* books, revealing Americans cheated, masturbated, and were homosexual in shockingly high numbers for a society that liked to think of itself as prudish.

There was no eagerness for leaving it all behind and getting back in uniform, or for passing the saber to another generation, to fight and die in Korea, a country most Americans couldn't point to on a map, or Germany, where plenty of American blood had already been spilled just three years prior. But at Purdue and campuses all over the country there was, inevitably, nervous talk of the possibility of the Cold War turning hot.

Neil Armstrong was intensely interested; he was bound to be in harm's way if war broke out, and he had to have been simultaneously thrilled at the prospect of being part of the action and horrified at the thought of being caught in what would be a bloody, vicious maelstrom, into which the Chinese would hurl countless numbers of troops (he later reflected on his Korean experience with sheer horror), and where there would be the constant specter of nuclear war if the situation escalated out of control.

In any event, the United States was ill-prepared for any major conflict. The army that had numbered twelve million in World War II could barely muster one million of all rates. Equipment hadn't been updated since the end of the war, and in fact arms such as antitank weapons, which had failed miserably against the German panzers, were still stockpiled for use in the next armored conflict.

But Armstrong was training hard to be a fighter pilot and knew that wherever the shooting started air power was going to be a very important part of the strategic mix, and would give him the chance to learn how to fly jet fighters off the deck of an aircraft carrier under extreme conditions.

Chapter Four

Early in January 1949, as Neil was about to settle into a fourth semester at Purdue, the summons came from the Navy Department. He was to report for active duty on February 16, to be transferred to the Naval Air Station in Pensacola, Florida, for intensive training over a period of a year and a half to fly aircraft carrier–based fighter planes. Despite the coming danger, it was a dream come true for a nineteen-year-old boy who lived to fly.

Pensacola, Florida, at the western tip of the panhandle on the Gulf Coast, was a shock to the system for Midwestern farm boys. Bars were open-air affairs, where people sat on stools practically on the sidewalk, not dark, discreet places, hidden from sight, like back home. Country music spilled out onto the street. The air was sometimes spiked with the caustic smell of oil "cracking" when the wind blew from nearby refineries.

In Pensacola, Neil and other Midwestern boys would see so-called "racial restrictions" in force for the first time, and several would be reprimanded for sitting in the black section of city buses.

The plethora of Confederate battle flags on bumper stickers, fluttering over stores, houses, and even public buildings was a surprise. "It was pure culture shock for us, a lot to get accustomed to," recalls Kansan Robert Kaps, who arrived in Pensacola with Neil. "The first thing we learned off the train was how quick Southerners were to refight the Civil War. I remember writing a letter home about that. Neither of us had much been out of our home states, so it was all new to us."

But once safely inside the Pensacola Naval Air Station, where most every object had its name stenciled on and the streets were as orderly, shipshape, and unreal as the set of a movie studio, things seemed more comfortable. The smells there were of jet fuel and disinfectant; the sounds—the indignant reports of jet engines and the squeal of rubber tires on hot tarmac—pure excitement.

The men's quarters were in squat redbrick buildings, shoehorned into small rooms accommodating six young men. "It was like being on a ship, we got pretty well acquainted, and formed quite a camaraderie," says Kaps.

About one hundred men arrived to form classes of twenty for preflight training on February 15, 1949. They were issued khaki work clothes, books, and slide rules right away, and put to work learning to fly a new generation of planes, including jets that would with luck be ready for the next conflict, wherever it might break out.

"The first six or eight weeks, we weren't allowed off the base at all because we didn't have our dress uniforms yet, so there was little to do but hit the books and get going," said Robert Kaps. Even after uniforms were issued, the young cadets were restricted to weekend leave. But they made the most of it, visiting the rowdy bars of Pensacola, catching movies like *On the Town* with Frank Sinatra and Gene Kelly, and Orson Welles's Cold War spy thriller *The Third Man*. They congregated in city parks, spent as much time as possible on the beach, swimming in the tepid Gulf waters. "Neil always liked to paddle way out until he was just a spot on the horizon," recalled Kaps. And the future airmen flirted with the local girls, dated them, and, in a few cases, eventually married them.

After sixteen weeks, Kaps and Armstrong passed their preflight training exams, were graduated and sent on to basic, and then advanced, flight training, which took another eight months. Theory was then put to practice aboard the aircraft carrier U.S.S. *Wright,* where the two men were eventually certified combat-capable, and deemed able to accomplish two of the hardest, most dangerous tasks in aviation: landing on and taking off from an aircraft carrier heaving and pitching in the open ocean, at night and in stormy seas.

Proudly wearing their shiny new wings of gold, the emblem of a Navy fighter pilot, the pair drove Kaps's car on the long journey across the Gulf Coast, through New Orleans, taking in exotic Bourbon Street and the French Quarter for the first time in their lives. They passed through Houston, where Armstrong would spend an important chunk of his life, and arrived at Corpus Christi, another oil-refining coastal town, for advanced training in fighter aircraft.

Following a hard year of intense instruction, Kaps and Armstrong were both given the reward they had fervently wished for and worked for: selection to the elite corp that would pilot the new F-9 Panther jets—and membership in only the second carrier-based jet squadron to deploy. Electrified, they returned to Pensacola for their first shot at the future of aviation.

The Navy's first jet trainer was called the TO-1 Shooting Star, which, compared to the World War II–era propeller craft they replaced, was "analogous to climbing out of a Model T Ford into a '95 Cadillac with the NorthStar system," according to John Moore, who was Armstrong's first jet instructor (Moore got the job because he was the only pilot in the Navy training command at Pensacola who had ever flown a jet). The trouble with the Shooting Star was that it was a single-seated plane, meaning trainees had to solo on their first jet flight, a daunting assignment. It would be nearly a year before the Shooting Star was replaced by the "great" T-33 two-seater jet, which would train a generation of flyers.

The TO-1 was far from a perfect craft, but nevertheless a pleasure and a thrill to fly for the men. The take-off was quiet and smooth, though the craft was worrisomely sluggish until well airborne. Another concern was how small the trainer's tanks were, and how rapidly it burned fuel. The upside was, it forced young fighter pilots to quickly learn "cruise control," meaning keeping a constant, accurate accounting of fuel use and supply remaining. Once the TO-1 was at cruising altitude, it had power to spare, inducing some of the young aces, including Lt. Donald Engen—later an admiral and Deputy Commander of the U.S. Atlantic Fleet—to briefly disappear for some fun in the clouds once in a while.

"Although we had little unsupervised flight, on occasion I sneaked time to fly in the brilliant white cloud mountains and valleys that developed. The airplane was a dream in which to perform acrobatics. The increased thrust with speed in the TO-1 seemed staggering and provided power in a way that I never before thought possible. I felt free!"

Training lasted just thirty days, including ground school and thirty hours of flight time. But there could be no dual instruction, practicing "touch-and-goes with an instructor yelling obscenities from a rear cockpit." Incredibly, Moore says that in two and a half years, teaching a class of twenty students every thirty days, there was not a single mishap, despite some foolish mistakes by green flyers.

Next stop on the way to Korea was Naval Air Station North Island at San Diego, where Armstrong and Kaps met the rest of the men who had been chosen to be among the aviation pioneers ushering in the era of carrier-based jet fighters. The twenty-nine men originally assigned to serve under Lieutenant Commander Ernest Beauchamp in fighter squadron VF-51, were—unlike in war movies—not a particularly diverse group ethnically or culturally. All the men were white, almost all were from either the South or the Midwest. There were two Catholics, Robert Kaps and Chad Cheshire, the rest from various Protestant denominations. Neil Armstrong, who had always been the quiet boy, the boy who was too inward and nearly incapable of small talk, had finally met a group of guys who saw things his way. "He was an engineer and so was I," says crewmate Bill Bowers. "We were more comfortable with technical things than general bullshit."

They would fight the enemy together, flying Panther jets off the often rolling, pitching, sometimes fog-enshrouded deck of the aircraft carrier *Essex*. And they would mourn together when their comrades died fiery deaths. The VF-51 men were bonded in war and remain like brothers a half-century later. Robert Kaps says, "The reunions are amazing. Feeling the old feelings and reliving the emotions we went through together in combat is quite incredible. As long as I can walk, I won't miss one."

Home for the unmarried midshipmen was the spartan Bachelor Officers' Quarters at North Island, drab one-story brick buildings. Across the street was Victor's bar, where the flyers gathered after work each day. For dinner, drinks, and a dance with local girls, there was the always raucous Mexican Village, which fifty years later is still a magnet for Navy flyers, and hosts the vets' reunions from time to time. Kaps, a lifelong teetotaler, who feared if he drank he might like it too much, was VF-51's designated driver. "The Mexican Village was the favorite hangout. It was quite small; always crowded, smoky and noisy. It was Neil's favorite. People who have only heard about how standoffish he is might be surprised, but he fit in really well there. He wasn't a crazy drunk, but he certainly liked his drinks. There would be singing, telling of tales, and general revelry. I didn't mind, but I spent much of my time driving guys home."

Dean Armstrong had been complaining loud and long that he had never been separated from his big brother for so long—particularly when he was doing such neat stuff—and desperately wanted to come to California. Neil missed him as well, so as soon as Dean's school was out in early June he bought a train ticket to the coast, partially with money he had saved from after-school jobs, partially subsidized by Neil and their parents.

"Neil was the youngest guy in our group and Dean was about fourteen years old," recalled Ken Danneberg, who became VF-51's intelligence officer and a lifelong friend of Armstrong. "Dean was sleeping in Neil's room in the Bachelor Officers' Quarters. One morning a senior officer came through and saw Dean, and he said, 'My God, these ensigns get younger every day.'

"We got a kick out of that. But it made Dean's day. He was a pretty tall kid, and for the rest of his stay he was just strutting around acting like a young officer. Neil never kidded him. He just let him have his fun."

For three months, long days were devoted to familiarization with the new Grumman F-9 Panther, the jet they would fly into combat in Korea. The Panther was modeled after World War II propeller-driven fighters; it was equipped with four 20mm cannons and proved very effective at strafing troop concentrations, blowing up oil depots and trucks, all while flying barely fifty feet above the ground. Men with World War II combat experience, who were making the transition to jets, like Don Engen, fretted over the Panther's flaws, particularly its excessive thirst for jet fuel, given the fact planes sometimes faced long delays getting clearance to land on aircraft carriers due to weather or heavy traffic. Worse, the plane had no ejection seat when it was first put on line in 1949, an oversight responsible for numerous deaths. Engen personally prevailed on the Navy to add a Martin Baker ejection seat, and volunteered to be guinea pig when it was first deployed. In order to blast a pilot up and safely away from a crippled jet traveling at great speed, the equivalent of a 40mm shell filled with slow-burning powder was installed under the pilot's seat. The bailing pilot pulled a curtain over his face and shoulders, then ignited the charge under his posterior. The canopy flew off, quickly followed by the pilot, who would then, it was hoped, free himself from the chair and parachute to safety. It was rudimentary and dangerous, but mostly it worked.

Unfortunately for Engen, his first land trial of the device cost him a compressed spinal disk when he pulled the escape cord too hard and apparently ignited the powerful charge much faster than required. But Engen never regretted the experiment, considering the seat, through many modifications over the years, was credited with saving the lives of more than six thousand flyers.

In June of 1951, the U.S.S. *Essex* was moored in San Diego Harbor, refurbished, World War II damages repaired, worn equipment replaced, and electronics updated. The venerable old ship was ready to carry another generation to war. VF-51 had one more stateside mission to accomplish before boarding her, a four-week gunnery and bombing training program in the California desert at Naval Air Station El Centro, a ghastly, hot patch of land just above the Mexican border.

Located nearby was the Navy's main parachute training school, a fact not lost on Neil, who was well aware of the vulnerability of the Panther and was very interested in learning how to survive an emergency bailout, an interest that proved to be prescient. VF-51's commanding officer, Lieutenant Commander Ernest Beauchamp, an easygoing career Navy man, could see the value in familiarization with parachutes and ejection seats, but shared the Navy's wary skepticism of the new gear. Neil was granted permission to go and have a look, but Beauchamp was adamant that he be careful, and not risk life and limb.

When the young midshipman—he still hadn't been elevated to ensign due to a paperwork snafu, and wouldn't be until the squadron reached Korea—returned, apparently intact, Beauchamp breathed a sigh of relief and asked him to brief the other pilots. Apt pupil that he was, Neil meticulously demonstrated parachute packing, the use of leg and shoulder harnesses, ripcord location, and the unhappy effects on the human body of being blasted out of the cockpit of a jet plane. The more detailed Neil's descriptions got, the more suspicious Commanding Officer Beauchamp became. Finally, when Armstrong was demonstrating the fancy footwork it took to land without breaking a leg or getting painfully dragged, he exploded.

"Armstrong, did you make a parachute jump when I distinctly told you to be careful?" he thundered, angrier than the men had ever seen him.

"But, sir, I *was* careful," piped Armstrong, knowing he had parsed his commander's words carefully enough to avoid being guilty of disobeying a direct order.

After cooling down, Beauchamp shook his head and told John Moore, "Isn't that kid something?"

The carrier *Essex* set sail from San Diego for Hawaii en route to the war zone at dawn on July 5, 1951, a hot, cloudless day with a stiff desert wind. Laden with 3,000 men, 399 tons of ammunition, and 157,688 gallons of aviation fuel, on top of immense quantities of supplies of all types, the immense ship lay heavy in the sea.

Armstrong and his VF-51 crewmates, plus some from VF-172, altogether twenty-five junior officers, bunked down in claustrophobically small quarters on the forward fo'c'sle deck, three levels down. The men quickly settled into a routine and were assigned jobs, aside from the primary one of being fighter pilots, that would hopefully aid morale, and perhaps even accomplish something useful. Early on the cruise, the C.O. appointed Neil education officer at his request, an assignment that often carried little or no actual responsibilities. Midshipman Armstrong, however, took it very seriously, teaching a class of thirty sailors algebra three nights a week, casually, informally bantering with the men who serviced aircraft about how planes fly off carrier decks so they would have a better understanding of their jobs, and made himself available to any seamen wishing to improve themselves. The experience clearly reinforced the love of teaching he had developed tutoring (often older) students back at Blume High in Wapakoneta.

"Neil's taking the time to teach enlisted men typifies him in my mind," says Beauchamp. "Rather than spending his time playing cards or other kinds of recreation, he spent his time helping the men learn."

Chapter Five

On June 25, 1950, the Soviet-equipped North Korean army, 100,000 strong, crashed across the 38th parallel into the Republic of South Korea, capturing the critically important port of Inchon and, three days later, the capital, Seoul. If Communism was to be stopped in Korea, the United States would have to make a massive commitment of men and treasure. Harry Truman turned to the brilliant, testy, sometimes reckless General Douglas MacArthur and charged him with commanding the United Nations forces, which consisted of contingents from sixteen nations, though the bulk of the fighting men and matériel were from the United States.

Called by its own people Choson, or "land of the morning calm," Korea was a brutally administered colony of Japan during the first half of the twentieth century. In the final days of World War II, the Soviet Union, with the assent of the United States, invaded northern Korea, accepting the surrender of Japanese troops above the 38th parallel. A month later, on September 9, 1945, the United States received the Japanese surrender south of the parallel. At that moment the country was effectively divided, and despite United Nations–administered general elections held throughout Korea, and an order recognizing the elected government as the only legitimate authority, the Soviets refused to allow U.N. officials to enter North Korea. Instead, they held elections Communist-style, with no opposition candidates to the parties' choices. On September 3, 1948, the Democratic People's Republic of Korea was announced, and a Cold War flashpoint created.

Truman, who had the last word on World War II—unleashing the nuclear genie—had his hackles up again: "By God, I'm going to let them have it," he vowed. Officially, and disingenuously, called a "police action" by spin doctors of the day, the conflict would drag on for three years and one month, from the North Korean invasion to armistice on July 27, 1953, and cause four million casualties. MacArthur's brilliant military career became a casualty as well, when an army of more than one million Chinese drove his forces to a disorderly retreat nearly into the sea. The old general's reaction, which came to be fairly universally discerned as reckless, was to argue for an invasion of China and the introduction of at least tactical nuclear weapons.

When the U.S.S. *Essex* steamed into the Sea of Japan and took a position about forty miles off the coast, the flyers were ready to do battle in the sky with Russian-made MiGs, as they had trained to do back in California, flying months of intercept missions against Air Force attack airplanes. But Neil and his crewmates were informed there were virtually no MiGs operating within range of the fighters aboard the carrier. In a sense that was good news, but the job in lieu of aerial combat with MiGs was going to prove dangerous and difficult: bombing bridges, strafing military targets, disrupting North Korean supply lines, and generally harrying the enemy.

Naval Aviation News described the mission as including "mundane chores such as chopping up railroad lines, bombing bridges and cratering roads." To fight back, the North Koreans made the most of their main resource, which was human beings, to move war matériel into place. "Whole populations of towns and villages are conscripted as human pack animals to carry all they can in one-night treks."

Using the Panther jet, at the time one of the fastest, most powerful war planes in the world, for what amounted to close-in ground support was risky and extraordinarily dangerous, particularly since Armstrong and his mates had not trained for it during their accelerated program. The charge was low-altitude warfare, flying the Panther low and slow, attempting to take out bridges, railroads, and gun emplacements, often in the face of heavy anti-aircraft fire. Casualties were certain to be heavy.

Fortunately, improvisation was to become a banner characteristic of Neil Armstrong's career—one of his strongest suits. Despite his youth and relative inexperience, he became one of the aces of the wing, flying seventy-eight successful missions under circumstances that were like nothing previously experienced by fighter pilots. He was awarded an Air Medal with two gold stars, a national defense service medal, Korean Service Medal, the Syngman Rhee Medal, and a United Nations Service Medal.

It was an outstanding record for such a young flyer, but was also extraordinary considering the then almost chaotic state of the nascent jet technology. Despite the fact that both sides in the conflict were well into the jet age, carrier technology, tactics, and thinking lagged far behind. According to the late Admiral Engen, the *Essex* and her sister ships were "strictly World War II."

There were "crewmen standing behind transparent plastic boards writing backward to show aircraft position and tactical plot for intercept officers standing in front of them." Worse, the so-called Combat Information Center, or CIC, had little training and even less understanding of the jets. "CIC poorly understood the specs, turning radii, and altitude capabilities of jet airplanes. Some controllers were good, but most were poor."

The result, despite dire warnings by astute pros like Engen, was unnecessary injury and death. And the failings hurt both pilots and crew. One of the most egregious examples was the unavailability of jet fuel, or JP-1 kerosene. Standard aviation fuel, which cost twice the price, twenty-two cents versus eleven cents, burned in jet engines gave off inordinate amounts of toxic lead that fouled turbine blades and spewed poisonous exhaust, creating an immediate health hazard. Fortunately, before too much harm was done Yankee ingenuity solved the problem. Sacks of walnut shells were thrown through the engine intake, which scoured both ends and largely mitigated the problem.

By late summer of 1951, the men of VF-51 and the other squadrons aboard the *Essex* had fallen into a pattern of launching around one hundred sorties over enemy territory each day. Well before dawn, squad commander Beauchamp briefed the pilots in the ready room on their assignments, which generally included hectoring and attempting to stop the antlike stream of transport south. The routine was periodically shattered by the death of a flyer. On August 26, a propellor-driven, single-seat AD-3 Skyraider attack plane used for extremely low flying burst into flame minutes after it was launched. Before the pilot had a chance to turn back to the carrier, the plane crashed into the sea and almost immediately sank. Pilots and crewmen watched in stunned silence as their comrade disappeared forever. But there was no time for sentiment; reports that the enemy's daylight traffic was increasing meant there was no time to waste. After a few minutes, the launches continued until ninety-four planes were sent into combat.

On September 3, the *Essex* lost its fourth pilot when Lieutenant Frank Sistrunk was hit by anti-aircraft fire while bombing a bridge. Seriously shot up and trailing smoke, Sistruck pulled away from the fight and desperately headed back to safety. Halfway home, at an altitude of just two thousand feet, the plane suddenly pitched nosedown and slammed into the ground, exploding in a ball of fire. There was no chance to bail out.

At about the same time, Neil was intently listening to Intelligence Officer Ken Danneberg brief the flyers in the ready room on weather conditions and known anti-aircraft positions. Finally Danneberg handed out maps and charts of the target areas. Topside Neil found his Panther, climbed into the cramped cockpit, began to strap in, attaching transmission and reception radio wires, slipping into his parachute, tightening shoulders belts, and pulling on three sets of gloves, first nylon, then rubber, and last thin, strong leather flyer's gloves.

Feeling a calm settle over him, a preternatural calm that drowned out extraneous thoughts and noises, making the tasks ahead and the tools at hand seem hyper-clear, he prepared to launch. *Essex* was turned into the wind, which was blowing a bit stronger than twenty knots, just enough to give the jets the sharp lift they needed. Suddenly "white flag" was barked over the radio, and the first Panther was catapulted roughly into the sky, reaching a speed of 125 knots in two seconds. Donald Engen remembered the experience as, "one hell of a rough way to wake up in the morning."

Armstrong howled off the *Essex* toward the west and the all-important Korean harbor of Wonsan. He banked hard to the left, checked instinctively to make sure no bogies were hiding in the blood-red orb above—the North Korean air force was said to be stillborn save for the rare, suicidal heckler, but it took only one—and began a low fast run with three wingmen toward the enemy's main oil refining factory, supply railhead, and transfer points. The four Panthers streaked northeast across the Sea of Japan with the sun at their back, then dipped even lower over rice paddies and agricultural land to the south, suddenly appearing out of a cloud bank, glistening silver and bristling with armaments to pound their rich target. The harbor was filled with large ships and steaming trains headed in all directions, offloading war matériel. But those targets were for the slower-moving propeller-driven workhorse ADs and F4-Us, which could shower thousand-pound bombs capable of sending the ships and their cargo to the bottom of the harbor, creating dangerous obstacles and further slowing resupply.

Adrenaline coursed through the veins of the four pilots, even as they cooly planned the attack. Neil screamed out of the sun number two of the four, strafing boxcars and enemy troops in the Wonsan freightyards—a vital target the Americans struck time and time again, only to see it miraculously rebuilt and teeming with supplies the following morning.

But the four young fighter pilots were determined to do their best, inflicting maximum possible damage. The 20mm cannon in the nose of Neil's Panther spat fire furiously, finding its marks over and over, as he made passes across the now-flaming depot. The big shells ripped into freight cars loaded with Chinese- and Soviet-made guns, rockets, and ammo meant to kill American boys, caused huge explosions that shook the earth and sent angry tongues of orange fire lapping toward spilled gasoline and fuel oil, which rent the air with thundering booms that thumped Armstrong's solar plexus, but encouraged the pilots to continue swarming around the flaming depot like angry wasps. Again and again, the Panthers made tight circles and returned, hurling 250-pound explosives on target and scattering defenders with nonstop machine-gun fire.

But as he made one last turn, flying at four hundred knots just two hundred feet above the railhead, Neil's luck ran out. A burst of black anti-aircraft fire peppered the nose of his Panther—despite the hellish attack, the North Koreans hadn't completely cut and run after all. The impact pitched Armstrong violently downward and within twenty feet of the ground. The elevator controls had been shot out, so he used the trim tabs, tiny flaps on the wings, to gain stability. But it was too late; before he could pull out, the Panther hit wires or cables and a telephone pole, shearing off two feet of starboard wing, as well as the port tip (fuel) tank. Two weeks into his twenty-first year of life, Armstrong was closer to death than to life.

From the moment Armstrong was hit, and in serious trouble, his three flight mates broke away from the battle zone and "gathered round his plane like mother hens," in John Moore's words. First, after disengaging, the fighter pilots escorted their wounded brother to the relatively safe Bay of Wonsan, where he would have at least a few moments to evaluate the seriousness of his situation. It was immediately obvious the wounded Panther was very heavy with unexpended weapons, which was going to make it difficult to reach a high enough altitude to bail out. Neil quickly jettisoned two cannons and 20mm ammunition. He flipped up the safety and released the firing switch to launch the port high-velocity air rocket (HVAR), which was adding much unwanted weight. It clicked satisfactorily into place. Nothing. Quickly he tried to fire the starboard rocket. Nothing. The twin stubby rockets, packed with enough high explosive to blow the crippled Panther to kingdom come, clung to the wings, mocking him. Apparently the arming wires had been ripped out in the collision, meaning he had two live rockets on his wings he couldn't do anything about. The acrid smell of an electric fire filled the cockpit, making his nostrils flare. Would the hopelessly fouled electrical system cause the HVARs to blow? There was no time to think of that. There was only time to think of solutions.

Working quickly but methodically, he dumped fuel from the damaged port tip tank, lessening the weight burden measurably. Struggling to bring the wings level and steady the speed at 170 knots, he started a slow but steady climb and gained a glimmer of hope, but then the engine violently bucked into a stall. Armstrong throttled up the engine again and tried to lower the flaps, which would have given some stability and helped control speed. But like most every other system on the doomed jet, they were useless. One hundred seventy knots is far too fast to land on an aircraft carrier, or anywhere, but at any lesser speed the plane would stall. A mayday plea to air traffic control elicited a crisp, matter-of-fact instruction to vector due south 170 miles to an emergency field behind United Nations lines, a destination Neil knew he would never reach.

The final, crucial failure was aileron control, the movable back edges of the wings that keep the plane level or help it turn. That made the situation utterly untenable. He could fly only with full left rudder plus elevator trim tabs; otherwise the plane would pitch over and power-dive into the Korean firmament, which it was threatening to do regardless. It must have seemed ironic that the ejection training Lieutenant Commander Beauchamp had forbidden because he feared losing a flyer to training injury was all that was between Neil and fiery death.

But bailing out over enemy territory was not an option. Falling into enemy hands would mean torture and likely death. Few captured pilots survived. With a combination of luck and skill, he held the broken bird together using what little hydraulic control was left, coaxing the plane along, climbing to 13,000 feet. Every warning system was screaming for help; the engine wailed an out-of-control high-pitched whine, desperately sucking oxygen. The damage was so severe there was no suggested way to survive. The rule book said: Bail. But friendly territory was just over one more set of green hills, if Neil could just hold on. Several times the plane nearly stalled, shuddering violently and pitching back to the right, but Armstrong managed somehow to keep it aloft.

Neil was prepared for most any contingency should he bail out and have to survive on his own for an extended period. Like the other Navy flyers, he had a .38 to make a desperate stand against capture. He was wearing a cold-water exposure suit, which would keep him alive a remarkably long time in near-freezing water, shark repellant, penicillin, a compass, cigarettes, vitamins, and even a change of underwear. He hoped none of the Navy's thoughtful emergency supplies would be needed.

But he was rapidly running out of rope and soon it was obvious there was no choice; the jet was going in. A moment's delay and it would be impossible to even bail out. Gingerly pulling the pre-ejection lever and tossing precious maps, kneepads, and finally his helmet—which could get snagged and tear one's head off—he pulled the ejection-seat face curtain safely into place and banged a fist down on the eject button. The explosive charge beneath the seat launched him out of the plane with such force he felt crushed and had to struggle to take a breath. Quickly recovering, he kicked away the seat as he was trained, so that it wouldn't get tangled in the parachute or, just as bad, crack him in the head.

Despite a clean ejection, the torments of the day were far from over. First, the oxygen "quick disconnect" stuck and had to be removed manually. Then for four thousand feet he tumbled end-over-end, sickeningly pitching through the thin, frigid sky. Grappling for purchase, he finally managed to "attain a horizontal, face-down spread-eagle attitude," in the words of the official Navy report. "After which he pulled the ripcord. From this position the jolt was not severe and all survival and light gear was restrained." His was the first successful ejection-seat bailout made by an Air Group Five pilot.

The great yellow silk parachute burst from his back and danced above him like a giant squid; suddenly it caught the air and snapped turgid, reeling Neil Armstrong heavenward like a celestial fish. But the mile-long ride back to earth—minus the Panther, which had already slammed into the earth three miles to the north, and was nothing but blackened, smoldering detritus scattered over the countryside—was far from trouble-free. In the dry language of the official Navy report, "He experienced extreme difficulty with oscillation in the chute," meaning because the chute failed to fully inflate, Neil was spinning like a top—an unpleasant characteristic of the round chutes in use at the time. To correct for this, he pulled at the toggles to "dampen" and smooth out the ride to a two-point landing in a rice paddy.

Armstrong was sure that he had bailed well south of enemy territory; in fact the K-3 U.S. airstrip was nearby. But nevertheless the sight of a Korean man dashing through the rice paddy carrying his discarded helmet had to have sent a slight chill up his spine. Fortunately, the man turned out to be a South Korean peasant determined to reunite the flyer with the helmet, which had come hurtling out of the sky, nearly killing him. Armstrong thanked him profusely and accepted the damaged gear.

Two days later, he was safely back aboard the *Essex,* in the ready room preparing for his next sortie. "Neil was slightly shook up about having come within twenty feet of the earth at that speed, but otherwise he dismissed it as just doing his job," recalled Ken Danneberg. "Naturally we had to rough him up a bit. He had that broken helmet in his hand and a smile on his face. We didn't say good to see you back, glad you're alive. John Moore and I jumped right on him. 'You know Neil, you're going to have to pay the government for that helmet.' John and I were examining it gravely. 'About a hundred bucks for one of these,' he said. I agreed, shaking my head. Of course, the damn thing had fallen ten thousand feet; it was a wonder there was anything left of it. We had him going for about thirty seconds."

VF-51 pilots flew three days, then had one day on ship liberty. And as the day after he returned wasn't a scheduled day off, Neil was in the air over Korea at dawn.

Chapter Six

Flying missions day after day from an aircraft carrier in wartime is about the most intensely stressful job in the world. Every bomb-burdened takeoff is a miracle, and landings, particularly at night, require Zenlike concentration as well as skill and daring. Several of the first astronauts, including Apollo 13 commander Jim Lovell, who brought his ill-fated capsule back with a superhuman aplomb, came from the ranks of these carrier jockeys. A flyer astute and skilled enough to land on carriers was an excellent candidate for astronaut duties. Flying to the moon on a balky craft, with no way to turn back, was a kind of challenge Lovell and Armstrong had faced in Korea.

The *Essex*, as well as the other carriers on duty in the Sea of Japan to the east of the Korean peninsula and the Yellow Sea to the west, served thirty days on line, then sailed two days to the port of Yokosuka on the Chiba peninsula, southeast of Tokyo, to allow the men to rest and relax and to refill the ship's vast stocks. The carrier spent ten days in port, received 133.8 tons of ammunition, among many other supplies, then steamed back to the line.

Neil and his VF-51 mates' first trip to the resort was on September 20, 1951, a well-deserved first break from combat. According to the *Essex*'s log, the great ship passed the Mitsuhima light to port, which put them far enough from the war zone to turn on the running lights for the first time in months. The ship's course passed through a series of submarine nets in a fog bank and moored in Yokosuka on the twenty-first.

Visiting the former Imperial Japanese Empire just five years after

Hiroshima and Nagasaki, it was a thrill for American soldiers to actually see the vanquished, evil empire they had grown up hating and fearing, and finally pitying.

"It was something of a surprise that there was no sign of devastation or even rebuilding after all we had heard," recalled Neil's flight mate Herschel Gott. "We traveled all over the country; Neil particularly was fascinated by it. Even Tokyo, which had clearly been firebombed over and over, practically razed, had been totally rebuilt by the time we got there.

"And also, somewhat surprisingly, given all the bitterness of the war, we were treated extremely well. There was no anger on their part that we could detect. It was strange after having hated those people when we were in high school. They were basically very subservient, bowing and backing out of rooms. You couldn't help but think that was part of what got them into such trouble in the first place; it was a national culture whose credo was to obey whoever was in charge, no matter what. If the emperor said it, they obeyed without question. They were a bit that way toward us; whether it was just show or not, that was the way they acted. It was rather unnerving."

Despite the strangeness of Japan, or perhaps in part because of it, the men of VF-51 remembered their days there, as well as other ports of call in the East, fondly. "The U.S. Army had taken over several large hotels on a lake with a view of towering Mount Fuji, and renovated them in a style where Americans boys would feel at home," recalled Harold Schwan. "I remember really good American food, ski trips and visits to little Japanese villages that looked like they were out of a storybook about ancient Japan. It seemed worlds away from World War II, and worlds away from our war as well."

Robert Kaps remembers accompanying the future astronaut on liberty trips aided by faded sixteen-millimeter home movies made with a Kodak camera won in a poker game.

"I have movies of us in Japan, skiing and swimming on different trips. And pictures of a day I remember most vividly on a ferryboat in Hong Kong harbor. Neil and I had spent the day shopping for tailor-made suits and wonderful shoes, like nothing we had ever seen before, at prices even junior Navy officers could afford. We also bought a portable record player to play the new LPs, as they called them, the big long-playing records. They were new and just terrific as far as we were concerned. Back on the *Essex* we could listen to our favorite music, like

Peggy Lee, Ray Coniff, Rosemary Clooney, and Harry James. The hip new stuff in those days," Kaps laughed.

None of Neil's buddies remember any fraternizing with the young women of Japan. "We pretty much kept to ourselves and kept out of trouble," says Kaps. Some of the *Essex*'s men weren't so discreet; numerous seamen, the ship's log notes, were sentenced to two days on bread and water for various infractions at a captain's mast disciplinary hearing after visits to the rest-and-recreation resort.

Neil was interested in Japanese culture, gathered souvenirs, wrote home enthusiastically to his parents and siblings of his experiences in Asia, and became something of a casual afficionado of Japanese civilization. During the waves of intense scrutiny he suffered not so gladly during his space missions, reporters picked up on the Japanese garden in the family's Houston house and made more of it than suited him. Responding to a comment that a red-painted beam indicated he was a practicing Buddhist, Armstrong slapped the query away with undisguised pique: "I believe you would find a Buddhist family would have a red-painted beam that would traverse the entire home." Smugly assuming his succinct and knowledgeable retort had knocked that theory down, he forgot about it until the next morning, when much was made in the papers about his devotion to all things Japanese, which would become a staple of the Armstrong thumbnail biography, repeated ad infinitum to add a bit of color to a man the reporters found maddeningly logical and, therefore, bland. It was one of ten thousand tiny cuts that drove him to avoid the press nearly all the time, quickly winding up being, absurdly, labeled a "recluse," despite the fact he was constantly out and about, as engaged with the world as a person can be.

The winter of 1951 was bitterly cold and frustrating for the unfortunate Americans serving in Korea. Both sides had returned to virtually the same lines they had held when the war started, despite a horrible loss of life. Cease-fire talks were under way, but the reality was an ugly stalemate that would hold for fifty unhappy years.

Armstrong had, since he was a small boy, built model airplanes assembled from balsawood, with .032 gage wire for the landing gear and propeller shaft, tissue paper, which was shrunk and strengthened by "dope" for covering of the fuselage, model wheels, and cement, or model glue. At sea aboard the *Essex,* that material was more or less impossible to find. So instead he taught himself to carve model planes, and eventually ships, out of wood. His ships were replicas of the battleships, destroyers, and frigates that served in the *Essex's* battle group. And he carved models of the peasant fishing craft of antediluvian design. At Christmas, Neil set aside time to carve a few special model ships for gifts. One he sent home for his brother Dean, a few others he decided to award to the winners of a lottery. The names of the men of VF-51 with children were placed in a bag and the winner chosen. The skillful, meticulously made and painted models became increasingly valuable to the recipients over the years as their creator's fame grew. "Most importantly, it was an incredibly thoughtful thing for a young man to do," says Robert Kaps. "It was emblematic of who he was, the kind of young man Neil was, and it's the kind of thing we remember about him."

Sunday afternoons aboard the *Essex* were generally quiet, civilized days during which the junior officers dined on steak served by Filipino stewards on white linen tablecloths. In early November, Armstrong was late arriving for dinner, having taken time to write long letters to his folks. He joined John Moore, Ken Danneberg, Herb Graham, and some others who were working on their coffee and pie. The civilized reverie was suddenly shattered by an unusual alarm. Six pilots were needed in a rush to clear the landing deck so that a badly shot-up Banshee jet fighter could make an emergency landing. Being junior among the men present, Neil leaped to his feet, despite having just been served dinner. Moore waved him off and headed topside double-time. Uncharacteristically, the man who had taught Neil Armstrong to fly jets cut a safety corner, skipping double gloves and even his fire-retardant flight suit, a lapse that would prove nearly fatal.

With three minutes before the Banshee was due to touch down, Moore gunned his jets and rolled the Panther across the deck, supposedly to safety. But before he could emerge from the cockpit and scramble away, the damaged plane slammed onto the carrier deck, ricocheted horrifically high in the air, then crashed back down, missed the tailhook, and skidded sideways, smashing into Moore's jet. There was an immediate explosion and the young lieutenant was engulfed in a blazing inferno. The force of the collision nearly blasted Moore's

Panther clear off the deck, which would surely have drowned him. Instead, in the split-second he had to act, Moore shoved off and dove clear of the fire and into the Sea of Japan, just ten feet from the giant ship churning past him at twenty knots. The four-story fall and second-degree burns on his face and hands were not good enough to do in a tough hombre like Moore, however; he would live to fight another day. But three men lost their lives, eight jets were lost, and eight thousand gallons of the newly available but still precious jet fuel burned with a red, smoky fury that melted and twisted portions of the deck grating.

The *Essex* was scheduled to sail to Naval Air Station Yokosuka a few days later for resupply, so Moore and the other injured men were taken to the naval hospital and the *Essex* was repaired at the Japanese port.

In May 1952, with the Korean conflict was still far from resolved, retired General Dwight Eisenhower was campaigning for president and vowing he would personally go to Korea and bring an end to what had become a pointless, bloody war of attrition. It was a promise that resonated; Ike was swept into office, and the following July an armistice was signed. But for Neil and the rest of VF-51, their tour was finished and the war was over that hopeful May day as the *Essex* proudly steamed back into San Diego harbor.

Back living at the B.O.Q. at N.A.S. San Diego, Neil and a number of his mates were assigned to Air Transport Squadron 32 and the easy, pleasurable job of ferrying planes. "Basically, it was a chance to fly about every plane in the Navy's arsenal," said Herschel Gott. "We might fly the oldest prop fighter plane in the fleet over to Texas, then fly the newest jet to Chicago, and come back to San Diego piloting a freighter. We got to fly a lot of hours and a lot of variety, and nobody was shooting at us anymore."

Armstrong spent much of his free time around the men he had bonded with in Korea. Danny Marshall had a beat-up old twenty-one-foot sloop, in terrible shape but salvageable. The guys were determined to make it seaworthy so they could join the fleet of weekend leisure boaters who crowded San Diego Harbor. "Neil, my wife, and I went to work and got it back in shape, all sanded down, waterproofed, repainted, everything. It still was far from a thing of beauty, but it was good enough," said Ken Danneberg.

"We spent about every free hour sailing. None of us knew anything about sailing, absolutely zero about the rules of the road. We'd be out in the Pacific, drinking beer, getting tangled up in the lines, narrowly avoiding getting bopped in the head every time the boom came around.

"One of the favorite trips was down the coast to Mexico, where we had picnics, got sunburned, drank too much beer, and had a great time. A couple of weekends we could see a storm was coming. There was a brief discussion both times, but we decided the hell with it and sailed anyway. A couple of times the Coast Guard stopped us, searched the boat, and were appalled to find none of the most rudimentary safety equipment. They gave us hell, but let us go knowing we weren't going to do anything about it. We were fearless, not to mention a bit crazy. How we got back to base in one piece I have no idea. But it was a memorable time."

On one occasion, the intrepid if unskilled mariners found themselves tacking back from south of the border as night descended on the Pacific. Too late, they realized the boat was totally unequipped for a nighttime voyage. There were no running lights at all. "Neil finally found a flashlight," laughed Danneberg. "He stood on the bow holding that very weak flashlight, trying to guide us back to San Diego. He held on a lot tighter when the beam picked up a big shark's fin circling the boat."

With all the revelry, Armstrong's pals were concerned at the paucity of his love life and were often attempting to set him up, though to no avail. "In the year and a half we were in San Diego, I never saw Neil go out with a woman once," said Danneberg. "The closest he came was our landlady's daughter. She hung on him like a puppy, had a major crush. Unfortunately, she was just a high school girl, so the relationship didn't have much of a chance."

Chapter Seven

Coming home after war has been through the ages a staggering experience for combatants. War changes everything, and it often seems to the soldier that much of what he bled for on godforsaken foreign soil is no more upon his return. Odysseus returned from the Trojan War to find his home filled with dozens of reprobates trying to seduce his wife; Robert E. Lee's family estate had been turned into a Union Army graveyard, as if to assure his house would be haunted by the men his army had slain.

But war's end also marks renewal. It is no coincidence that so many American businesses and other institutions were founded in 1865, 1919, and 1945. But Neil Armstrong's conflict was the so-called "forgotten war," and had it not been eponymously named, latter-day American college students might just as well guess it happened in Tibet or Lebanon or France.

The future astronaut came home to the merely disquieting. Transistor radios blared pop music, the newspapers carried the story of an ex-GI named George Jorgensen, who had been surgically changed into a woman called Christine Jorgensen. Even Mom and Dad bashfully showed off their new television, which occupied a place of honor in the family living room.

With unsettling change looming on the home front, Neil returned to Purdue after two years at war flying jets, just twenty-two and more determined than ever to make aeronautics his life and to get to the moon one day. He was a different person from the boy who had ridden the Greyhound bus to Florida. His hair was still sandy-blond and the cowlick as mulish as ever. But there was a sadness in his eyes from the memory of the friends he had lost and the carnage he had seen, and caused. Aircraft had, in his then short lifetime, gone from a diversion for daring young men, a rather dangerous but speedy way to deliver the mail, and a tool for aerial jousting with no effect on the outcome of the war, to a weapon of mass destruction that could well be an instrument of mankind's collective suicide.

When Armstrong left N.A.S. San Diego for the last time, he was flush with Navy pay, squirreled away during nearly three years in the service. Anxious to return home and get on with the rest of his life, which meant getting an aeronautical-engineering degree from Purdue, and somehow getting involved in America's nascent space program, he shared the drive home with a VF-51 buddy on his way to Chicago. The two naturally took the legendary, and soon to be lamented, Route 66. Driving nonstop through the night, taking turns at sweaty, jerky road sleep, the two vets roared up California's Highway One, saying good-bye to the hazy shoreline, hung a right on 66 in Santa Monica, and headed for the long, winding road through the high desert of California and into northern Arizona, where they passed Meteor Crater.

Almost two decades later, Neil again visited the spot, this time taking considerably more time to check out the enormous rent in the earth's surface in preparation for Apollo 11. The crater was the closest thing on earth to the tortured moon crust.

Heading toward his future, Neil and his former squadmate bounced over the sometimes buckled and deeply pockmarked highway through New Mexico, the panhandle of Texas, through Oklahoma, the south-eastern tip of Kansas, across the Mississippi at St. Louis, and finally, on the last leg, north through Illinois. Route 66, which would be romanti-cized by a song and TV show, was at points almost too narrow for two cars to pass without sideswiping. In some states across the prairie it was made of brick, which produced a gut-jarring, conversation-killing vibration; other places it was gravel or even dirt, which turned into deep muck in rain and produced choking clouds of dust in summer heat. All in all, travelers like Armstrong felt no love for the 1926 road, touted as the first "all-weather" link among the industrialized Midwest, rural

West, and booming Southern California, and were thrilled with the prospect of the planned interstate highways replacing it with limited-access divided roadways.

Neil spent a few days in Chicago, sightseeing and visiting friends, then grabbed a train to Ohio, where his grateful and relieved parents, siblings, friends, and relations greeted him as the returning war hero.

First on his list of things to do was the purchase of an indulgence: a 1952 Oldsmobile Super 88 convertible, bright red with cream trim, a car that made him beam with pride. The uncharacteristically flashy car was enough to draw small crowds when he cruised the streets of Wapakoneta. But Neil had earned it, to say the least, agreed his amused parents, so let him enjoy it.

Most of the summer was spent prepping for his return to Purdue, hunkered down in the library, dutifully poring over books on engineering, math, and aviation to get a head start on the coming semesters.

Purdue was every bit as bustling and crowded as it had been when he left for Korea three years earlier; only the World War II veterans he had looked up to in awe were mostly graduated and gone to various versions of Levittown across the country, and were being replaced by vets of Neil's war. He looked around and decided he wanted to be a member of a fraternity, which was the center of much of campus social life. Settling on Phi Theta Delta, he came hat in hand to apply for admission.

"Right away we thought Neil seemed like a good guy, somebody who would fit in," says fraternity brother Ronald Pierce.

"He was no teenager, but clearly a grown man, kind of quiet and obviously quite bright. We understood he had been in the Navy, but he gave no details, so we assumed that like most veterans he had served quietly aboard a ship and seen limited action, if any.

"Hazing existed in those days, in a low-key way, but he was clearly two cuts above anything like that. But he accepted the chore of doing some heavy house-cleaning as a condition of pledging and cheerfully went about his chores.

"Then one day after he was a fully pledged member, he came bounding down the stairs in a full-dress naval officer's uniform, just bristling with decorations and medals. It was a shock. But he just kept going, and if he noticed our surprise, didn't react to it, just said 'Got a reserve meeting' and walked out the door. We were surprised and quite impressed to find we had a jet ace and a genuine war hero as a brother."

In 1954, sixty-nine young men were members of Phi Delta Theta at Purdue University. About half the members lived in the three-story brick Georgian house at 503 State Street in West Lafayette, Indiana, that was fraternity headquarters. Opposite the student union building, the big house with imposing white pillars was built in 1904. Entering Phi Delta Theta, one saw the long dining table that centered the building. To the right was the music room, with a baby grand that was often in use, and shelves of trophies won by the brothers over the years. On the left were two small card-game rooms, a ladies' lounge, and a comfortably old-fashioned house-mother's room, which was unoccupied during Armstrong's tenancy—despite which the former brothers remember their house as "always immaculate." Above were two floors, plus an attic with dorm-style rooms, four on a floor and each occupied by three young men.

Within a few months of joining, Armstrong, the newly minted leader of men, began to shape the social life of the fraternity. "Neil took part in all the normal pastimes; he was quite good at bridge, and knew his way around a keg of beer," recalled Pierce. "He enjoyed golf, an occasional spur-of-the-moment game of basketball, and was a good quail hunter. But he felt we needed to do more socially, particularly with the sororities. One of his first projects for us was a variety show event co-sponsored by Alpha Ki Omega, which happened to be the sorority his future wife Jan Shearon belonged to.

"He insisted that we have 100 percent participation; even those of us who pleaded tone deafness weren't excused. When he heard how poorly I sang, he said, 'Just pantomime it.' Neil wrote the lyrics and music, and took charge of seeing that the show was put on. Pretty soon it became a regular thing and transformed fraternity life for us."

There appears to have been little resentment over the newcomer taking over. "Neil was an excellent role model. He was mature, older, and brought more decorum than we had before he arrived," said Ronald Snyder.

In 1954, Neil wrote and directed the Varsity Varieties show in a "clever satire on our campus." It was a large music-hall concert featuring members of the Kappa Kappa Gamma sorority as well as Phi Delta Theta. Along with his brother Dean, who came to Purdue in 1956,

Neil sang with the Purdue Choir and toured the Midwest with them for a time.

With so much to learn and so many potential worlds to explore, sleep was a necessary annoyance to young Neil Armstrong. Each hour spent asleep was an opportunity missed, a lesson not learned, a tune unsung. As a boy he seemed never to sleep, burning the midnight lights until ordered to desist; even during the years spent at the family farm in St. Mary's Neil rose before the rooster. In his later college years he determined to take on the dark sleep beast for once and for all.

Hazing was not in the vocabulary of Purdue fraternity boys, but there were certain rites associated with pledging. At Phi Delta Theta, new recruits were assigned a "pledge dad" to whom they were bound in gentle servitude for a time. Dale Birtch was assigned to Neil.

"Neil was convinced he could get along with almost no sleep if he just reduced his dependence on it in increments," recalls Birtch. "He believed it was a question of just conditioning your body, like working out to build muscles. My duty was to wake him up a few minutes earlier each morning. It went on for a couple of months until he was sleeping just a few hours a night. But even that was too much. Finally it was down to two hours a night, and, incredibly, he still seemed alert and functional. I was starting to believe he was on to something, though it definitely wasn't something I was interested in for myself. Then, one day, he just collapsed like a rag doll and slept coma-like—it was impossible to wake him—for two solid days. I think he was still convinced the theory was sound, but he felt he had pushed it a little too far."

While the future astronaut was developing into a leader in many ways, he still appeared slightly tone-deaf socially. His Phi Delta Theta roommate and fellow Eagle Scout Tom Heidenreich recalls: "My future wife came to visit occasionally and would come up to our room. No matter how many broad hints I dropped, Neil would just sit there in the corner, drinking a beer and chatting away. Apparently it just didn't occur to him that we might want to play kissy-face. He was still quite naive despite being a war hero and a fearless flier."

One of the perks of being a decorated Naval Reserve weekend warrior was access to training planes, and even jet fighters on occasion.

"Even back then there was a tradition of going to Florida for spring break," says Ted Dunn. "During the cold winter of 1954 a bunch of us were sitting around discussing how many could pile into different guys' cars and drive all night to get to the sunshine. Neil didn't say anything; he was studying and looking a bit too smug. We should have known he was up to something. As it turned out, he flew a jet fighter down to Florida. He showed up in full fighter-pilot gear, partied with us a few days, and jetted back. No long, all-night drives for him. We were pretty impressed."

Occasionally he was able to take his fraternity brothers for a plane ride that almost fifty years later would still be memorable. One Sunday morning following a particularly boozy night's revelry at the frat house, Neil shook his roommate Tom Heidenreich awake and announced he had a plane reserved that they should take for a quick spin. Queasy and groggy, but still up for some fun, Heidenreich tagged along. A bit later they were in a tiny J-3 two-seat Piper Cub, soaring through the clouds, enjoying a sensational view of the meandering Wabash River and the pastoral Indiana countryside.

Heidenreich remembers thinking of his roommate as a young man possessing a certain gravity, even a bit of world-weariness beyond his years. Armstrong was an engineer at heart, and not a slap-happy frat boy given to dangerous stunts. So he was taken completely by surprise when Neil suddenly turned the little plane upside down, leaving him hanging precariously and very uncomfortably from his seatbelts.

"All of a sudden he pointed out a flock of ducks way below us. 'MiGs! Those are MiGs!' he shouted. Neil put that flimsy little plane, made of little more than canvas and fiberglass, into a power dive toward the Wabash that threatened to tear it apart. It scared the hell out of me; I was terrified, I couldn't believe he was doing a maneuver like that with a plane meant for nothing more than leisurely cruising. I was afraid the wings would rip off, it seemed to be way beyond its capability, but he just kept pushing it, screaming through the air. He was one helluva pilot, that was obvious.

"But before I could complain, I threw up all over the plane, all over Neil. I guess that taught him!"

Heidenreich's confusion over Armstrong's character was a contra-diction that seems apparent in most men who challenge the gods by flying faster, higher, and in newer, untested machines. At once they are engineers, by aptitude and training cautious, but predisposed to "push the envelope," as Tom Wolfe famously phrased it.

Another contradiction was Neil's continued work delivering the *Lafayette Courier* newspaper in the predawn hours of each day. But it served to get him closer to a girl who had caught his eye during rehearsals for the various musical shows he had participated in. She was a tall, lank girl with short, cropped hair, a quick smile, and the toned body of swimmer—which indeed was one of her passions in life. She was an early riser like Neil and took a 6:00 A.M. laboratory class three mornings a week. Fortunately, Janet Shearon didn't suffer from Neil's sometimes overwhelming reserve. They spotted each other most mornings, and walking and talking together became a regular thing. Happy at the prospect of having a boyishly handsome fellow to share her daily walk in the predawn gloom, she fell into step and peppered him with questions, drawing him out. For the next two years they shared their early-morning walks through the changing seasons, talking nonstop about their hopes and fears. Soon, he was sufficiently comfortable to talk about his mission to go to the moon. Janet listened attentively, then demurely let drop that her daddy, a doctor in suburban Chicago, had his own plane and was teaching her to fly. Her mother and two older sisters had also learned to fly. Neil was impressed.

Nonetheless, he took forever getting around to asking her for a formal date. Without a trace of petulance or irony, Janet reflected later in life, "Neil is not one to rush into anything." He had met his natural partner, a soulmate who would stand by his side from their twenties until their sixties, when the marriage dissolved, perhaps in part because of a reserve he never overcame.

"Jan was a very charming lady, and was a lot like him," recalled Ronald Pierce. "The thing I remember most about them was their cheerfulness. They were both the kind of people who always had a smile and a good word. Plus, she seemed to understand Neil's temperament and when he needed to be drawn out and when he needed to be left alone."

When the couple finally did start to date, Neil had made up his mind and knew Jan was the girl for him. "He pinned her and got most of his fraternity brothers to come to her sorority for the obligatory serenade. That was a first step to getting married, and was something he took very seriously. When she said she wasn't quite sure, Neil turned to his engineer's training and gave her a prepared, detailed list of logical reasons why they should marry. Apparently the reasons were so logical and sound she couldn't argue the other way and they became engaged," laughed Pierce.

Neil's method of telling his mother on a weekend at home in Wapakoneta was a bit more oblique. He said, "You know, Mom, there are some really pretty swimmers at Purdue." Viola Armstrong caught on immediately and insisted upon meeting the pretty swimmer.

Chapter Eight

After graduating from Purdue in January 1955 with a bachelor's degree in aeronautical engineering, Armstrong applied for work as a flight engineer/test pilot at the newly formed National Advisory Committee on Aeronautics (NACA), which would become NASA. He hoped to be stationed at Edwards Air Force Base in California's Antelope Valley, the only place in the world young men with Neil Armstrong's particular ambitions wanted to be. At Edwards in the mid-fifties, America was testing the fastest, most advanced, experimental, top-secret—and occasionally harebrained—flying machines. It had been home to the first generation of X-1 rocket planes since 1947, and was ground zero in what would eventually morph into America's space program. Chuck Yeager broke the sound barrier for the first time in the fall of 1947, proving that speeds high enough to escape the earth's hold were possible to achieve, without causing an apocalyptic catastrophe, as some scientists had predicted. Near the base's gate was the fabled Happy Bottom Riding Club, run with panache by the legendary female daredevil flyer Pancho Barnes. Record breakers were routinely rewarded with a free steak dinner and lost test pilots were immortalized with portraits hung behind the bar. The place and its pilots were the inspiration for Tom Wolfe's *The Right Stuff.*

The brightest and best with the most brass was the byword at Edwards. This included the brilliant, notorious rocketman Wernher von Braun and his team of ex-Nazis in an all-out effort to reach space.

The Antelope Valley is a brutal stretch of high desert about sixty miles from Los Angeles, where searing summer sun parboils residents' brains and gale-force winter winds howl like tortured souls, stirring up vast sandstorms that blind and choke.

John Wayne, whose Christian name was actually Marion, presumably to toughen him up, was born there in 1907, and attended a one-room schoolhouse where the Space Shuttle now lands. He thrived. But most folks don't have constitutions so leathery. It is a place where people dance on the razor's edge of madness.

Edwards had to wait nearly a year for Armstrong, who would become a legend at the High Speed Flight Facility, as it was originally known. His first job out of Purdue was with their Lewis Flight Propulsion laboratory at 21000 Brookpark Road S.W. on the southwestern edge of Cleveland, part of Hopkins International Airport.

Neil moved all his belongings in his Olds convertible and settled into a dreary boardinghouse in a dismal neighborhood. But what mattered was that he was a part of the space program, his vision was on track.

The $100 million state-of-the-art facility, dedicated from the start to developing advanced propulsion and space-power generation, was run by a visionary of manned space flight, Abe Silverstein, who quickly saw in the young Armstrong an engineer who would, literally and figuratively, go far. Silverstein, in the late fifties, left Lewis to head NASA's Office of Space Flight Programs, where he named the nascent project Apollo after the Greek and Roman god of music, light, and poetry.

Jan continued at Purdue, studying home economics during the winter of 1955, her last semester. On weekends, Neil frequently, happily, made the nearly six-hundred-mile return trip from Cleveland to Lafayette. The two spent romantic, care-free days sledding, sharing mulled cider at Purdue Boilmaker football games, and cheering along with the world's largest mascot—a twenty-four-foot tall, 10,800-pound re-creation of an old-time locomotive. And since the tradition, which dated back to 1939, was the responsibility of his old club, the Reamers, Neil could occasionally be coaxed into wearing the Reamer beanie for old times' sake.

Following graduation in the spring, despite their troth, Jan accepted a job as camp counselor and swimming coach at the northern Wisconsin camp she had attended throughout her youth. She would stay there or at her parents' home in Barrington, Illinois, until her marriage to Neil the following January.

Lewis, with its high-level security, caused a lot of talk and rumors in a period when UFO sightings and movies about space invaders were prevalent. Clevelanders were frequently subjected to blinding flashes in the night sky, punctuated by rumblings that rattled the china cabinet. Lewis spokesmen were constantly explaining away "flashes like balls of lightning" and a disturbing phenomenon that the *Cleveland Plain Dealer* on December 31, 1955, quoted a concerned citizen describing as "mushroom-shaped light that turned pink to red with a subsequent rumble."

To quell citizen fears, NACA officials at one stage held an unprecedented open house. The public-relations people went to lengths to categorically deny rumors that captured UFOs and little green men were being experimented on at the facility, instead describing the work as "attempting to solve problems of high-speed flight."

Other agitated complaints included calls to the *Plain Dealer* of strange "flashes that came from the ground and hung in the air momentarily before disappearing."

The men who were aiming for the stars were unwittingly treating the good burghers of Cleveland to a dollop of the "age of anxiety."

Research conducted at Lewis during Armstrong's year-long stint included deliberately crashing old C-82 Boxcars and C-46 Commandos—veterans of the Berlin Airlift—and then carefully studying the wreckage for clues to increase survivability odds. Another group was developing the jet reverse-thrust device to brake a plane on its landing roll, which is now used on virtually every jet in service, commercial or military. Research was under way to develop stronger airplane skins that would hold up under sustained supersonic speeds. The laboratory was experimenting with new jet fuels that would be more efficient and provide extra boost. And far more exotic research was going on as well, including the planning and development of an atom-powered jet engine, billed as capable of round-the-world, nonstop flight. Touting the proposed new powertrain, officials at Lewis rattled Cold War sabers, saying bluntly that an atomic bomber held the key to air superiority in the postwar world.

Assistant director Eugene Manganiello called the nuclear project "of extreme urgency and necessity from the standpoint of national security." Nuclear power also held out the promise of ending military dependency on fossil fuels, an application that would have had astounding implications. "New and powerful means have been uncovered for increasing greatly the performance of military aircraft," said Manganiello. "Some of these improvements are revolutionary, instead of evolutionary. The use of nuclear energy is the obvious way to extend the range of supersonic aircraft. The fission of a single pound of uranium will produce as much heat as the burning of two million pounds of gasoline."

The key problem, as NACA scientists saw it, was metallurgical. Under Defense Department guidance, researchers at Lewis began the search for a metal strong enough to contain the enormous heat generated by nuclear fission, able to protect passengers from deadly radiation, yet light enough to make a practicable jet engine. And they needed new metals that would stand up to the stress and heat of flying at supersonic and hypersonic speeds for extended periods.

Early in World War II, propeller-driven pursuit planes like the P-38 Lightning were approaching the speed of sound in combat dive situations that often resulted in cataclysmic breakups, presumably due to extreme shock waves. No one knew the extent of the stresses or the degree of the heat involved; it was all new and each new day held new surprises. For Armstrong the challenges were just what he had envisaged: a brave new world where anything that could be imagined in aerospace could be tried. Atomic energy was the genie that would power the new world; it would defend, provide warmth, supply clean, nonpolluting power, and, along with hypersonic-capable craft, it would take man to the moon and beyond.

At his request, Armstrong was soon transferred to Lewis's free-flight rocket group, where he quickly discovered that his sense of optimism wasn't universally shared. John Sloop, the head of rocket research at Lewis, believed, and frequently publicly said, that rocket travel was fifty years in the future, a prediction Neil did not want to hear. "Present aircraft engines took fifty years to perfect; rocket power will require a similar period," said Sloop.

It was particularly galling—and unnerving—coming from a man who had been honored by being elected a fellow of the American Rocket Society, a group Armstrong had belonged to and believed in since early boyhood. Pioneers like Armstrong seemed to be getting whipsawed, on one hand pumped up wildly by the bottomless technological cornucopia that atomic energy supposedly promised, then jerked rudely back to earth by pronouncements like Sloop's, suggesting their dreams were foolish. It was a given that, unlike the heroic journeys of their predecessors in exploration, whose achievements took a relative handful of stout men and money to accomplish, space exploration would take the will of an entire people to achieve. And in the mid-fifties the will was not there. President Eisenhower saw rocketry as a means of delivering a warhead—preferably nuclear. He had no interest whatever in going to the moon; unfortunately for Armstrong and his fellow dreamers, that was the consensus almost across the board. In short, as William Burrows writes in *This New Ocean*: "No politician or general wanted to go to Saturn to count rings."

Sloop agreed with the commander in chief that the worthwhile work lay in purely military applications—surface-to-surface, long-range missiles as weapons. The other "down-to-earth application," as Sloop put it, was providing auxiliary power for large bombers and transports, capable of supersonic delivery of nuclear weapons. NACA was then testing such an aircraft at the High Speed Test Center in California. Called the Douglass Skyrocket D558-2, it was the world's first truly transonic plane, capable of reaching Mach 2, nearly fifteen hundred miles per hour. (Mach, named for the nineteenth-century Austrian physicist Ernst Mach, is a measure of the velocity of an object traveling through fluid, such as a plane traveling through the atmosphere.) It flew on normal jet power at low altitude, then would fire its rocket engine and climb as high as seventy thousand feet. Though Neil came to Edwards in the last days of the Skyrocket, which first flew on February 4, 1948, he was very nearly killed launching one from the belly of a decrepit B-29 over the Mojave Desert.

Neil Armstrong traveled with a group of Lewis engineers to the NACA facility at Langley Research Center in Hampton, Virginia, on a blustery March day in 1955, and found his ticket to the California desert, and eventually the space program, in the person of Stanley P. Butchart. "Butch" Butchart was one of the original four research pilots—along with A. Scott Crossfield, Robert A. Champine, and John Griffith—at the High Speed Flight Station, having been there since 1951, flying X-1s, Skyrockets, and Skystreaks. By the time Neil arrived in 1956, Butch was mostly flying the big planes, like the reconfigured B-29s that lifted experimental rocket planes to altitude. It wasn't as sexy as flying the one-man rockets, but the job required a skilled World War II veteran like Butch, who had earned the Distinguished Flying Cross and Presidential Unit Citation flying Avengers in a torpedo-bomber air group off the aircraft carrier *San Jacinto*. The New Orleans–born aviator's best friend aboard the *San Jacinto* was another ace flyer, a fellow who would go far in life—George Bush. Butchart arrived at Langley for a series of aerospace lectures with some of the top test pilots around, including Jack McKay, who was flying Skyrockets. It was a group Neil knew by reputation, had a lot of respect for, and hoped one day to join.

"I first met Neil in the Langley chow hall at noontime," recalls Butchart. "He was introduced to me by the head of flight operations at Lewis. He said, 'I've got this young fellow I just hired out of school. I had no need for him, but I couldn't pass him up because he's a damn fine flyer and an excellent engineer. Have you guys got any room out there? Of course I knew we did, but I just said I'll ask Joe when I get back."

After a long lunch during which Butchart and McKay quizzed the young flyer on his experience and career goals, the pilots flew back to Edwards Air Force Base in California and highly recommended Neil to Acting Chief of the High-Speed Flight Station Joseph Vensel, for a slot as a test pilot/engineer.

One year earlier, NACA had moved its operations to a new $3.8 million headquarters, Building 4800 at the center of the Edwards Air Force Base complex. Over two hundred engineers, test pilots, and support personnel of various stripes were laboring there, testing variable swept-wing craft like the X-5, the forerunner of today's B-1, as well as supersonic planes including the X-3 Flying Stiletto. Soon to roll down the tarmac was the legendary X-15, which would make an enormous impact on aviation for all time, and prove that manned rocketry was not only a possibility, but could be a practical and safe day-to-day enterprise—a giant step toward Armstrong's small step.

And there would be the last-gasp effort to meld a fixed-wing aircraft with landing gear to a rocket ship. With the amusing moniker "Dyna-Soar" (for Dynamic soaring), X-20A was the greatest early space effort, designed to be lofted into orbit by a Titan III booster, then maneuvered back to earth to land like a conventional plane, the precise idea of the Space Shuttle.

Neil packed his Oldsmobile convertible with all his belongings, once again, and began the long trip west, but before hitting Route 66 he had business to take care of in northern Wisconsin. Showing up unannounced, since there were no phones at the wilderness camp, Neil surprised and pleased Jan, though she remained coy and somewhat aloof about agreeing to move to the California desert. Years later, Jan remembered Neil's coaxing and her reluctance: "He said if I would marry him and come along in the car to California, he would get six cents a mile for the trip. If I didn't, he'd only get four." Apparently she was less than thrilled with the prospect of living in the desert while her husband defied death daily, because she said she would have to think it over, though they talked dreamily about a wedding the following January.

Discomfited by the possibility that he might be faced with the torture of choosing between his lifelong passion and the woman he loved, Neil headed for California, worried but excited.

Forty-eight hours later, bleary-eyed and bedraggled from his usual nonstop, no-sleep marathon drive at his usual breakneck speed, Neil showed up at Butch Butchart's bright little ranch house in Lancaster, in the shadow of the High Speed Flight Test Center on the Edwards base.

"Neil was very worried that Jan was going to refuse to come out," recalled Butchart. "He asked me if I thought she would wind up coming all the way across country and live with him in the high desert, and would she stay after she got a load of the winds, the heat in summer and the cold, cold winters. It certainly isn't the kind of weather most people think about when they think about California. I told him my wife had come all the way from the East Coast when we moved to the desert five years earlier. 'Neil, if the girl really loves you, and knows you've got the need to be a test pilot, she will come out here. Get settled in, then go back, marry Jan, bring her out here, and raise a family together. She'll be fine with it.'"

For more than six months, Neil lived alone in a small apartment at East 50th and L streets in Lancaster. He was a frequent visitor—and practically became a member of the family—at the Butchart house. Afternoons, he often tutored Butch's grade-school daughter in math, and stayed on to enjoy a welcome home-cooked meal.

Finally, Janet agreed to a January wedding back in Barrington and to move to California. Ebullient, Neil left California just before

Christmas, drove back to Wapakoneta for a large family reunion, then led his clan to Illinois, where he and Jan wed on January 28, 1956.

When Janet and Neil Armstrong arrived in Lancaster, California, for the first time in late January 1956, pulling a trailer crammed with their belongings, Dwight Eisenhower was about to embark on his second term in office. The space race was well under way. Elvis was King, topping the charts with "Heartbreak Hotel," and Grace Kelly became a princess by marrying Prince Rainier III. At theaters in Lancaster, hometown boy John Wayne was starring in probably the best film he ever made, *The Searchers,* director John Ford's epic Western about a tough, taciturn man's quest for revenge against Indians who had kidnapped his niece (played by Natalie Wood). When he finally finds her and discovers she has "gone native," adopting the ways of her captors, Wayne vows to kill her, thus ending what he sees as a subhuman existence. The film spoke volumes about the horror many Americans felt that their society was being changed into something foreign to them, and inescapable. Two science-fiction films, *Godzilla, King of Monsters* and *Invasion of the Body Snatchers,* were reflective of a growing anxiety with technology and the unknowns that man seemed determined to explore.

Jan gradually was welcomed into the company of test-pilot families, a close-knit society where strict rituals were observed, few outsiders permitted, and few secrets kept. Most everyone lived in the same neighborhood, ate at the same restaurants, and sent their kids to the same schools.

For a time they complied, but found the atmosphere too close for comfort. Driving through the heights surrounding Juniper Hills, they found an old forest ranger station at an elevation of more than a mile high. The towering pines filled the thin, cold air with the aroma of sweet sap and a blanket of snow covered the ground in the winter. But it was pretty primitive; the nearest neighbors were miles away, and black bears foraged through the trash at night if it wasn't kept well out of their way. But it was perfect for them, the price was right, and there was plenty of room for home-improvement projects, which the couple enjoyed.

Once ensconced in their mountain aerie, Neil was living in the twentieth century by day and well in the past by night. Hanging laundry to dry on a line, Jan would often wave to Neil as he shrieked by in the latest experimental flying machine, sometimes passing at an altitude below her.

"Neil was a friendly guy and genuinely liked people, he just didn't like too much of them, too much of the time," laughed Butch. "He had to have time out on his own; that's why he moved way out there, all the way to the top of the hills. He was very social, though. We were often at each other's houses for dinners, barbecues, and parties. And Neil started a glee club at the Test Center, just as he had in college. There were five or six of us that joined. He played the piano, which he was very good at, and taught us how to harmonize and use our voices. He took it very seriously. We even put on performances for the families. The truth is he was never any kind of a recluse. Neil was just a man who needed a lot of breathing room."

Nevertheless, Armstrong's reputation as a square peg in the flyers' determinedly round holes was established and would last through his long career with NASA. Occasionally the couple could be coerced into attending one of the nearly nightly parties. To get past the most painfully abashed moments, they played piano duets and led group singing, but never exactly became part of the crowd and never wanted to be.

What Neil had always wanted to be was the best flier possible. He had proven beyond a doubt in Korea that he was already a jet ace, but at Dryden he had the opportunity to prove he could be a supersonic or transonic ace, able to instinctively be proactive in dealing with potentially catastrophic events. Over the next few years, he proved over and over that he possessed those skills that would be essential for a space pioneer.

On March 22, 1956, shortly after his arrival at Dryden, Neil was assigned as Butch's co-pilot on the B-29 (or P2B, as the World War II workhorse plane was designated by the Navy) with a D558-2 Skyrocket manned by Jack McKay attached to its bomb bay. The Skyrocket and its sister craft, the Skystreak, were experimental rocket planes that constituted what was referred to as "Phase One" of the road to space.

The Skyrocket was at the time the fastest, highest-flying plane in the world. During its years in service the research plane was sometimes configured with both jet and rocket engines; sometimes it took off conventionally from a runway and sometimes it was launched from under a mother ship. In 1951, NACA pilot Bill Brideman had reached Mach 1.88 at 62,000 feet without the violent rolling previously associated with such speed and altitude. Then, on November 20, 1953,

Scott Crossfield exceeded Mach 2 for the first time in another Sky-rocket.

Launching the Skyrocket was an arduous task, and just as danger-ous as flying the rocket plane, mainly because the B-29s, originally purchased by the Navy for relatively undemanding low-level sub patrol, were barely up to the job of lifting the relatively heavy rocket. "Those little twenty-nines took a beating," says Butchart. "You were at climb power for at least an hour. And if the pilot wanted to get a little higher—thirty-four to thirty-five thousand feet, we spent another thirty minutes on the last three to four thousand feet." Given that strain, it was no great surprise when one of the plane's four engines quit. Neil and Butch were at 31,000 feet, somewhere over Palmdale, California, when engine number four suddenly belched black smoke and died. Butchart immediately tried "feathering" the engine, pushing a hydraulically connected button that rotates the blade so that it is parallel to the airflow, reducing wind resistance, hopefully allowing it to restart. But it was useless; after three attempts he gave up and decided to unload the Skyrocket.

"I wasn't too worried because we were at altitude, and we'd made drops before where we'd had engines quit on us," recalled Butch. "Neil was flying, so I turned to the flight engineer and went through the checklist of things to restart the engine, but nothing worked. So I directed Neil to get us in position for the drop and to get into a dive so we could get up enough speed—about 210 miles an hour—for the drop. I figured we'd just get it over with and limp home. But then Jack McKay called and said, 'Butch, you can't drop me.' A valve down at his side that jacked up some of the nitrogen pressures for the engine had broken. He said, 'I felt it break off in my hand.' I said, 'Jack, I've got to drop you.' I told Neil to push [the nose] over. We had to get into a dive quickly so we wouldn't stall. As soon as we were up to speed, I reached up to pull the emergency handle. It was a T-handle on the dash. I reached up and pulled and nothing happened. The other way to sepa-rate from the Skyrocket was to hit two toggle switches. That worked and away he went. And just a few seconds after he departed, that engine blew—big time."

The explosion rocked the ship, filling the cabin with thick black smoke. Shrapnel from the engine ripped through the bomb bay, where Jack McKay had been minutes before and that would almost certainly have cut him to ribbons. Rapid depressurization then quickly sucked the choking smoke back out.

Butch knew McKay was disappointed over not getting to ride his Skyrocket, but knew he would be able to safely glide down to the lakebed.

"Neil said it looked and felt like everything but the kitchen sink had hit us. The nose dome was torn off the plane, and the [propeller] blades went in all four directions. Unfortunately, one blade went right through us and completely cleaned off one of the other engines. Another went though the bottom of engine number three."

Butch tried to help Neil fly the plane, but discovered the cables connecting his wheel to the controls were completely severed.

"I just turned it and nothing happened. I looked over at Neil and said, 'Have you got lateral control?' He said, 'Yeah, a little bit.' But he had about six inches of free play in his wheel. It had cut part of his aileron cables. The frayed cables were sticking out." The badly damaged B-29 was quickly pitching to the right and toward what could easily have become a sharp graveyard spin, a tight spiral downward, nearly impossible to pull out of even with fully functioning controls, that would have likely caused the plane's wings to shear off. Carefully, and with great difficulty because of the resistance, Neil pulled the frayed cables out through the guide holes—called by their nautical term "fair leads"—and little by little gained some degree of control.

As Neil struggled and gradually began to right the B-29, the number-three engine quit. A nimbus of sparks erupted from the burned-out engine, and the plane lurched violently, but he stayed with it, refusing to relinquish control. Flight engineer Joseph Tipton shouted out: "Butch, you've got to feather number three." The engineer had discovered to his horror that the damage was worse than they dared imagine.

"Shrapnel had hit the plane in so many places that one had cut through our fuel line, our throttle cable, oil pressure, everything on the engine. So, essentially, we had lost control of engine number three. But fortunately it feathered all right. That left us with two engines on one side. The only nice thing was we were at thirty thousand feet. So we glided out over the desert and headed straight for the lakebed. Then Neil kind of got into an argument. He said, 'You'd better get your gear down.' I said, 'Wait a minute.' 'We're getting closer, better get your gear down.' Well, nobody had ever made a thirty-thousand-foot approach to the lakebed in a B-29. He kept thinking we were going to overrun it. And I wanted to make certain we got there, because I could only use one engine. In the end we landed it, both of us struggling with the elevators, both of us on the rudders, and Neil on the ailerons."

The two pilots proved in the end that working with a fraction of normal control it was possible to bring a catastrophically damaged old bomber more than five miles in the air to a relatively safe landing in the desert.

"Of course, the fact we had that huge, practically endless lakebed made it possible," said Butch. "You wouldn't want to have to try hitting a short city runway under those conditions."

But despite all the precautions and the favorable geography at Dryden, men died. On September 27, 1956, Air Force Captain Milburn G. Apt flew the X-2 to Mach 3.2, well over two thousand miles an hour. The extraordinary and historic flight ended in tragedy when Apt lost control of the plane and crashed in the Mojave Desert. Some of the experimental planes were just horribly flawed. The Bell X-5 variable swept-wing was a classic example. The design of the plane's tail and vertical fin were simply wrong, and caused "violent stall-spin instability." Armstrong agreed that the plane had "truly vicious characteristics." Test pilot Joe Walker critiqued the Bell Aircraft plane in the unemotional language of an engineer: "As the airplane pitches, it yaws to the right and causes the airplane to roll to the right. At this stage, aileron reversal occurs; the stick jerks to the right and kicks back and forth from neutral to full right deflection if not restrained. It seems that the airplane goes longitudinally, directionally, and laterally unstable in that order." In other words: The damn thing was a lemon and a death trap. Eventually it would claim Air Force test pilot Ray Popson.

Despite its killer flaws, the X-5 was considered a success. It proved that swept-wings were viable, and, because they could be adjusted, it allowed study of the range of swept-wing positions. All of the planes Neil and his colleagues at Dryden flew were demanding, and most of them required high levels of piloting skills, and potential death was always part of the mix.

Life at Dryden was punctuated by experiences very few men ever dare, let alone survive, but mostly it was composed of the daily minutiae of life, including, of course, report-writing and domestic concerns.

Most of the pilots, men who loved the danger and were addicted to going faster and higher, regularly doing what no man had ever done, lamented the paucity of opportunities to fly the research planes. The veteran pilots, like Butchart, Milt Thompson, and Scott Crossfield were lucky to fly experimental planes once a month. Thirty lifetime flights was about average for most of the veterans.

Chapter Nine

By the spring of 1957, Jan had grown into a rather proficient pioneer woman/test pilot's wife, which was well because she was pregnant with her first child, a boy they named Eric (Rick) Alan, who was followed in two years by Karen Anne, nicknamed Buffy, and four years later, in 1963, their son Mark was born.

Like most government employees, Neil carpooled to work each day. One of his fellow employees was Betty Love, a researcher who was married to a NACA project engineer. Though retired some years ago, as of this writing she still works as a volunteer in the NASA history division at Dryden.

"I met Neil when he first came to Dryden, and was living at a little apartment in Lancaster," recalled Love. "Soon after he married and brought Jan to California, they bought the forest ranger cabin. They had spotted it cruising around the mountains in his Olds convertible. It was way up the Pear Blossom Highway where it loops around the Juniper Hills. It had a great view of the valley and the dry lakebed facing north. The place was just a little cabin when they first moved in. But they both went to work on it and turned it into a very nice, rustic house. It had two stories with one big room on the first floor and two bedrooms upstairs. The downstairs was a comfortable living room with fiber weave squares of carpet covering the floors and beige walls. The kitchen area was cleverly done, so that when Jan wasn't actually cooking it didn't look like a kitchen at all. They had installed a Frigidaire stove that was popular back then for people with limited kitchen space. The electric burners were built into the wall; when you weren't using them they folded up and disappeared. Jan had a beautiful antique tea cart of solid oak in the room. Not the kind of thing you would have expected to see in a mountain cabin, but she put it to great use serving food and drinks, and then just wheeled it out of the way.

"Outdoors, Neil had a wonderful old-fashioned player piano that needed work. For a long while he kept it outdoors and covered with a tarpaulin. On weekends he tinkered with it until it finally worked good as new. When it was fixed, Neil kept it outside in the nice weather and would play ragtime songs like "Shine On, Harvest Moon," and we would all sing along out there around the manzanita bushes. It was absolutely expected that everyone would join in and sing. That was the way an evening at the Armstrongs' usually went.

"Neil was a private person, but once you got to know him he relaxed and was very friendly, very sociable. One of the first things he confided was the fact he wanted to be an astronaut and go to the moon. We had never even heard the term astronaut when he first started telling us that was what he wanted to be and that was what he was doing in the California desert. He was so enthused about going to the moon and had such confidence, it was infectious, he made us all believers."

Armstrong had even mentally dealt with the consequences of fame that would surely follow a pioneering space mission. Carpooling through the desert on the way to work one predawn winter morning, through patches of thick fog, the astronaut-to-be spoke—fifteen years before the triumph of Apollo 11—to his drowsy companions, as though he had finally reached the deductive conclusion of a long-considered inner monologue: "I don't blame Charles Lindbergh for being so private; I would be that way, too." It was a comment that would resonate with his car-pool mates for many decades.

Lindbergh was obviously already something of a role model, a person whose life Armstrong admired and whose feats in aeronautics and ecology he aspired to emulate. In later years, the men would meet on numerous occasions, though never truly become friends. There is no evidence of correspondence between the two in the Lindbergh Collection at Yale University's library. But the intrepid air pioneer lent his name and support to favorite projects of Armstrong's, including the Society of Experimental Test Pilots, which Neil cofounded with Stan Butchart over beers at Alex's restaurant in Lancaster.

"Lucky Lindbergh," as he was known, was also a visitor several times at Cape Canaveral before launches, and he privately lunched with the crew of Apollo 11 the night before the first moon flight.

At age twenty-seven, Neil was by all accounts a dutiful husband and a dedicated and loving father, but he was a young man with a need for speed, whether in the air or on the highways, and his driving was often hair-raising. "I used to tell Neil his driving was like his flying—relaxed and supersonic," laughs Betty Love. "He was always involved in helping Jan with her projects. She taught Red Cross swimming and lifesaving at a pool south of Lancaster on Route 138 near Little Rock. All of the car-pool kids, including mine, were in Jan's class. So when they graduated from the swimming pool to a lesson in righting an overturned canoe in a lake, we organized a pot luck and all went along. Neil was going to drive his Olds convertible and naturally all the kids wanted to go with him."

The trek across the San Gabriel Mountains to Jackson Lake on the way to Wrightwood was a potentially treacherous journey even in summer without ice and snow. There are hairpin curves and switch-backs with vertiginous dropoffs all along the narrow, then-unpaved road, but Neil knew the geography well and went very fast, as was his habit, deftly accelerating out of turns, putting the big Olds through its paces, sending a huge plume of dust in his wake. When he arrived at Jackson Lake, he screeched to a stop and hopped out, as confident of his skills driving on mountain roads as jetting over them. But to his surprise, the kids were nowhere in sight. Glancing in the backseat, he could see they were glued to the floor, clinging desperately. Used to their parents' timorous driving on mountain roads, they had been ter-rified, sure Mr. Armstrong was going to miss a turn and spin out into the abyss.

"When it came time to go home, not a single child would go with Neil," recalls Love. "They whispered that Neil was not a very good driver as far as they were concerned. For years kids, and adults as well, gave Neil a wide berth when it came to accepting the offer of a ride."

The Air Force Police, or "AP," as they are known, who patrol the grounds of Edwards Air Force Base and its related facilities, also had brushes with Neil's sometimes very distracted driving, when he was arguing the arcana of aviation with his car-pool mates.

"One night on the way home from Dryden after a snowstorm, we were driving the detour around the flood track of the base. It was a long, dark blacktop through the base and there was almost never any traffic, so you didn't really have to pay much attention as a rule. I happened to ask Neil, who was driving, that if he took the wing of his plane and flew along the snow pattern on the San Gabriel Mountains, would the altimeter stay the same? It was the kind of questions we bantered back and forth on our long commutes. Before long everybody in the car was busy debating the point; we were looking at the snow-capped mountains south of us and having a lively chat. All of a sudden a truck was coming straight at us; before Neil could do anything, it swerved to avoid us and ran right off the road. Neil stopped, and to our horror we realized it was an AP truck. Neil got out and showed the none-too-pleased officer his badge and apologized. When he realized it was one of the pilots, heroes in these parts, he saluted and said, 'Please be more careful in the future.' We never did resolve the question of the altimeter being tricked by snow; the conversation for the rest of the ride was focused on how fortunate Neil was not to be spending the night in the brig."

In the course of over one hundred interviews conducted for this book, the author was unable to elicit any truly negative comments regarding the character and competence of Neil Armstrong from anyone, ranging over seventy years of his life, from schoolmates in Wapakoneta to neighbors in the Cincinnati suburb where he lives at this writing in semiretirement. The single exception is retired Brigadier General Chuck Yeager, one of the few people who declined to be interviewed about Armstrong. In his eponymous 1985 biography, the Air Force pilot, who over the years became nearly as famous for his hubris as for being the first human to travel faster than sound, accuses Armstrong of being headstrong and very foolish. (To his credit, Yeager makes it clear he loathed the NACA pilots from the start and is incapable of judging their work fairly: "I rated them as high as my shoelaces; they were sorry fighter pilots.")

In *Yeager: An Autobiography* he wrote: "Neil Armstrong may have been the first astronaut on the moon, but he was the last guy at Edwards to take any advice from a military pilot." He then relates the hotly disputed tale of his being asked by Paul Bickel, then head of NACA at Edwards (according to Yeager's account), to fly a T-33 jet trainer with Armstrong to Smith's Ranch Lake two hundred fifty miles across the lakebed, which was under consideration as an emergency landing site for an X-15 flight, to determine if it was dry enough for a landing. Yeager contends in his book that he responded he had flown over the area "recently and it was soaked from the winter rains." Bickel said he had heard from other pilots that it was dry. "I laughed," wrote Yeager, " 'Well, then, be my guest.' . . . He then asked if I would fly Neil up there and attempt a landing. 'No way,' I said. 'Would you do it in a NACA plane?' he asked. 'Hell, no. I wouldn't do it in any airplane because it wouldn't work.' He then asked, 'Would you go up there if Neil flew?' 'Okay' I said, 'I'll ride in the backseat.'

"I tried my damndest to talk Armstrong out of going at all. 'Honestly, Neil, that lakebed is in no shape to take the weight of a T-33. . . . But Neil wouldn't be budged. He said, 'Well, we won't land. I'll just test the surface by shooting a touch-and-go,' meaning, he'd set down the wheels and immediately hit the throttle and climb back up in the sky. I told him he was crazy. 'You're carrying a passenger and a lot of fuel, and that airplane isn't overpowered, anyway. The moment you touch down on that soggy lakebed, we'll be up to our asses in mud. The drag will build up so high, you won't be able to get off the ground again.' He said, 'No sweat, Chuck, I'll just touch and go.'

"And that's exactly what Armstrong did. He touched, but we sure as hell didn't go. The wheels sank in the muck and we sat there, engine screaming, wide open and the airplane shaking like a moth stuck on flypaper. I said from the back, 'Neil, why don't you turn off the sumbitch, it ain't doin' nothin' for you.' He turned the engine off and we sat there in silence. Not a word for a long time. I would have given a lot to see that guy's face. It was cold and the sun was moving behind the mountains in the late afternoon. Very soon it would be dark and the temperature would drop below freezing. We were only wearing thin flightsuits and the nearest highway was thirty miles away. 'Any ideas?' I asked him. Neil shook his head."

Yeager's version of events is that he cleverly radioed a DC-3 pilot sent to search for them and suggested he touch down on the edge of the lakebed, taxi until they jumped aboard, then take off again. Back at Edwards, everyone had a good laugh at the foolish, incompetent Armstrong and Yeager was the prescient genius.

Stan Butchart was at NASA (not NACA) at Edwards at the time and remembers the incident quite differently. Butchart also makes it clear he rates Yeager little higher than shoelaces, and ranks his credibility rather dismally as well, comparing him to a certain finger-wagging U.S. President, who "didn't have sex with that woman."

"Neil was going on a routine mission to check the conditions of the lakebed. Yeager never advised against it; that's nonsense. He made a low pass over the lakebed and it looked dry, so he came back and landed, then as he rolled out to the end that part of the lakebed was muddy and they got stuck. A lot of times all you had to go on was coloration to guess how wet it was. The point is that it was far better for a T-33 to get temporarily stuck in the mud than to land the X-15 in mud at high speed and have a serious mishap. Yeager's description of the incident is sheer nonsense."

Astronaut Gordon Cooper says another explanation was Yeager's bitterness at not having been selected for the space program. "Some fellow pilots, especially those who hadn't been selected for the program—like Chuck Yeager, who hadn't met the criteria for selection, partly because he wasn't a college graduate and was too old—were left with sour grapes. They joked about us being nothing more than 'Spam in the can.' "

Chapter Ten

The sphere which now revolves in the heavens above us is the guarantee that man can soon break completely the fetters of gravity which hitherto bound life to this tiny planet. The long road to the stars is now open.

—*The New York Times*, October 7, 1957

Blinding flames swirled about, and a deep rolling thunder was heard. The silvery rocket was instantly enveloped in clouds of vapor. Its glittering, shapely body seemed to quiver and slowly rise up from the launch pad. . . . 'She's off. Our Baby is off.'

—Evgeny Riabchikov, *Russians in Space*

On October 4, 1957, Neil was attending a symposium of the Society of Experimental Test Pilots (SETP) in Los Angeles when he heard the news that would change the world forever and propel him toward the heavens. The Russians had rocketed a twenty-three-inch-round, 184-pound aluminum sphere called Sputnik into space, and it was now orbiting the earth. Many in the space program were thrilled, though careful not to let anybody see them smile. The feeling was that it was the shock therapy needed to make America wake up and get moving. The political humiliation of being beaten into space by the Soviet Union electrified the country in a dozen ways. But most important to Armstrong, it accelerated the space program to a degree previously unimagined.

"Those of us at Edwards High Speed Flight Station were working on projects we thought might lead eventually to spaceflight, so Sputnik was of extreme interest and concern to all of us in that business," Armstrong recalled in 1987. "What it came down to was: The Russians had one and we didn't. We got one and then went on to the moon."

After the initial shock wore off, there was a national mandate for a space race that would finally provide Wernher von Braun and company with the billions needed to put a man on the moon.

Two months later, the urgency and sense of national shame was underscored when an American Vanguard rocket carrying a tiny 3.5-pound capsule exploded on the launchpad as the world watched and the Russians gloated. The ensuing debate roiled from bedrooms to boardrooms, in schools and the halls of Congress. The consensus was not only that the space program was a shambles, but the entire educational system of the country needed to be massively overhauled. Science, math, and chemistry had to be rigorously taught. And the canon put forth by the popular culture that science was the domain of the oddball, egghead, or the buck-toothed Nutty Professor played to horrifying perfection by Jerry Lewis, must be changed.

The Soviet triumph that eclipsed the 1957 World Series (the Milwaukee Braves defeated the New York Yankees 4–3) as well as, ironically, Neil's long-planned SETP symposium was in many ways the milestone that begat the United States space program as surely as the severe insult of Pearl Harbor roused the somnolent American colossus to enter World War II. On the twenty-fifth anniversary of the Sputnik launch, Neil McAleer wrote in *Space World* magazine: "Sputnik 1 did nothing less than change our world, and most historians concur that it is one of the most important events of the 20th century. Had the United States been the first nation to launch a satellite during the International Geophysical Year (and both nations had announced plans to do so), it is very possible that there would have been no Apollo voyages and no human footprints left on the moon."

Shortly before leaving Edwards for Houston and the space program, Neil and a few of the other X-15 test pilots were honored at the 1962 World's Fair in Seattle for having exceeded 100,000 feet in altitude. The surprise was the long line of folks who had already achieved that feat. "We were properly humbled when we realized we were well out-numbered by balloonists," Armstrong noted wryly.

The X-15 program was an essential step toward space travel. It was an attempt to master control of a craft flying above the earth's atmosphere, where traditional wings would be of no use, necessitating small rocket engines for maneuver. It was also a means of testing whether men and ships could withstand temperatures exceeding 1,400 degrees. These and dozens of other technical problems had to be quickly solved if the United States was to have a prayer at catching up with the Soviet Union's seemingly insurmountable lead.

For a craft that could fly with a human pilot twice as fast as a bullet, the X-15 was disarmingly small, just fifty feet long, with a wingspan of twenty-two feet. It had thin, stubby wings and a wedge-shaped vertical tail. Empty, the craft weighed 14,000 pounds; fully fueled, approximately 34,000. Only three were built; number one is in the Smithsonian's Air and Space Museum in Washington, D.C., number two is on display at the Air Force Museum at Wright-Patterson Air Force Base in Ohio, and number three disintegrated on reentering earth's atmosphere, killing pilot Michael Adams. To this day, the X-15 is the fastest throttle-controlled craft ever flown; it developed 60,000 pounds of thrust, reached an altitude of 354,200 feet or 67.08 miles, and made a speed nearly seven times that of sound, 4,520 miles per hour. The ship was made of Inconel X, a nickel-chromium alloy slightly heavier than steel, which had been selected for its ability to withstand extreme heat. Each eighty-five seconds of powered flight devoured 18,000 pounds of liquid oxygen and anhydrous ammonia.

Neil was the seventh man to ride the rocket, making his first trip of just ten minutes on November 30, 1960, throttling up to a mere 1,131 miles per hour at 43,840 feet. The following April 5, he nearly lost his life in an X-15, and a few minutes later first touched the edge of space.

Jan bathed her babies and watched nervously over her shoulder as a B-52's eight long contrails marked a path through cloudless blue desert sky. When it became a mere speck on the horizon, she imagined it would soon be high enough to release her husband's rocket plane, which clung to the bomber's left wing. Wrapping the babies in terry-cloth towels, she went about her business. There was nothing to do but wait.

When the moment came, Armstrong was ready. He had gone

through the steps to detach and activate the rocket engine a thousand times and was anxious to begin. Set loose, he experienced a slightly sickening feeling like an elevator in free fall. The B-52 immediately banked steeply to the left to avoid catching the X-15 in the vortex of its wake, which could spin the little plane out of control. It was immediately obvious to Armstrong and the mother-ship crew that something was terribly wrong. The X-15's engine was programmed to fire immediately upon separation. Instead the craft was continuing to fall. Slowly, methodically counting through the checklist, Neil released a red safety cover and pulled a toggle switch marked IGNITION, wincing slightly in anticipation of the rocket's awesome thrust. The reply was silence. There was nothing but the increasingly shrill howl of the wind as the plane's descent quickened. Immediately he repeated the ignition procedure, finding all systems apparently functioning. The plane had already plunged seven thousand feet. A red ignition light glowed, uselessly, while the earth pirouetted insanely below. He had plummeted two miles through the sky. Armstrong pulled the damned switch once again and a controlled explosion roared behind him, the little black plane abruptly ripping a path through the indigo sky. When the fuel was finally spent and the 60,000-pound thrust engine licked its hot chops with one last flicker of ammonia, Neil had pushed the balky plane to a peak speed of 2,830 miles an hour and an altitude of thirty-four miles, or 179,000 feet.

He probed deeper into the veneer of the deep purple realm that is the edge of space just fourteen days later, on April 19, 1961, with Jan and their then four-year-old son Eric anxiously watching from the NACA control center at Edwards. The future astronaut stepped into a silver reflective pressure suit, which helped keep the temperature down by reflecting sunlight in the cockpit, and climbed into the tiny cockpit of the X-15, which was attached to the wing of a B-52.

Jan and little Eric watched him wave as he disappeared into the cabin; then they retreated to the control center. At that point he had about forty-five minutes to run his checklist before the mother ship would roll. The next fifteen minutes were devoted to strapping in and going through all the switches, while inspectors stood around watching and triple-checking every system. When the canopy was locked in place, the claustrophobic aspect of the craft became painfully obvious. There was barely a few inches between his helmet and the two tiny windshields, though the view was surprisingly good due to experimental planar-flat window glass that cut out the distortion of curved windshields. Another half-hour was spent starting all the B-52's engines and rolling three miles to the takeoff end of the runway. Nestling under eight huge, throbbing jet engines was a trial even for an experienced test pilot. After takeoff, the gradual forty-five-minute climb to 45,000 feet and the drop site 250 miles uprange in Nevada began. With the countdown to launch officially under way, Neil ran down his checklist. He thoroughly checked the pressure suit, tested the steam rockets that would enable him to control the ship when it passed out of the earth's atmosphere, firing them briefly to make sure they hadn't frozen. Next he expelled some cryogenic propellant to cool the lines, reducing the risk of catastrophic vapor lock once he launched. Finally, the B-52's captain asked if he was ready to be dropped. He glanced at the two T-33 chase planes close on his flanks. Both gave a thumbs-up signal, indicating that visually everything looked good. The sudden drop was disconcerting; he was plummeting toward earth in an unpowered plane. Then there was a deafening roar and the plane surged ahead insanely, as though it meant to leave him behind. The needle-nosed machine seemed to be colliding with the atmosphere, bullying its way more than flying through it, pinning Neil to his seat with a punishing 4 g's.

But in a few years as the space program got under way 4 g's would seen positively benign. "Original Seven" astronaut Gordon Cooper experienced eighteen g's in a simulator, making his body feel as though it weighed eighteen times normal, or an astonishing 2,700 pounds. "It felt as if a Mack truck had been parked on my chest. I lost my vision completely and I stepped away wet with blood from broken capillaries up and down my arms, legs, and back." Such g-levels were never tried again.

Another peculiarity of the X-15 was the "phantom pitch rate" caused by the pilot losing his horizon reference during the steep acceleration path. A pilot tends to feel that "down" is where the acceleration is coming from. Therefore the sensation was of flying almost straight up. Neil, and the other pilots, were alert to the phenomenon, and kept a steady eye on instruments, which assured them it was only an illusion. But there was no way to shake the feeling, and it made for a rough ride.

Trembling was so severe it seemed the plane would disintegrate—a very real concern that the X-15 was going to answer one way or the other; the pilots obviously were counting on the craft maintaining its integrity. Then, suddenly, the ride started to smooth out. The airspeed indicator confirmed it was continuing to accelerate through 3,000 knots, but as it blustered through the sky, climbing at a giddy 35-degree angle, resistance ebbed to mild chop, then disappeared altogether. At last there was burnout and an incredible rush of freedom from the earth's tyrannical clench. Armstrong came to agree with Milt Thompson's assessment that "the X-15 was the only aircraft I ever flew where I was glad when the engine quit."

The checklist binder slowly floated off his lap and hovered in the air; experiencing zero gravity for the first time, he couldn't help but play. A dropped ballpoint pen similarly floated; only his shoulder harness kept him in his seat. The earth below was a curved blue ball, lazily turning in its lacy white cocoon of fluff. Above and ahead was the black, twinkling panoply of the heavens.

One of the goals of Armstrong's late-April flight was to test—for the fourth time—a new autopilot system integrating the maneuver rockets with the tail. As the craft streaked through the rapidly thinning atmosphere, the tail would be raised to its maximum-up position to help the rockets keep the X-15's nose up, and control of the wing and nose jets would be automatic, adding stability over the previous manual control. If the autopilot was as effective as hoped, it would be installed on the upcoming Dyna-Soar orbital glider.

Neil leveled off at 207,000 feet, thirty-eight miles high, just 10,000 feet shy of the record. Land speed was 3,818 miles per hour, also just below the record of 4,093. Once again, a NASA pilot had demonstrated that spaceflight was possible and that the tools to achieve it were within grasp. He experienced no nausea or other untoward symptoms in weightlessness. Controlling the craft in the vacuum of space using the maneuver jets was not only possible, but relatively easy. For the few minutes he spent in space that day, Armstrong was, in effect, practicing the landing of the *Eagle* at Tranquillity Base that would occur seven years later.

Having achieved the goals of the mission, Armstrong carefully aimed the once-again powerless craft—now a glider—back into earth's atmosphere, carefully choosing the exact angle that would let him reenter gradually enough not to burn up. He started a long left turn over Nevada and headed back toward the dry lakebed, and applied the upper speed brake, which peeled away excess energy and allowed him to enter into an acceptable landing pattern.

Back in the control room, Jan listened warily as her husband calmly related speed, altitude, and other calculations. Suddenly there was a sonic boom far louder than any she had heard in five years as a test pilot's wife. Startled by the ferocity of the crack, she audibly gasped, causing little Eric to look at her hard, registering his mother's alarm. Just as quickly she forced the reassuring smile that she had assumed many times before and would have to repeat countless times in the future.

When the X-15 was visible in the northern sky, some NASA officials nearly gasped; Neil was coming in very hot and alarmingly fast. Unpowered reentry into the earth's atmosphere wasn't normally as demanding for the pilots as controlling the plane's fierce acceleration. But it was hard on the pilot's body; for a mercifully brief period less than thirty seconds long, Neil experienced an unacceptably brutal 5 g's, meaning his body would feel as though it weighed nearly a thousand pounds. As soon as the plane's fall was broken, the weight was lifted. But on that April morning Neil had miscalculated; from the NASA control room he appeared to be coming almost vertically for a crash landing on the dry lakebed. Jan and the other onlookers were speechless. Then, at the last moment, he pulled out of the dive and slammed the craft to the ground on its landing gear, which somehow held up. He had missed the landing mark by about three miles, and skidded down the lakebed for two miles before finally coming to a safe stop. Once again the long, forgiving lakebed had saved a life.

It was taken for granted that the work being done at Edwards was extremely dangerous; the miracle was that out of 189 X-15 flights, only one resulted in a fatality. Despite the obvious dangers, the work—seen by the government as strictly military defense research—was going to be accelerated, not slowed; events on the other side of the world were ensuring that.

In August of that year, the Soviet Union began building an enormous brick wall that would seal Communist East Berlin off from the West, effectively making its citizens prisoners. The area immediately to the eastern side of the wall became a dead zone, fortified with antipersonnel mines, barbed wire, and enforced by soldiers ordered to shoot to kill East Berliners attempting to flee to freedom. It was seen as an egregious, ugly, and brazen act of aggression, a crime against humanity, and, chillingly, an iron-fisted mien the Soviets were not ashamed of displaying to the world. The space research Armstrong and his colleagues were doing in the California desert became more urgent daily.

On the very day that Armstrong was suffering a razzing over his too-hot landing and several-mile-wide miss of the landing mark, he got more bad news. The Air Force announced that Captain Robert H. McIntosh, who had just completed an eight-month test-pilot training program at Edwards, would likely be the first man to walk on the moon. McIntosh had much in common with Armstrong, despite his lack of test-pilot experience. He was also a decorated Korean War pilot in his early thirties who had dreamed all his life of space travel. But, unlike Neil, he was a military officer and an Annapolis graduate. The Air Force generals in charge of the project selected a total of eight officers for their moon project because they were determined a military man would be first on the moon. The intention was that the eight would be the next group to follow the Mercury astronauts at NASA. "The new group are all graduate engineers," said an Air Force spokesman, "and have quite a bit more background than the seven astronauts in the civilian space program."

Asked to evaluate his chances of going to the moon, McIntosh was optimistic. "The chances are getting better. I hope they are one to one." None of the eight ever flew in space.

In the wake of NASA's great success and leap forward in knowledge with the X-15, the agency prepared for "Round Three," the Dyna-Soar, which was the closest they would come at Edwards to the model that would eventually land man on the moon. Dyna-Soar was designed to be boosted into earth orbit by a Titan III rocket. It would allow pilots to spend extended periods in space to determine what effect it had on their functioning, and to acquire useful data on reentry to earth's atmosphere. In the end the craft was never fully deployed, and the project was canceled in December 1963 because thinking on spacecraft design was rapidly changing. But it was considered a useful design exercise.

Neil Armstrong was maturing into one of NASA's most creative analytical engineers, as well as an unusually adept test pilot, and the challenges of the Dyna-Soar program allowed him to further demonstrate his powers of deduction.

One of the chief safety worries over Dyna-Soar's design was what procedure to follow in the event of an abort—specifically, how to save the pilot and spacecraft in the event of a launch-pad booster explosion. Dyna-Soar was designed with a small abort rocket that would disengage it from the booster and supply sufficient power to escape an explosion. The question was how to land the Dyna-Soar safely after it was blasted away from the booster. Armstrong took on the problem and began experimenting using the F5D-1 Skylancer, an aircraft with a similar configuration. After a few weeks, working first on paper, then with the Skylancer, Armstrong told his superiors he had a solution. The flight path to safety was not for the faint of heart, nor for the novice pilot. But its concept was a thing of beauty, and it worked every time. He flew the Skylancer in a vertical climb reaching five thousand feet, pulling it into a half-roll, then turning upside down, nose to the horizon, finally rolling 180 degrees and landing on the lakebed in an area that had been marked like the 10,000-foot escape landing strip at Cape Canaveral.

Another innovation Armstrong endorsed was a strange hybrid flying machine called the Parasev—called the "space-age kite," or the "Rogallo wing" after its inventor, NACA engineer Francis Rogallo. Armstrong and fellow X-15 pilot Milt Thompson felt the wing could be stowed in a spacecraft and used to maneuver through the atmosphere. It would give the pilots a large measure of control over their otherwise unpowered craft and would eliminate the need for dangerous, and sometimes sickening, ocean splashdowns. While the idea had little appeal to the NASA Flight Research Center technical staff, Thompson and Armstrong had considerable clout and were able to get a research version built. Parasev I, as it was known, was an odd-looking beast indeed. It was essentially a big tricycle with a single seat. Attached was an angled mast and a thirty-square-yard parawing. The whole "research plane" cost less than five thousand dollars; it was the first and only craft built totally in-house by the space agency. At first it was towed at sixty miles per hour behind a utility vehicle across the dry lakebed, sending choking clouds of dust into the face of the unfortunate pilot. Parasev's first flights were to an altitude of a few dozen feet, but it worked. Parasev I-A, with a reconfigured stick-and-rudder control system and an improved-design wing, was lifted nearly one thousand feet skyward by a rented Stearman biplane. Armstrong, Thompson, and Gus Grissom all flew Parasev I-A, felt they had mastered the device, and wanted to see it deployed. But NASA engineers were still unconvinced and apparently weren't moved by the future astronauts' wishes not to be plunked into the sea at the end of a journey to outer space.

X-15 pilot Bill Dana says NASA used an unfortunate accident as an excuse to scuttle the project. "Neil, Gus, and Milt had no problems flying Parasev. It was a very successful project. But when a guy far less skilled than they were had an accident, the whole project was killed as too dangerous. Neil was disappointed and cursed that it wasn't incorporated into the space program every time astronauts had to be fished out of the ocean at the end of a trip. But to me it is one more example of the way Neil thought. Neil had the ability to come up with a solution to a problem before we even knew we had a problem."

Chapter Eleven

Jan Armstrong grew increasingly concerned in the hot summer of 1962 about their three-year-old daughter, Karen. She seemed to be running fevers all the time. Cool baths, aspirin, and medicine the doctor gave her had minimal effect. In desperation, she and Neil drove the child to Cedars of Lebanon Hospital in Los Angeles to see specialists. After a battery of X-rays and tests, doctors came to a terrible diagnosis. Karen had an inoperable tumor on her brain, which would inevitably kill her. Reeling with shock, utterly poleaxed, the dauntless test pilot cried and trembled with grief.

Despite the hell he was going through, Neil soldiered on and rarely spoke to his colleagues of the grief his family was suffering. Betty Love recalls the occasional hopeful updates Neil would share with his carpool mates, inevitably followed by days when he was so grim and so pained inside it hurt just to look at him. "He would tell us when there were new tests, new possibilities that one specialist or another could offer a glimmer of hope. But it was a slow, torturous ache that Neil mostly kept to himself. That was his way; he wasn't one to talk about things like that. It was mostly kept inside."

When Karen died a few months later, the Armstrongs seemed to friends aged far beyond their years, ragged and damaged. "It took Neil a great deal of time to understand how God could do such a thing to a little child," said Viola. "But in the end he accepted it. Neil and Jan could never have survived their ordeal without a lot of help from God."

A few years later, close friends who had known Armstrong since

INDIAN PRAIRIE PUBLIC LIBRARY
401 Plainfield Road
Darien, IL 60561

Purdue saw a rare display of the still-raw emotions just below the surface, usually so carefully contained and hidden. "Neil came to Purdue for homecoming and the football game, as he usually has over the years," recalled Sally Lugar. "He came alone; Jan wasn't with him. He was subdued, but not terribly. Of course we all knew what had happened, what they had been through, but Neil wouldn't say a word, so it wasn't mentioned. Then, one afternoon, we were at my sister's house in West Lafayette, having a casual afternoon with some of our old classmates; cocktails, chatter. I remember my sister's little girl was there. She was about four or five, and all dressed up in a pretty green party dress, just the age Karen would have been. Neil noticed her and smiled, then all of a sudden he just broke down and sobbed. It was the most horribly painful thing you can imagine."

Another friend said that, in addition to the searing pain, there was guilt on Neil's part that he was not present when the end came for Karen. "Jan was alone when she died," said Ken Danneberg. "It hurt her badly that he wasn't there."

After they buried their child at Joshua Park Cemetery near Lancaster, Jan and Neil's life in their mountain home was certainly soured. Neil had been examining other challenges, particularly applying to be an astronaut.

The Houston Space Center, the spacecraft being developed there, and the program the test pilots had scorned gradually were coming to be seen as the wave of the future. It was becoming evident that Edwards was no longer the place to be. Things were changing in the space race, and everyone was talking about a new facility opening up near Houston—a "space center." Most scientists were convinced that fixed-wing planes were the wrong approach to space travel. The X-15 had been both a failure and a success. It had touched the face of space as it was meant to, but it was becoming evident that a multistage rocket with multiple tons of additional thrust was necessary. Our ablest scientists had grossly underestimated Mother Earth's tenacious grip.

Most test pilots had scorned the notion of riding a capsule fixed on the tip of a rocket as "monkey's work." But after years of flying exotic fixed-wing rocket craft like the X-15 and Dyna-Soar, Neil and his colleagues were wavering. Wernher von Braun felt the key was to launch a multistage rocket with a second craft on its nose that would blast free of the earth, then use the moon's own gravitational field to pull it through space. When it reached the moon, it would insert itself into orbit and dispatch a third craft with a tiny rocket engine to visit the surface, which was all that would be needed in the relatively slight gravity and nonexistent atmosphere. After a visit, the lunar module would lift off and redock with the orbiting craft. Reserve rockets would fire to break free of the moon and get far enough away that earth's gravity could pull it home. It was a simple, even elegant plan, yet horribly complex in the details. The first phase of the project was to be called Mercury, and its champions were convinced it would get the United States into space, and quickly. And since speed was of the essence in the politically charged space race, their strategy was given the thumbs-up by Congress and President Kennedy.

Von Braun asked for volunteers to go to the new space center in Houston to prepare for a flight to the moon. During the summer of 1962, Armstrong was still apprehensive. "We had spent years developing the rocket airplane concept, and Mercury looked like a dark horse to us," he wrote in a 1964 *World Book* article. "We tended to regard Mercury people as inexperienced intruders in our business. I am frank to admit I gave them too little credit. As a pilot accustomed to full control of the X-15, I didn't relish the Mercury concept of relinquishing control to people on the ground. Also, like most flight-test people at Edwards, I wasn't convinced that the Mercury ballistic configuration NASA had decided on would ultimately be the most practical and economical shape to use in space exploration. But as the moon program became a reality, I could see we were beginning to move much faster into space than I would have dreamed possible."

In the spring of 1962, there were two competing United States space programs. Dyna-Soar was still a fully funded, operational project, and Neil was a senior pilot, guaranteed command of one of its earliest spaceflights. But the window of opportunity to apply for the upcoming Gemini/Apollo program in Houston was narrow, lasting only that April and June. By mid-June, Neil was still straddling the fence, despite pleas from friends on both sides of it. Finally, days before the deadline for the next group of astronauts, he made the wrenching decision, which in the end boiled down to the difference between possibly only skirting space, or fulfilling what had come to seem his destiny: a walk on the moon.

"I deliberated until June, during which I balanced my desire to participate in deep-space work against continuing with the near-space programs in which I was so deeply involved. I decided to make a clean break and apply for Gemini and Apollo."

Shortly after Armstrong's formal application arrived at Houston, Deke Slayton phoned with the welcome news he had been accepted and should move to Texas to begin astronaut training immediately.

The media response came shortly after the family's arrival at Houston, and was as puzzling at the time as it is prophetic now. The August 18, 1962, *Washington Star* carried a story on its front page quoting unnamed official sources as saying: "Neil Armstrong will be the first civilian selected for training as an astronaut. Conceivably he could command America's first attempt to land men on the moon." In the report's third paragraph, D. Brainard Holmes, then director of NASA's Office of Manned Space Flight, is quoted cautioning that the final selection of astronauts had not yet been made. Yet the *Star*'s editors felt confident enough of their information to lead with the news that the first moon walker had been at least tentatively picked, seven years before the event. This incredibly prescient report, later officially denied, was the first sign, officially or otherwise, that Neil Armstrong, thirty-one years old at the time, had been selected for the astronaut program, let alone chosen to be first on the moon. In NASA's files the original clipping is marked "later denied" and the line "Holmes did not identify any of the men likely to be named" is underlined. At the time, NASA had no way of knowing whether it would ever send any man to the moon, and it certainly wasn't in a position to know which man would go through the rigorous physical and psychological training required and emerge as the right candidate. But the leak to the *Star* does offer a glimpse into the space agency's thinking at the time. Neil Armstrong was at least the kind of man it was after, and the notion of a civilian as America's first representative on an extraterrestrial body was likely set as well.

The headlines sent fame crashing through the Armstrongs' door that summer, and it would never again leave. Among the bizarre symptoms was a rambling letter addressed to President Kennedy signed Neal (with an "a" rather than an "i") Armstrong from a Louisiana man claiming to be the newly chosen astronaut's father. Assured that he had no relatives in Louisiana, NASA dispatched security personnel to investigate. It was a harmless, but annoying, example of the kinds of worms that would begin crawling out from under rocks.

Despite the unspeakable pain of losing a child in 1962, Neil recalls the period of 1955 to 1962 he and his family spent at Dryden as "wonderful years." At the fiftieth-anniversary ceremonies at Dryden in 1996, he spoke rhapsodically about the center: "I have enormous affection for this place—its people and its visions for the future of flight. The idea of flight research aircraft was not new—the Wright Brothers had done it—but the government had never funded one, at least not for the specific purpose of flight research. My years here were wonderful. There's an unbelievable willingness to test impossibilities here. I congratulate the institution."

Armstrong said the glory days spent at Dryden were about much more than fame for the pilots. "Speed records and altitude records were a very important way for the military services to demonstrate advanced technology and to engender the support of the American people and Congress for their budgets. The X-15 was undoubtedly one of the most memorable, most exotic of all the programs at Dryden. Advances in speed at that time were achieved with great difficulty. The X-15 seemed to be an enormous jump from what we were flying then. I'll be forever grateful I had a chance to be a part of that program."

In October 1983, writing the foreword to *On the Frontier: Flight Research at Dryden, 1946–1981,* NASA's account of its first twenty-five years, Armstrong proved he wasn't just a steely-eyed engineer, but also brought a poet's eye to his work.

"A stillness was on the desert. Daylight settled unhurriedly down the hilltops bordering the triangular valley. The indigo sky above and to the west was pierced with the gleam of a solitary planet and the flicker of an occasional second- or third-magnitude star.

"The valley bottom was an immense expanse of flatness. Miles of mirror-smooth clay were marred by neither hummock nor furrow. No tree or bush could be seen on this seemingly endless waterless lake. No sound from animal or bird punctuated the silence. Wild creatures found little to attract them on this vast empty platter. It was one of nature's quiet hideaways, an outpost of serenity.

"There were intruders. On the western shore of this 'lake,' figures scurried around a strange assemblage. A small shark-sleek craft was being attached to a much larger mother-craft. The shark's midsection was banded with ice crystals; puffs of ashen vapor wafted upward and disappeared into the clear sky. The juxtaposition of ancient geology and modern technology curiously seemed to fit.

"By mid-twentieth century, the science of aeronautics had grown to substantial maturity. Aircraft were speeding faster and faster and were threatening to outrace their own sound. The National Advisory Committee for Aeronautics had a trio of laboratories to study the fundamental problems of flight. They had a variety of test facilities and a cadre of bright, able and dedicated scientists who had performed with remarkable success over the years surrounding the Second World War. For the testing of very-high-speed aircraft, however, they needed a new laboratory: a laboratory in the sky.

"And so it was that researchers came to the Antelope Valley in California, a place blessed with clear and uncrowded skies, a sparse population and Muroc Dry Lake, a natural aerodrome where runway length and direction were, for most practical purposes, unlimiting.

"On the shore of Muroc, NACA established its High Speed Flight Station and began its challenge of the unknown. The mysteries were numerous and perplexing. The search for solutions was tedious, protracted and often dangerous. The research methods placed men and machines at the boundaries of understanding. On occasion, fine men were lost at those boundaries of understanding. Their sacrifices will be remembered.

"At the dawn of the Space Age, the researchers on the shore of the dry lake were already actively engaged in its planning. After NACA became NASA, their considerable contributions were of substantial significance in the evolution of America's manned spaceflight program."

John Kennedy was at his eloquent and inspirational best on May 25, 1961 when he delivered an address to Congress: "I believe this nation should commit itself to achieve the goal, before this decade is out, of landing a man on the moon and returning him safely to the earth."

Challenging a generation to take up the gantlet, he asked: "Why choose this as our goal? Why climb the highest mountain? Why twenty-five years ago, fly the Atlantic? We choose to go to the moon. We choose to go to the moon in this decade and do the other things— not because they are easy, but because they are *hard*. Because that goal will serve to organize and measure the best of our abilities and skills, because that challenge is one that we are willing to accept, one we are unwilling to postpone, one which we intend to win."

To the complete surprise and delight of Jan and the couple's friends, Neil's personality seemed to change drastically at the Houston Space Center. Uncharacteristically, he agreed they should live in a red ranch house at 1003 Woodland drive in El Lago near the Texas space center, which was a virtual astronaut enclave of cookie-cutter tract houses. But they were nearly new, with much-needed air conditioning during Houston's long, humid summers, a pool in the backyard, high cathedral ceilings, and neighbors who were also in the space program. After years of determined resistance, he was going to join the brotherhood and let his family become part of it as well. At the rowdy backyard barbecues favored by the flyers, Neil let himself go more than he ever had, even chugging down beers on occasion. Jan remembered the early sixties in Houston as the happiest period of their marriage. Through many terror-filled moments when her husband's life was in jeopardy, there was support from the other astronaut families, the only people on earth who knew exactly what it was like.

Just as the Armstrongs began unpacking, America was facing the most terrifying crisis of the Cold War. On October 14, a high-flying American U-2 spy plane flying over Communist Cuba took clear pictures of newly installed missile bunkers that Central Intelligence Agency analysts determined contained nuclear-tipped ballistic missiles capable of reaching the United States mainland in minutes. Like most Americans, Neil and Jan watched with horror as President Kennedy told the nation of the missiles, and his plan to place a naval embargo around the rogue island, challenging the Soviets to cross the line he had drawn in the sea. For the first time, the superpowers were engaged in a nuclear face-off. The space center's security was upped many times, guards with machine guns ringing the perimeter. In Florida, more than two hundred thousand troops stood at the ready. Neil had resigned his commission as a Navy reserve officer two years before, but was fully aware that he would certainly be sought after by the military for his skills and knowledge of flight in the event of war, unless the unspeakable happened—a nuclear exchange that could end in both nations' decimation.

The crisis ended on October 28, when Soviet Premier Nikita Khrushchev accepted a compromise. The United States pledged never to invade Cuba and to remove U.S. missiles based in Turkey, in exchange for the Soviets' removal of their weapons from Cuba.

While the world breathed a sigh of relief, Neil got word from NASA that he was about to be sent on a training mission to Panama, which was no surprise. Since the earliest days of the space program, NASA brass had been concerned that the astronauts could, conceivably, crash-land anywhere in the world—a jungle, desert, or mountaintop—and they had better be prepared to survive that eventuality, however disagreeable. In fact, the trip to the Panamanian jungle was just the first of many to some of the most hellish spots on earth. Neil's partner was fellow Ohio country boy John Glenn, who had become the first American to orbit the earth the previous February. The astronauts were flown to a U.S. Air Force base near Panama City, where they were lectured for two long days by Marine survival experts about what things in the jungle will kill you and how to avoid them, what will keep you alive and how to catch them. Buzz Aldrin, who attended the same school a few years later, was horrified at some of the cold-blooded advice. "We were told that if you catch an iguana, and are not particularly hungry, don't kill it and carry its smelly body around. Instead, immobilize it until you are ready to eat it. The front claws have nails, which you pull quite hard on until they come loose and hang by a tendon, which you can tie behind its head for easy portage. They told me it didn't hurt. I said it certainly looked like it did."

After the grisly tutorial on edible bugs, roots, and worms, Armstrong, Glenn, and the other men were transported by helicopter into the Choco Indian territory deep in the high-canopy rain forest armed with the standard NASA survival kit and sleeping hammocks to last out the rest of the week. Glenn remembered: "Neil had a sly sense of humor. After we had built our two-man lean-to of wood and jungle vines, he used a charred stick to write the name 'Choco Hilton' on it."

The most exotic creatures the astronauts actually ate were small fish they caught in a stream and cooked over a fire made of damp, hard-to-light kindling, which never got the fish quite done. It rained nearly the entire time they were in the jungle—torrential monsoon-type rains that kept them sopping wet and miserable. During brief respites from the downpours, mosquitos feasted on them. Both men struggled with the mosquito netting they had been given, winding up tangled, cursing, laughing, and falling down in the mud.

At the end of the training, there was another surprise. The scattered and mangy survivor trainees were issued life vests and told to wade out to a rapid stream, which led to a river. Holding on for dear life, they careened downriver, finally getting hurled into the Panama Canal. Cast into the great canal like tiny bits of flotsam, they bobbed in the water helplessly while enormous freighters and cruise ships steamed by. The astronauts' ordeal finally ended when they were fished out of the water by a NASA launch boat.

Back in Houston, the intense training rarely let up; but with the goal he had dreamed of for a lifetime nearly within reach, Neil became even more obsessed with his work, learning everything he possibly could about a technology that was being invented by the day. "Neil always gave his heart and soul to a project, but the Apollo mission completely consumed him," recalled Jan Armstrong. "He stayed on the job all night long, totally losing track of time. When he went to Cape Canaveral, he often forgot to call and tell me where he was staying. I'd get frantic. He was possessed by the project."

Always taciturn, Neil became even more withdrawn. "To Neil, silence is an answer, no is an argument," Jan summed it up at the time. "Usually when you ask him something he just doesn't answer," said their son Rick.

During the winter of 1963 Jan gave birth to Mark Stephen, giving her a preoccupation to match her husband's. "Jan was an absolutely dedicated mother," said Danneberg. "She devoted all her efforts to the swimming lessons, music lessons, helping with homework. You could tell she was happy doing it all. And she made the most of Neil's obsession with his work. Even when it hurt to be alone, to feel left out, which she often did, Jan never complained, never questioned it. She backed him one hundred percent."

Neil was busy and excited at the prospects of what lay ahead. By June he was regularly experiencing weightlessness in a training plane jocularly dubbed the "vomit comet." The plane would dive from a high altitude, then go into a steep climbing attitude until the aircraft achieved sufficient altitude for another steep dive, like a roller coaster path, the zero-g effect in the top part of the arc creating a reasonable simulation of weightlessness for about thirty seconds. Neil had been in a weightless environment during his X-15 flights, but this was much different. The huge hull of the cargo plane used for the exercise allowed the astronauts to actually waltz through space as though they were beyond earth's gravity field.

Meanwhile, Congress was about to earmark $5.5 billion dollars for NASA, which amounted to more than 4 percent of the total U.S. budget, to fully fund the Gemini project. The 7.5-million-pound-thrust Saturn V rocket, which, unlike the X-15 and planned Dyna-Soar, actually had the power to send men to the moon, was being developed at Marshall Space Flight Center in Huntsville, Alabama. And the concepts of establishing a permanent lunar base, as well as a manned orbiting laboratory, were being seriously studied.

With the Gemini program finally under way, there was little time for family and even less for rest. Typically, Neil and the other astronauts put in twelve or more hours a day and stumbled home bleary-eyed, barely able to gulp down a meal, kiss the sleeping children, and collapse into bed.

April 22, 1964, was a typical long night at the space center. Neil was exhausted when he arrived home and went to sleep quickly. Then, in the early-morning hours, he and Jan woke simultaneously with a start. The house was hot, not just because the air conditioner was on the blink, but truly hot; suddenly they both realized there was thick smoke swirling into their bedroom. Jan would never forget the nightmarish brush with tragedy: "Neil went out the bedroom door to see what had awakened us. He came back and said the house was on fire. So I turned on the light, fumbled for the telephone—and Neil told me to call the fire department. I couldn't get the operator on the telephone at 3:00 A.M. It was a long-distance call to the fire department; I couldn't call them directly. I tried dialing 116, because I had had a first-aid course in California. Then I realized that number was local only for the Los Angeles area. So I put the phone down, and Neil had gone in for Marky. I ran to the back of the house, and I was banging on the fence, calling for Pat and Ed White, who lived next door. Our air-conditioning wasn't working, and it was a warm night. I had closed the doors and opened the windows. Otherwise Mark probably would have been asphyxiated by the time we got to him. And there I was, banging on the fence. It was a six-foot fence. The Whites' air-conditioning wasn't working, either, and they heard me calling. Ed came bolting over the fence. I don't know how he did it, but he took one leap and he was over. He got the hoses out immediately, and by this time I had run around to the front of the house for Neil to hand Marky out the window. But no: Neil didn't do that. They were little windows, and Neil would have had to break one of them. He brought Mark down the hall, back to our bedroom, and out. He was standing there and he was waiting for someone to come and get Mark because he was—what, ten months old?—and he couldn't put him down because he was afraid Mark would crawl into the swimming pool and drown. By this time I could hear the fire engines on the way—Pat White had turned in the alarm. This whole wall was red, and the glass was cracking on the windows. I can remember Ed White calling me. He was saying: Here, you hold the hose; I'll get Mark. Neil had gone in for Ricky, who was just awakening at the time. And I was standing with the hose, the concrete was burning my feet, and we had to keep watering the concrete so we could stand there. And Neil came back with Ricky, holding a wet towel over his face."

One ironic, horrible footnote to the fire and Ed White: Four years later, in January 1967, Ed White was burned to death along with Gus Grissom and Roger Chaffee when faulty wiring turned their Apollo 1 capsule into an inferno.

Neil and the boys recovered quickly from the smoke they had inhaled, the house was rebuilt, and their neighbors pitched in to get the Armstrongs' lives back together.

Reluctantly, Armstrong began spending more and more "time in the barrel," as the astronauts called the frequent public appearances that were considered an important part of the job, because it was believed by NASA brass the only way to keep Congress passing billion-dollar budgets was to keep the public firmly in their corner. The week of July 6 through 11 was typical grueling barrel-time. On Monday Neil departed Houston on a NASA plane for a talk at a Staunton, Virginia, military academy. Tuesday was the National Youth Science Camp at Camp Pocahontas in West Virginia. Wednesday was a day in Washington organized by NASA headquarters. It began with briefings, then meetings with key congressmen and reporters—Neil was meant to charm and win them over to NASA's program. Friday was New York, and an appearance at the World's Fair in Flushing Meadows to pose for pictures in front of an X-15, and a press conference. Afterward was a long flight cross-country to Ames, Iowa, to address the Iowa State University Aerospace Workshop, then on to Drake University in Des Moines in the afternoon, and a speech before the Scientific Societies and Universities in the evening. And finally home to Houston.

The standard stump speech at these events covered NASA's basic priorities: the need for space research, a trip to the moon, and how much these expensive exercises would benefit folks from all walks of life. But it was always a welcome bonus when a question from the audience could elicit a headline-making response. At Drake, a woman teacher testily asked if NASA planned to have a female astronaut—pointing out that the Russians already did. Neil defended the agency, saying there were simply no qualified women around, asserting gender was not even considered in the selection process. Then he made headlines, merely predicting that "someday" there would be a female astronaut. In 1964, an X-15 test pilot suggesting there was room in the ranks for a woman—even "someday"—was news.

Although he didn't go into detail, the question of a female astronaut had been an issue at NASA for years, and was on the front burner since June 16,1963, when the Soviets sent female cosmonaut Valentina Tereshkova into earth orbit aboard Vostok 6. At the time, there were five woman cosmonauts in the program, a fact the Russians made a point of publicizing. As Armstrong pointed out, there weren't trained female pilots available to NASA. The United States armed forces allowed no women to train for combat, nor to attend test-pilot school, at least one of which was required as a precondition for applying to the astronaut program. A few women had taken some of the preliminary medical tests, but their applications had been dropped because they lacked those basic requirements of test-pilot or combat experience. American culture still envisioned commanding women, particularly Russians, as the famously lethal, poisoned-tipped-shoe-wielding K.G.B. operative Rosa Kleb (played to wicked perfection by Lotte Lenya) in *From Russia With Love,* the James Bond film that premiered that year. It wasn't until twenty years later, on June 18, 1983, when Dr. Sally Ride orbited the earth aboard the *Challenger,* that the situation was corrected.

Spending weeks "in the barrel," where pointed questions could be fired at him, would seem a daunting challenge for a soft-spoken farmboy with a reputation as an aloof recluse. But Armstrong not only survived, he became exceedingly adept, and in 1969, when the world was watching, it was Buzz Aldrin's choice to let Neil be spokesman for the crew on their world tour.

During the summer of 1964, Gemini, the most ambitious space program ever undertaken, was ready to begin. Its missions of earth orbit and rendezvous—coupling with another craft while circling the planet at 17,000 miles per hour—were the essential first steps toward the moon. And just as important, it was hoped they would reinvigorate American pride and confidence in our ability to compete with and surpass the Soviets in science. Billions of dollars had been allocated, hundreds of thousands of skilled men and women were at work; the nation was crying out: Let's go. The previous April 8, Gemini 1 had been launched from the Cape. But it was an unmanned flight of just three orbits carrying dummy equipment. Still, it was a start and proved the bird could fly.

But the program was bedeviled by problems beyond the control of NASA. In July, with Gemini 2 on the pad and ready for launch, lightning struck. Two weeks later, hurricane Dora threatened and the rocket had to be disassembled and stored. That was followed by yet another hurricane, Ethel, which likewise feigned a charge at the Cape sufficiently convincing to make NASA once again stow its multimillion-dollar rocket. Following glitch after glitch, it was conceded Gemini 2 would not be launched before the end of 1964, leaving Gus Grissom and John Young, in line for Gemini 3, which couldn't launch until Gemini 2 proved successful, sorely frustrated, as was the nation.

Finally, on December 9 the launch of Gemini's first manned flight was under way. But one minute after ignition there was a serious problem in a hydraulic valve, causing the automatic malfunction-detection system to shut the engine down immediately. The safety device, newly installed on Gemini's Titan rocket, may have saved the rocket from exploding, and untold damage to the program.

NASA tried again on January 19, 1965. This time was the charm. The first stage fired as planned and fell away; the second stage likewise was flawless. The capsule separated, then fired its maneuver rockets, which turned it around, fired retrorockets, and reentered the atmosphere as planned. At last manned shots could be scheduled; Project Gemini was a go. Amid the jubilation, Armstrong learned he had finally been assigned a slot by Deke Slayton, albeit as a backup. He was set to train as such, along with Elliot See, for Gordon Cooper and Charles "Pete" Conrad's Gemini-Titan 5, a seven-day orbital mission tentatively set for the fourth quarter of the year.

One of the first simulators Armstrong trained on for the mission was a diabolical machine developed at the NASA facility where his career had begun—the Lewis Research Center in Cleveland. Called the "Multiple Axis Space Test Inertia Facility" or MASTIF, it was designed to train astronauts to cope with an out-of-control space capsule spinning like a blender on puree—ironically, the exact near-disaster that would befall him.

The astronaut was harnessed to a reclining chair that revolved on three separate axes at a dizzying, sickening pace while he attempted to control all three: pitch (vertical), yaw (side to side), and roll (horizontal). Even NASA administrators thought the ingenious simulator was a bit over the top, and reckoned the arcane skills its mastery required would never be needed in actual space flight. "I don't know what the odds were," wrote Deke Slayton rather incredulously. Nevertheless, Armstrong worked hours without complaint until he could effortlessly manipulate the controls at even the highest gravity-force level.

In March, Virgil "Gus" Grissom and John W. Young were blasted aloft by a Titan II rocket, on Gemini 3, the first two-man orbital spaceflight. In their spacecraft, nicknamed "Molly Brown" after the famed, feisty survivor of the *Titanic* disaster, they orbited the earth three times at an apex of 142 miles, and performed orbit-changing maneuvers for the first time. After four hours and fifty-four minutes aloft, soaring at speeds over twenty thousand miles per hour, "Molly Brown" was steered back to earth by the astronauts—proving the space program was not making monkeys of the pilots—and splashed down near Bermuda, far closer to its target then had ever been accomplished.

That great success was followed on June 3 by James McDivitt and Edward White's Gemini 4, which orbited the earth sixty-two times and set a world record spending over ninety-seven hours in space, finally trumping the Russians. And an American, Ed White, finally walked in space, 135 miles above North America, tethered to the orbiting capsule by a twenty-five-foot lifeline. White was scheduled to stay outside for twelve minutes, which would have bested the Russians by two minutes. But the cocky, athletic astronaut, enraptured with the thrill of dancing a minuet in space as the blue earth revolved below and the panoply of stars glowed above, ignored the calls of Commander McDivitt and the pleas of Mission Command in Houston ("I'm not coming back in," he joked at one point), staying outside for twenty minutes, taking movies and still pictures.

Two months later, Gemini 5, which was designed to keep astronauts in space for a record eight days (as long as it would take to get to the moon and back) was launched. It was the second ride in space for Gordon Cooper, who had made twenty-two orbits on a Mercury mission in 1963. Gordo's good fortune was resented by some of the astronauts who had not been in space at all, as Armstrong had not, but there was certainly an awareness in the corps of his skill as an astronaut, and that most-admired quality, composure under conditions that would make most mortals come unglued. Cooper had been an engineer at Edwards, not a test pilot, and it came as a surprise to Deke Slayton and others in the program that he had been chosen in the first place. But Gordo's Mercury flight, dubbed "Faith 7," made him a hero and an inspiration. On the nineteenth orbit of his tiny, one-man capsule, 165 miles above the earth, soaring at 17,546 miles an hour, Gordon experienced total power failure. All on-board electronics, including automatic guidance systems, shorted out, followed by the cooling system, which was needed to purify the oxygen he was breathing. Carbon dioxide levels rose and the temperature soared to well over a hundred degrees. Displaying the perfect temperament of a space pioneer, Cooper didn't panic, but instead took control of the dead ship manually, estimating the correct pitch for the delicate job of reentering the atmosphere—not too deep so as to burn up and not too shallow as to bounce off. Rather incredibly, considering the complexity of the calculations, he did the job perfectly, saving his life and possibly the life of the space program, making the most accurate splashdown to date, just off the deck of the aircraft carrier U.S.S. *Kearsarge,* near Midway in the South Pacific.

Cooper was greeted as an American hero with a ticker tape parade in New York City, and, just as important to him, was considered a champion to his colleagues for proving, for once and for all, that astronauts in a space craft were not "Spam in a can," but highly skilled pilots. Most agreed he had earned his spot on Gemini 5.

Gemini 5 also had its moments of drama for Conrad and Cooper when the newly installed fuel cell–electrical system proved balky, causing the capsule to become uncomfortably hot. Conrad later expressed his fear that the retrorockets, needed to slow the craft and reenter earth's atmosphere when the mission was over, would have frozen after eight days in space, preventing their return to earth while there was still air and water left. Conrad later admitted he had decided he would slit his wrists rather than endlessly orbit, waiting to be asphyxiated when the oxygen ran out. Of course, the public knew nothing of the astronauts' dark thoughts, but heated television and radio reports about the mission's electrical problems got a rise out of a nation grown complacent over the seemingly routine and clockwork precision of the first four Gemini missions.

Cooper and Pete Conrad circled the earth a record 120 times and returned to earth none the worse for wear, proving man could indeed endure, for more than a week, weightlessness and the other vicissitudes space imposes on the human body.

Next up was the most ambitious mission yet—actually a double mission. Gemini 6 and 7 would be in earth orbit at the same time and attempt to rendezvous. Gemini 7 was first into orbit, on December 3, piloted by Frank Borman and Jim Lovell. It was to be followed a few days later by Gemini 6, piloted by Walter Schirra and Thomas Stafford, but 6 was bedeviled by failures, including two launch scrubs, and wasn't able to blast off until December 15, when its sister mission had already been in space for 162 orbits and twelve days. If Gemini 5 had been a wake-up call, the rendezvous flights really flirted with disaster. The fuel cells that had been trouble on Gemini 5 were constantly threatening to shut down completely on Gemini 7; thruster misfires causing the ship to spin were a continual annoyance and drained so much maneuver fuel there was barely enough left to fulfill the docking mission.

Frank Borman was a by-the-book West Point graduate who believed the mission was all that mattered, and Jim Lovell, who later commanded the ill-fated Apollo 13 moon mission, was also a tough and dedicated soldier. But after twelve days of frustration with technology that simply wasn't performing, and miserable conditions inside the spacecraft, they were barely holding on, wishing the journey they had dreamed of for a lifetime would come to a quick end. It was only the adept coaxing of NASA flight controllers like Christopher Columbus Kraft, a legend for his brilliant management of the men and machines of the space program, and the professionalism of the astronauts aboard the flight that brought the mission to a successful conclusion. Despite all their problems getting into space, Schirra and Stafford managed to catch up with Gemini 7, after a hundred-thousand-mile space chase, and came within six feet of exhausted, exasperated Borman and Lovell's ship, while both orbited earth at nearly twenty-eight times the speed of sound.

After thirteen days, eighteen hours, and thirty-six minutes, and 206 orbits, the bearded, bone-weary astronauts splashed down in the Atlantic, requesting a helicopter pickup because they couldn't stand to spend another minute in the cramped, malodorous capsule.

Chapter Twelve

On the balmy north Florida morning of March 16, 1966, two and a half years after John Kennedy's death, his words were still ringing in the ears of many of the 400,000 people working with the space program to fulfill his promise. Neil Armstrong, then thirty-five years old, gave the thumbs-up sign, grasped a hatch handle, and swung into the Gemini 8 capsule, which was about the size of the front seat area of a compact car, mounted on a ten-story, 400,000-pound Titan II. The rocket, which seemed enormous and unfathomably powerful at the time, was only a fraction of the size of its successor, the giant moon rocket Saturn V.

Gemini-Titan was originally designed and configured as an intercontinental ballistic missile with a nine-megaton nuclear tip rather than passengers. As a result, the ride was bone-crushingly jarring, and the vehicle's reliability was problematic; out of an armada of hundreds of nuclear missiles, losing a few to explosions in-flight mattered little. For NASA to adopt them for the space program had required an enormous, costly, and, most important, in space-race terms speedy effort. But by Armstrong's first spaceflight most everyone was satisfied NASA had a safe, smooth-riding powerhouse.

Armstrong's pilot was the handsome six-foot-tall Air Force Major David Scott, a West Pointer who finished fifth in his class and held a master's degree from the Massachusetts Institute of Technology in the arcane but pertinent subject of interplanetary navigation. Thirty-two years old, he was a square-jawed, all-business kind of a guy whose hobby was archeology; he had a reputation for being as reserved as

Neil. Scott was also considered one of the best of a very good lot and Armstrong was glad to have him along.

Five months after Gemini 6 and 7's troubled effort proving that rendezvous in space was possible, the space agency was ready to try again. This time it was to be the real thing, with Gemini 8 not only performing a space rendezvous, but actually docking with the unmanned Atlas-Agena.

The long countdown went smoothly for both Atlas-Agena and Gemini. Atlas-Agena roared skyward at 10 o'clock in the morning. The trajectory was at first low and to the south of the flight path until a supplemental-maneuver engine automatically fired hard to drive the rocket back on target. Six minutes after blastoff, the spacecraft had effectively broken loose of earth's gravity, so the booster fell away, tumbling back down to the Atlantic, and the Agena engine's propulsion system burst into life. Just as planned, it carried its payload smoothly into earth orbit 170 miles high, perfectly positioned for rendezvous.

While Atlas-Agena successfully coasted into orbit, Armstrong and Scott were completing their final checklist for blastoff. The flight-preparation crew—aided by Gemini 8's backup commander Pete Conrad and pilot Dick Gordon—feverishly righted minor glitches, including a potentially lethal foulup—glue in one of Scott's parachute catches, which Conrad and McDonnell Aircraft pad leader Guenter Wendt quickly dug out. Scott was seriously peeved, fuming to himself that the glue "might have cost us a launch." The famously profane Conrad was cursing a blue streak, sweat coursing down his prematurely balding head, as he labored over the job. Pausing to wipe his brow, the gap-toothed astronaut realized that over the din of Launch-Pad 19 he hadn't realized Armstrong and Scott were enjoying a raucous preflight laugh at his expense. Conrad barked an obscenity and got back to work.

Though neither man mentioned it, both Conrad and Scott were relieved to hear Armstrong's happy, staccato laughter. Three weeks prior, on February 28, Elliot See, who had trained long and hard with Neil as backup crew on Gemini 5, was flying to the McDonnell Aircraft plant in St. Louis for simulator training in the astronaut's usual getabout, a T-38 trainer. Arriving for an early-morning landing through thick clouds, See apparently realized he was coming in too slow and needed to circle around for another landing attempt; he hit the afterburners and made a right turn—directly into the building that held the crafts they were scheduled to ride into space. Both See and fellow astronaut Charlie Bassett were killed instantly. Armstrong had grown quite fond of the soft-spoken See, and his sudden death was a blow. He was near-morose and preoccupied since the accident. Men who daily live with death, whether skyscraper riveters or police officers, tend to deal with a fatality in their ranks as not preordained or an act of Providence, but an incident that can logically be traced to a flaw in performance or character and therefore avoided, at least in their case. The astronauts were not exceptions. Deke Slayton gruffly concluded See hadn't been aggressive enough as a flyer—a cardinal sin among men who put "high speed" before their job title. "Too old-womanish. I mean he flew too slow," groused Slayton. This too-neat assessment hadn't made Armstrong, or the dead flyers' other friends, feel any better about the loss.

As the launch window approached, Armstrong was informed the target Agena was on an excellent trajectory and would be awaiting his rear approach. He smiled and said: "Beautiful, we will take that one." Seconds later, Gemini 8's hatch was slammed and bolted in place from the outside, an "improvement" over the Mercury hatch, which had prematurely blown its explosive locks and nearly drowned Gus Grissom on July 21, 1961, when he splashed down his Mercury-Redstone mission.

Gemini 8 was ready for liftoff at 10:00 A.M., Eastern Standard Time. Countdown went smoothly and launch director Rocco Petrone gave a signal to light Titan II's candle at 11:40:59 A.M. Armstrong and Scott braced as a river of fire flowed out of Titan's engines, then felt the snap of the huge iron claws that had held them in place on the pad, while sufficient energy was generated for a clean liftoff of the ten-story behemoth. Once under way, the flight was surprisingly smooth, though acceleration seemed to continue, and continue, and intensify way beyond their wildest expectations. Even for test pilots who had flown at twice the speed of a bullet, the acceleration to 17,350 miles an hour was shocking. In less than ten minutes both stages of Titan were gone and the 8,351-pound Gemini 8 spacecraft had reached elliptical orbit 161 nautical miles high.

Armstrong and Scott were in space and on track, a goal a few years earlier that seemed so daunting that many doubted it could ever be accomplished. But on their mission it was only the beginning; the next challenge was catching the target, Agena, which had a thousand-mile lead. In the vastness of the purple void before them, finding a tiny pinpoint seemed hopelessly futile.

Less than forty-five minutes into the flight, they had crossed the African continent and were approaching Australia. In the inky blackness over the South Pacific, Armstrong and Scott looked in concern and mild alarm at the first untoward indication of the journey. Gemini, which at that stage should have been purely ballistic, was instead spewing a fountain of sparks from its thrusters. The ship appeared in the Australian sky as a flaming meteor, a miniature sun, causing late-night sky watchers some shock. The astronauts, and eventually the public, were quickly reassured by NASA's Carnarvon, Australia, tracking station that their radiator had vented slightly and the thrusters fired to realign their course. Carnarvon informed them there was no concern at Houston, as the incident was considered a normal automatic systems correction. Gemini 8 flight-operations director Chris Kraft had given the "go." In any event, by that point the ship had passed the Hawaiian islands, was back in daylight, and the astronauts could see the California coast clearly. After checking calculations and reassuring themselves they were on course to catch their prey, Armstrong and Scott took some more time to admire the quick-moving planet below. Neil's adopted home state, California, was below. He struggled to find Edwards and the dry lakebed, and admired the armada of merchant and pleasure ships that dotted the Pacific off the coast of Los Angeles: "Oh, look at all those ships!"

Soon Texas was in view and the astronauts strained to see Houston and their homes in Nassau Bay. Armstrong made the first flight-path adjustment, firing a five-second burst of the thrusters to slow the ship. In the process, he noticed the thrust cutoff was far from accurate. To Armstrong this was far more worrisome than the earlier radiator venting and thruster firing. Given the speeds and distance they were traveling, a fraction of a second less than precision in thruster firing could mean disaster.

Noticing it was time for one of the seven meals scheduled during the planned seventy-two-hour flight, Neil fished a freeze-dried chicken casserole out of the compact cupboard. The less-than-appetizing-appearing bag of food came attached to another smaller bag of water, which was to be squeezed to hydrate the food. Neil wouldn't like it, but he would choke it down. He smiled, recalling his mother Viola's admonition to remember to eat. She was, of course, right; it would be easy and dangerous to get caught up in the drama and detail of the mission and forget to eat and drink. It had happened on other missions with a resulting diminution of performance.

The Armstrong family had turned out at the Cape in full force, pleasing the astronaut. His brother Dean came down from Anderson, Indiana, with his wife and three children. His sister June, her physician husband, and six children drove to the Cape from Menomonee Falls, Wisconsin.

Viola Armstrong, then fifty-nine years old, had been concerned when her husband had taken Neil on his first flight at age six, and was heartsick when he enrolled in the Navy flight program, but after all the years of aching worry, she was, by 1966, resigned. She told the *Lima* (Ohio) *News* that she was only reluctantly going to Florida for her son's launch because she would have preferred to stay at home, where "I can have a good cry when I feel like having one." But she went along with her family and planned to stay at Cape Kennedy for the three-day mission anyway and vowed she would stay supportive. "If that is the life Neil wants, I'll be happy for him because I want him to do what he wants and be happy in life." Stephen, also fifty-nine, had encouraged his son's lifelong love of aeronautics from the start, but even he was rattled at the pending space mission, which they had had more than sufficient time to fret over. "It is only natural for a father and mother to worry about their children, but to have advance knowledge of their participation in dangerous missions makes it more pronounced."

A little over two hours into the mission, Armstrong had to adjust the orbit slightly to keep on a path to rendezvous with Agena. He fired the thrusters and cursed under his breath when they continued a slight but troubling residual firing that was enough to push the spacecraft into a higher orbit than was desirable.

Just shy of three hours after liftoff, in their second orbit, Gemini 8 had Agena on radar and was closing rapidly from about two hundred miles. Suddenly the very concerned voice of Capsule Communicator James Lovell crackled into the capsule, ordering Armstrong to fire the thrusters immediately, greatly increasing speed and changing orbital plane. The balky thrusters had sent them farther off course than had been apparent, and there was less than a minute to correct. It was the first test of Armstrong's ability to ad-hoc quick changes in space while under great pressure, and he performed with alacrity and precision. The problem was solved and Gemini 8 was again on course to couple with Agena.

Further adjustments were made over Madagascar with help from the tracking station there, and Lovell in Houston verified that Gemini 8 was still on course. As the astronauts squinted into the gathering darkness, they caught first a metallic glint dead ahead, then, after they picked it up and lost sight of it twice, Agena's bright running lights appeared unmistakably and comfortably in their path. At a range of sixty miles, Scott took control of the ship, switching the computer from the catch-up to the rendezvous program. In the pitch-black of space, all that could be seen of Agena were her twinkling lights, which slowly grew brighter.

Armstrong cautiously maneuvered Gemini 8 to a position slightly beneath Agena's docking platform, then pitched her nose up and slightly to the left. As the two spaceships moved closer to their historic celestial rendezvous, he fired his aft thrusters, making two small corrections. Nearly two hundred miles above the Caribbean, less than six hours into the mission, he damped the craft's forward motion to dead slow. At about a yard or two, Armstrong halted forward motion and fell into orbit with the Agena, balletically tumbling through space as one. For the next half-hour, Scott visually inspected Agena, making certain no obvious damage had occurred in flight that would compromise the safety of Gemini 8. When he reported everything seemed to be in order, Neil gave Houston the good news and was told: "Go ahead and dock."

The last part was the most delicate and dangerous. Never before had craft hurtling through space at 17,500 miles per hour attempted to couple. In theory it was workable, but as the two moved slowly, inch by inch, through the black sky, the question loomed of whether there would be some kind of static charge, a power arc, something generated by the tremendous forces involved in breaking free of earth's grip. Suddenly there was a solid sound of metal embracing metal and a slight but satisfying lurch forward. Armstrong broke the frozen moment of stunned silence, blurting gleefully: "Flight, we are docked! It's . . . really a smoothie—no noticeable oscillations at all." Another pregnant silence fell as a hundred minds in Houston grasped at once the implications of what had just happened. Then the flight-control room erupted in triumphant cheers.

As soon as the celebration ended, continuing glitches cast a pall. Capsule Communicator Jim Lovell reminded the crew: "If you run into trouble and the attitude-control system in the Agena goes wild, just turn it off and take control with the spacecraft." Armstrong and Scott would soon wish the problem were that easily remedied.

Less than a minute later, the astronauts knew they were in serious trouble. Scott had begun his chore of learning to control the cumbersome twin craft, first turning in a slow starboard arc, then reversing, gaining a feel for maneuvering the beast. The first indication was that it was slow to respond, but pretty much what he had been trained to expect. But just as he exhaled a slight sigh of relief, he realized something was terribly wrong. The horizon indicator showed Gemini and Agena were listing almost forty degrees. His heart began to race; the craft should not have been banking. Instinctively, Scott glanced out the window, searching for a visual horizon, but saw nothing but black.

"Neil, we're in a bank," Scott said, firing the thrusters once, a bit too sharply, reversing the bank and slightly overcompensating for it. Armstrong began a slow, methodical checklist, silently, efficiently going through the ship's various systems, searching for a problem that could with luck be corrected by the flip of a switch. Scott watched the horizon indicator with dread as it showed the list returning, ten, twenty degrees, then suddenly the craft did a 360-degree turn. Without a word, Scott carried out Lovell's order, shutting down the computer-controlled attitude-control system and reverting to manual control. Armstrong took over and leveled the craft, carefully correcting and lining up perfectly, even checking the earth dawn they were rapidly approaching for a visual horizon. They were back in control—the old-fashioned way: Old-fashioned flyboys doing what they did best. The men looked at each other and grinned; Scott had a spacewalk to do, and there were dozens of other important experiments to carry out. They were anticipating a busy and fruitful three days ahead.

Both men's thoughts turned to the extravehicular activity (EVA) Scott was scheduled to make the next day. Far more ambitious than Ed White's EVA the previous June, Scott was going to try out a new oxygen and propulsion system that included a "maneuvering gun." Neil was going to separate Gemini from the Agena so that Scott could shuttle back and forth between the craft, a dry run for future walks that would include repairing satellites in orbit and other space-handyman duties.

But their self-congratulation and reverie abruptly ended when they began to roll again, faster and faster. David Scott's concerned voice bit through the static with chilling words: "Neil we're in a roll." Instruments indicated the two craft were in a thirty-degree roll and quickly pitching further off course. Armstrong struggled to correct, but found it oddly very difficult; shifting direction should have been relatively effortless. Both men sensed something was terribly wrong; the craft began violently bucking and rolling, tumbling at the dizzying rate of one rotation per second. The fragile Gemini craft was in imminent danger of cracking and rupturing. They desperately checked all systems, yet nothing appeared out of order and the hellish spin was getting worse. If it wasn't brought under control, they were going to black out.

It seemed logical that the Agena satellite was the problem: Manufacturers McDonnell Aircraft and NASA had been repairing the ship's electrical systems after a short in the oxidizer led to an explosion during a ground test. Armstrong struggled to gain control of the conjoined spacecraft, firing the thrusters desperately. Scott pushed the button separating the craft, making the spinning worse.

"We're rolling up and we can't turn anything off," said Armstrong. "All we have is the reentry-control system." After a pause, he added, "And it's not functioning."

In Houston, flight director Chris Kraft, whose professional life was about calm and control, remembers being seized with "helplessness and fright."

Despite their desperate situation, Scott cooly pointed his Hasselblad camera out the window and snapped a few shots of the exterior of the two vehicles and their coupling. The pictures would later be invaluable in sorting out what had gone wrong and why. They shut both Agena and Gemini systems on and off, desperately looking for the glitch, but still found nothing. The first solid clue was when Scott noticed the fuel supply for the control thrusters had fallen to only 60 percent. It should have been nearly full, giving them enough fuel to maneuver for three days of experiments. It could only mean that one of the sixteen thrusters was stuck in the open position. They isolated the one that was firing, brought the ship under control for a few moments, then another thruster fired, starting the sickening spin all over.

As they passed Coastal Sentry Quebec, James R. Fucci, CapCom aboard the ship, was concerned because a red blinking light on his console indicated the craft had undocked with Agena for some reason.

In addition, radio contact with Gemini 8 was sporadic and getting worse. He had no way of knowing the reason: that Gemini's spinning was pointing the antennas all over the heavens. Concerned, he called the crew.

> **Fucci:** Gemini Eight, CSQ CapCom. Com check. How do you read?
>
> **Scott:** We have serious problems here . . . we're tumbling end over end up here. We're disengaged from the Agena.
>
> **Fucci:** Okay. We got your SPACECRAFT FREE indication here. . . . What seems to be the problem?
>
> **Armstrong:** We're rolling up and we can't turn anything off. Continuously increasing in a left roll.
>
> **Fucci:** Roger. [Thirty-seven seconds later] Gemini Eight. CSQ.
>
> **Armstrong:** Stand by.
>
> **Scott:** We have a violent left roll here at the present time and we can't turn the thrusters off, and we can't fire it, and we certainly have a roll . . . stuck hand control.

Armstrong and Scott began having trouble seeing the panel dials. They were going to black out soon if a solution wasn't found. "All that we've got left is the reentry-control system," Armstrong said. With a superhuman effort, he reached the control panel above him and shut down the system that fueled the thrusters, then activated the reentry-control system. Slowly the two-ton capsule stopped whirling and the astronauts were able to regain their senses.

Carefully, Armstrong fired the maneuver thrusters and steadied the ship. Using the reentry-control thrusters meant mission abort. But there was no choice. It was, of course, heartbreaking for him, and for Scott. But there was nothing else to do. After less than twelve hours and seven orbits, the mission was over. Gemini 8 was streaking over central Africa when Houston gave the order to fire retrorockets and prepare for a splashdown about six hundred miles south of Japan.

A big chunk of the truly mind-boggling cost of sending men into space was due to the fact that a very large portion of the United States Navy was required to be on alert and essentially at the disposal of NASA. A fork in the road had occurred at Edwards several years prior, when Neil, Milt Thompson, and others had championed the Parasev, or "space-age kite," as it was called, which would have allowed space crews to glide back to earth rather then land in the sea. But NASA chose to take the far more expensive fork.

As the astronauts fired their retrorockets and descended, burning white-hot into the atmosphere, Gemini 8 dropped out of orbit and began a fiery decent. Armstrong was fighting to keep the craft within the extremely narrow two-degree angle that would allow survivable reentry. Too steep an angle would mean incineration; too narrow and Gemini might bounce far into space, possibly irretrievably. Staying on course, the little ship bounced through layer after layer of atmosphere, announcing its return with an auroral sky fire visible to a quarter of the planet's people. Navy recovery forces in the Pacific were ordered to make for the splashdown point. In the dawn sky over Asia, Gemini 8 streamed long, angry red tails as it sharply braked and plunged toward earth, its men hoping NASA's calculations for their emergency return to earth and recovery at sea would fall close to the mark.

Years later, Armstrong admitted to a fear that seemed strange for a man so enamored with the dream of traveling to foreign worlds, and who seemed so fearless in the face of death. His nightmare was over the possibility of being lost where rescuers could not find him. He said he had read desperate accounts of travelers adrift at sea or wandering aimlessly through a jungle, unable to get their bearings, and he was quite anxious about the possibility of finding himself in such straits. Three years later, a quarter of a million miles from home on the surface of the moon with Buzz Aldrin in the impossibly frail, spider-like *Eagle*, such thoughts must have returned.

Descending over the coast with China and the Pacific Rim glimmering over the horizon, Neil seemed to suddenly have a crisis of confidence. "I keep thinking there's something we've forgotten about," he said, "but I don't know what it is." Scott was confused. In the many months he had worked with Armstrong preparing for the mission, self-doubt was not a trait that had been evident. After a brief hesitation, he answered, "We've done everything, as far as I know."

Remarkably, given all they had endured mentally and physically in the course of the ten-hour, forty-five-minute journey, the men guided Gemini 8 to a near-perfect splashdown within three miles of target, the most accurate to date.

Despite having a Navy flotilla steaming toward the area at flank speed and two HC-54 Rescuemaster planes en route, one from Tachikawa Air Base, Japan, and another from Naha, Okinawa,

Armstrong and Scott bobbed in a rough sea—suffering agonizing seasickness—for forty-five minutes. When the HC-54 from Naha base arrived, two gung-ho young pararescuers, Larry Huyett and G. M. Moore, immediately parachuted to the sea-tossed capsule and quickly found themselves in rough water filled with potential trouble—the seas, which hadn't looked terribly bad from the air, turned out to be twelve- to fifteen-foot swells. Eventually they were able to secure a flotation collar to the capsule, greatly adding to its stability and the comfort of its occupants.

For the next three hours, there was nothing the Gemini astronauts and their rescuers could do but ride the waves and the waves of nausea. When the U.S.S. *Mason* finally arrived, Gemini 8 was secured with lines and a ladder was dropped. The climb, with both the capsule and ship heaving and powerful wind gusts buffeting them, proved one last challenge.

Immediately whisked past a deck filled with cheering sailors, Armstrong and Scott, looking white as ghosts, were taken to the sick bay. They were treated for slight dehydration and found to be otherwise unfazed. The U.S.S. *Mason* sailed into Okinawa Harbor, where the astronauts were greeted as returning heroes—their first taste of the adulation to come. Despite heavy rain, a crowd of many thousands of Americans and Okinawans turned out. Marching bands played and ships sent spouts of water high in the air.

The next days were a blur. The men, dubbed "cosmic twins" by the media, were bedecked with traditional leis in Hawaii, then flown to Cape Kennedy, where they were debriefed and deliberately kept away from the clamoring press, pausing only once before the shouting reporters to pose with their hands together prayerfully, indicating, presumably, that if they hadn't been fully aware of how close they had come to disaster at the time, they now were.

After a weekend at the Cape going over the details of the near-disaster, the men flew back to Houston for a reunion with their families and a press conference during which they would finally fill the world in on exactly what had happened. When the time came, they appeared in the briefing auditorium wearing suits and sporting matching "exceptional service" medals to dispel any notion that NASA thought pilot error was involved. President Lyndon Johnson personally approved both the medals and pay raises for the astronauts on the night of March 22, 1966, just six days after the flight. In a memorandum from presidential aide Joseph Califano (who in later years successfully led the government's antismoking crusade), Johnson signed off on Scott's promotion from Air Force major to lieutenant-colonel. In Armstrong's case, Califano pointed out that his civil-service rank was already a GS-16, step four "earning $21,653 a year . . . a grade comparable to a general or flag officer." Therefore a promotion to the next grade wasn't recommended. Instead, he was given the more modest "one-step-in-grade promotion amounting to a $700-a-year raise to recognize his 'meritorious achievement' on the Gemini 8 flight."

In addition, being a civil servant, Neil was eligible for a per diem for his time out of town during the brief, aborted flight. Normally it would have been $16 per day at his pay grade. But since food and billeting were included, the per diem was just $2. Nevertheless, it was reflected in his next paycheck.

The presidential citation lauded Armstrong for "exceptional piloting skill in the face of great danger . . . advancing the technology of manned space flight immeasurably . . . in a moment of great peril, when failure of an electrical system caused his vehicle to go out of control, he displayed great heroism and physical endurance in regaining control of the spacecraft."

During the press conference, the astronauts denied they had suffered "blackout" or "grayout," but described the "bucking bronco" ride Gemini 8 had given them and the tumbling "at the rate of one revolution every second." Hewing to NASA's political line, albeit one that they certainly shared, Armstrong and Scott emphasized their continued confidence in the space program and expressed their regret at having to return early.

Reflecting the restive national mood over a nearly two-week wait to hear the astronauts' story of what went wrong, United Press International used the line VEIL REMOVED in their caption of the picture of Scott and Armstrong at their news conference. The immediate aftermath of the journey had been a delicate time for NASA. The official rendering was that a catastrophe in space could have killed Gemini and meant Apollo would be stillborn. The fact that Armstrong and Scott managed to skillfully avoid disaster and limp home alive made them heroes. That the men had been equally adept at handling the crucial public-relations aspect of their jobs was also much appreciated, at NASA as well as in the Oval Office.

Five years later, when the world was praying for the safe return of Apollo 13, the Jim Lovell–commanded moon mission that nearly ended in tragedy when an overheated oxygen tank exploded 200,000 miles away from earth, crippling the ship and aborting the moon landing, Armstrong reflected about Gemini 8: "I've heard people say [that] when they got in a tough spot, they had their life story flash in front of their minds. I didn't experience that. It was like a pilot getting into an inadvertent spin and recognizing that he absolutely must solve the problem and correct the spin before hitting the ground. All his attention is directed toward that end. You don't wring your hands. You just try to decide what the best course of action is. But the possibility of not getting back from a crippled ship is a very real one. It always exists in the back of your mind."

The space program's critics, including Senator Edward Kennedy and civil rights leader Ralph Abernathy, were searching for an excuse to reel the agency in, and while their motive was stanching what they considered profligate spending that was better directed to social welfare, safety concerns would do if they were sufficient to sway public opinion. As was pointed out often in the press, the Gemini program had, by March of 1966, cost more than $1.4 billion. Unfortunately NASA saw the problems that aborted Gemini 8 in public-relations terms rather than as a warning of systemic trouble and possible danger to the lives of the astronauts (a misperception that led to disaster the following January).

Having put the press ordeal behind him, Neil was able for the first time in a year to take a vacation with his family and spend time around the pool with Jan, the boys, and the family mutt, Superdog, who was known to wear a cape from time to time. It was well that Neil had some downtime, because the next year would be spent traveling the world, touting NASA's accomplishments and its future plans. That would segue directly into the Apollo program and training for the moon shot.

After a few weeks relaxing and avoiding his newfound fame, which grew to be as persistent and as unwanted as a cowlick, it was time to go home to Wapakoneta and a celebration that would include almost the entire Armstrong clan and really rock the proud little burg.

NASA encouraged hometown tributes for the All-American images they created and was not about to pass on a town like Wapakoneta. Jan and the boys received their summons from the agency authorizing government transportation to Ohio on April 13 and a per diem of twenty-five dollars each. The letter assured them their "participation will make these activities more meaningful." Everyone was meant to pitch in. Neil, Jan, Rick, and Mark flew from Houston to Ohio in style in a NASA Gulfstream jet. They were greeted at the Allen County Airport by a crush of local officials, relatives, press, old friends, and folks from miles around. Most important, Neil's mother and father were at the front of the crowd, beaming with pride, and certainly with a large measure of relief. Beating his dad to the punch, Neil congratulated him first. Stephen had recently been appointed number-two official in charge of prisons and mental-health facilities in the state of Ohio.

The family was quickly hustled into a waiting car and driven to the Wapakoneta Fairgrounds for a press conference before more than a hundred reporters and photographers representing the world's press. The *Wapakoneta News* reported "Neil made his way through a tangle of wires and cable to the platform and a mass of microphones. Questions were flung at him rapidly." Squinting into the furiously flashing cameras, Neil surveyed the sea of heavy-hitter-media–type faces, passing over correspondents from the wire services, the *Times* newspapers of New York, London, and Los Angeles, as well as the three television networks, and puckishly pointed to sixteen-year-old Susan Harsh, editor of the *Wapakoneta High School Lantern,* deflating the balloon of the world's press. In a clear, confident voice, Harsh asked what he had felt when his capsule had "gotten out of control." Armstrong replied that he had been trained for such a crisis, the standard answer, but then he paused, surveyed the room beyond the clamoring newsmen, and changed from techno-speak into country-boy talk, adding, "Anyway, it wasn't any worse than some of the scares I received when driving in an automobile." Friends and family familiar with Neil's driving recall smiling and saying "amen" to his last remark.

When the press conference was over, the governor of Ohio, James Rhodes, announced the award of a $100,000 grant to Auglaize County for construction of the Neil Armstrong Airport. He then led the party out, with help from a state police escort, to a waiting motor cavalcade assembled from police cruisers marshaled from near and far. It would be the biggest parade in Wapakoneta history, a statistic that lasted just three years—until Neil returned from the moon.

"Bands playing 'Star Spangled Banner,' floats and cars, gaily decorated, moved down the streets under overcast skies," reported the *News*. "The closer the parade got to downtown, the denser the crowds and the louder the yelling and cheering. Neil and his party were besieged with confetti and serpentines rivaling a Wall Street welcome. Cameramen, riding on two trailers attached to convertibles in front of Neil's car, ground out yards of film for viewing that evening . . . of this once-in-a-lifetime occasion."

Police and journalists in rural Ohio circa 1966 had no training at crowd estimates. There was no need; the only time large groups gathered was for the state fair or a high school football game, and tickets would account for all but a few kids who skulked in under the fence. But most people there that chill, happy April day recall there had never been such a crowd gathered in Wapakoneta in living memory.

At the end of the parade route, dignitaries, guests, relatives, and many of the town folk repaired to the cafeteria of Neil's alma mater, Wapakoneta High School (formerly Blume High) for a banquet. Newsmen were prohibited from entering the school—most importantly because it was a family gathering, but also because there wouldn't have been room. But Wapakoneta showed it was a town with manners; each media representative was given a free box lunch.

The banquet was followed by a gathering in the school gym, where Neil and Jan appeared on a stage festooned with flags—American flags, a Rotary Club flag, Kiwanis, Lion's Club, and the flag of St. Paul's Evangelical and Reformed Church, spiritual home to the Armstrongs for generations. The brass band of Wapakoneta High played patriotic songs and St. Paul's Choir sang the "Battle Hymn of the Republic."

Neil looked out over the crowd come to honor him and said, "There are a lot of people here, and most of them are my family." The truism was greeted by polite applause, which ended unevenly when the Armstrong kin realized they were clapping for themselves. After his brief remarks, a NASA representative showed a "color" (as was noted in the *Wapakoneta News*) movie of the liftoff of Gemini 8, and an animated simulation of the docking; those hoping for an animation of the "bucking bronco ride" were disappointed.

But the bronco ride made Neil famous the world over. Astronauts were no longer seen as "trained monkeys," but flesh-and-blood heroes who mastered balky machinery while screaming through the heavens at unfathomable speed, bravely risking life and limb. They were cowboys, swashbucklers of the new ocean.

NASA intended to take full advantage of the publicity—meaning Armstrong and Scott, particularly, were looking at a great deal of "time in the barrel." High-profile events saturated by media coverage were first priority, because they gave the most bang for the buck. A few weeks after the hugely successful parade in Wapakoneta, NASA's public-relations wizard, Julian Scheer, who favored Armstrong as a symbol because he was a civilian, sent the astronaut to the Montreal World's Fair opening. Amidst the internationally flavored pomp and circumstance (which, in the Cold War era, meant huge expenditures on exposition halls built by the Soviet Union and the United States touting their respective technology and political systems), Armstrong played well.

In between public appearances, considered by NASA as important as any other work the astronauts were engaged in, the work of training for Apollo was under way in earnest. In February 1967 the first three-man crew—Ed White, Gus Grissom, and Roger Chaffee—were scheduled to go into earth orbit for fourteen days aboard Apollo 1.

But before settling down to the enormously complex and exhausting business of training for the moon flights, Neil was assigned the longest stint "in the barrel" an astronaut had yet been subjected to. More a State Department goodwill trip than a NASA funding drive (though important to the cause because it might help create goodwill in the executive branch, where budgets were written), the October 1966 trip took two astronauts on a journey through eleven Latin American countries. Traveling more than fifteen thousand miles, they met presidents, senators, cabinet members, generals, and mayors, held fourteen news conferences, gave twenty-five lectures, and rode in countless parades.

Armstrong's partner on the trip could hardly have been a less likely match. Dick Gordon was known as one of the more bombastic, cocky, and dramatic astronauts, as well as being such a hard-partying, unapologetic ladies' man that his Gemini 11 crewmate Pete Conrad unflatteringly dubbed him "animal."

The trip began on October 6 with a flight from Ellington Air Force Base in Houston, where much of the Apollo training was being conducted, to Washington, D.C. At the State Department, the astronauts and their wives were briefed on proper protocol, ranging from how to address the various leaders they would meet, as well as warnings about the possibility of attack by anti-American groups. Most important, they were filled in on all the good things the United States space pro-

Neil, seated, was vice president of the school council in 1946, his senior year. The council solved traffic problems and made money from scrap and paper drives. *Courtesy of the Wapakoneta Public Library*

Neil *(top, second from right)* at a rally in high school, 1946. *Courtesy of the Wapakoneta Public Library*

Neil as a U.S. Navy pilot during the Korean War. *Courtesy of the U.S. Naval Institute*

Midshipman Neil Armstrong of VF-51 on the beach near Barber's Point NAS, Hawaii, in 1951. *Courtesy of Cdr. John Moore, USN Ret.*

Neil Armstrong, Air Commander Marsh Beebe, William Mackey, and K. C. Kramer of VF-51 during the Korean War, preparing for the mission in the ready room. *Courtesy of William Mackey*

After the mission, being debriefed, are Squadron Commander Ernie Beauchamp, K. C. Kramer, William Mackey, Neil Armstrong, Air Intelligence Ken Danneberg, and Air Commander Marsh Beebe. *Courtesy of William Mackey*

VF-51. *Courtesy of William Mackey*

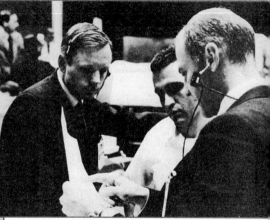

Mission Control Center. During the Apollo 10 mission, Neil *(left)* and Buzz Aldrin *(right)* discuss the lunar orbit activities in progress with astronaut-scientist Jack Schmitt. *Courtesy of NASA*

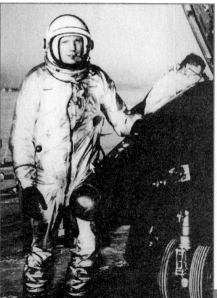

Neil suits up for his first space flight for Gemini 8. *Courtesy of NASA*

Pilot Neil Armstrong standing next to the X-15, 1960. The X-15 was a rocket-powered aircraft 50 feet long with a wingspan of 22 feet. *Courtesy of NASA*

Neil Armstrong in X-15 cockpit. NASA research pilot Armstrong is surrounded by ground crew and NASA research pilot Bruce Peterson *(right)* following a mission in the first X-15 rocket plane in 1960. *Courtesy of NASA*

NASA Research Pilots, circa 1962. Seven test pilots at NASA's Flight Research Center lined up in front of the retired X-1E rocket plane for a group photo: Neil Armstrong, Joe Walker, Bill Dana, Bruce Peterson, Jack McKay, Milt Thompson, and Stan Butchart. These NASA fliers were among the elite group of test pilots who flew the early rocket and jet-powered aircraft involved in the original NACA-NASA research airplane program, which investigated transonic and supersonic flight, the X-15 hypersonic program, and the wingless lifting bodies. *Courtesy of NASA*

Some of NASA's sixteen astronauts participate in tropic survival training from June 3 to June 6, 1963, at Albrook Air Force Base, Canal Zone: Unidentified trainer, Neil Armstrong, John Glenn, L. Gordon Cooper, and Pete Conrad. *Courtesy of NASA*

Neil Armstrong at the Lunar Landing Research Facility, 1969. In the background is the infamous Lunar Landing Training Vehicle, also known as the Flying Bedstead. *Courtesy of NASA*

Neil Armstrong during training for Apollo 11. *Courtesy of NASA*

The Apollo 11 crew: Neil A. Armstrong, commander; Michael Collins, command module pilot; and Edwin E. Aldrin, lunar module pilot. *Courtesy of NASA*

Kennedy Space Center, Florida. Apollo 11 rises past the launch tower at pad 39A to begin man's first lunar landing mission. Liftoff occurred at 9:32 A.M. EDT. *Courtesy of NASA*

Astronaut Aldrin poses for a photograph beside the deployed flag of the United States during the Apollo 11 EVA. The lunar module is on the left. The astronaut's footprints in the soil of the moon are clearly visible in the foreground. *Courtesy of NASA*

President Nixon as he telephoned "Tranquillity Base" and the astronauts Neil Armstrong and Edwin "Buzz" Aldrin.
Courtesy of NASA

Photograph taken by Armstrong of Aldrin walking toward the lunar module.
Courtesy of NASA

The Apollo 11 lunar module ascent stage photographed from the command service module during rendezvous in lunar orbit. The LM was making its docking approach to the *Columbia.* The LM descent stage used as a launch platform was left on the lunar surface. This view is looking west. The earth rises above the lunar horizon.
Courtesy of NASA

Apollo 11 Pacific recovery area. A Navy para-rescueman and one of the three Apollo 11 astronauts close the spacecraft hatch while the other two space pilots watch from the life raft. The para-rescueman helped the astronauts from the spacecraft and disinfected them after they donned biological isolation garments. *Courtesy of NASA*

After a successful moon landing, the three happy astronauts, in their quarantine trailer, talk with President Nixon. *Courtesy of NASA*

The Apollo 11 crewmen, still under a 21-day quarantine, are greeted by their wives as they arrive at Ellington Air Force Base after a flight aboard a U.S. Air Force C141 transport from Hawaii. The astronauts are *(left to right)* Armstrong, Aldrin, and Collins. The wives are *(left to right)* Mrs. Collins, Mrs. Armstrong, and Mrs. Aldrin. *Courtesy of NASA*

The Agriculture, Customs, Immigration, and Public Health form signed by the crew of Apollo 11 upon returning to the U.S. from the moon

The Neil Armstrong Air and Space Museum in Wapakoneta, Ohio. *Photo copyright Leon Wagener*

Neil Armstrong speaks at the National Press Club in Washington, D.C., February 2000. *Photo copyright Leon Wagener* gram would do for the rest of the world, including the provision of vastly improved weather data and communications capabilities, which would be made available to any country that installed "a simple and inexpensive receiving station."

At the last minute, the traveling party, which included five Air Force crewmen as well as assorted NASA and State Department officials, were given the bad news that they would be traveling not on a luxurious government jet, but on a Convair prop plane, considerably more cramped and vulnerable to weather. Departure day, Friday October 7, got off to a rocky start when Gordon overslept, making the group miss their scheduled takeoff at Andrews Air Force Base. The old workhorse plane lifted off several hours late, only to suffer an immediate electrical problem, necessitating a return to base. When the plane was finally under way to Miami for a brief fuel stop before winging on to Caracas, it was discovered that the dramatic space-program slides Armstrong and Gordon were planning to use in the lectures were damaged beyond redemption. Then, traveling over the southern Caribbean, heavy turbulence sent Gordon and the Bloody Mary in his hand crashing into the ceiling, bruising him and spraying everyone else with tomato juice. Luggage, including many NASA souvenirs brought along as gifts, was also strewn around the cabin and damaged.

Moderate turbulence continued until heavy thunderstorms over Caracas buffeted the plane, resulting in an hour spent circling the city, bouncing and lurching so violently that Neil jokingly compared it to the ride he and Scott had endured on Gemini 8. When they were mercifully on the ground at long last, the travelers—most of them decidedly queasy—were greeted on a rain-drenched red carpet by Venezuelan and American officials.

The rest of the goodwill mission went far more smoothly. Though the Americans were somewhat disconcerted at the omnipresence of soldiers bristling with automatic weapons, they found their reception warm and enthusiastic everywhere, both from government officials and the tens of thousands lining the streets to greet their motorcades. The personal letters from President Lyndon Johnson and the signed Gemini memorabilia were likewise accepted with gratitude. Most important in Armstrong's mind was the enthusiasm over his message about space technology. In lectures to the continent's intelligentsia, he made sure they understood that the satellites NASA was building and launching were going to change the lives of their countrymen forever.

Latin Americans would be able to access information that would spare their nations the devastation of unforeseen storms, supply them with accurate weather forecasts, increase farm production, and unite the region through instant communications.

Neil, who found the traffic in South American capitals more vexing than in Washington or New York, took to the skies for his sightseeing, soaring with a local gliding club in Santiago, Chile. The rest of the group spent what little free time they had shopping and sightseeing.

Most of the ceremonies, speeches, and motorcades were well covered by the local press, often live on television and splashed on the front pages of newspapers. The trip was considered a great success by President Johnson, who invited the space pioneers to the White House to thank them personally, and by the State Department, which concluded that astronauts, with their panache, were a valuable tool of foreign policy.

The trip home was less successful. Sputtering out of Panama on the last leg of the trip back to Houston, the old Convair once again blew a circuit breaker, necessitating an emergency return that was rather embarrassing for men who were billed as masters of the skies.

In January 1967, with only two and a half years to go before man would set foot on the moon, the Apollo program could only be described as a mess. John Moore, Neil's old friend and first jet instructor, was by then manager of Apollo test operations for North American Aviation and responsible for the safety of the equipment North American was supplying NASA, including the Apollo 1 space capsule. Moore was so unsure of that capsule that he pleaded with Apollo 1 commander Gus Grissom to delay a simulated countdown on the pad at Cape Kennedy. There were serious issues over the hatch, which NASA had ordered North American to design to swing open inward, so it wouldn't accidentally open—as had happened, ironically, to Grissom while awaiting recovery after the splashdown of his Mercury 4 flight. Another problem was the use of pure oxygen in the capsule. If there were a spark, a pure-oxygen environment would greatly intensify the flames. Pure oxygen was a necessary danger during spaceflight because in order to stretch supplies as far as possible, the capsule had to be pressured very low—no more than five pounds per square inch. But, on the ground, not using a nitrogen-oxygen mix was basically careless—simply a question of not bothering with the extra equipment. Considering the miles of wiring contained in the new Apollo capsule, it was something that should have been rethought.

Grissom, at forty the senior astronaut, was thought by many to be a shoo-in as first man to walk on the moon and lead-off man as commander of Apollo 1. He thought he'd be the first moon walker, too, and he wanted it to happen sooner rather than later. Grissom liked Moore, but knew that Moore (who had been nearly burned to death in an aviation accident) might be overly cautious. After listening to Moore's arguments, Grissom smiled, thanked him, and promised to take them up with NASA. The North American position, probably lukewarmly delivered by Grissom, was promptly rejected; several days later, the Apollo 1 team was strapped in the Apollo 1 capsule with the inward-opening hatch bolted shut. The simulated countdown had been delayed over and over again due to glitches, and the always-combative Grissom was at the end of his tether. Even communications between the capsule and launch team bunker two hundred yards away weren't working properly. Grissom complained they might as well have two tin cans connected by string. "I can't hear a thing you're saying. Jesus Christ, how are we going to get to the moon if we can't talk between two or three buildings?"

Shortly after Grissom's frustrated outburst, he, Ed White, and Roger Chaffee were dead. At 6:36 P.M., a spark shot out of some frayed wires underneath Grissom's couch, ignited barely perceptible fumes from a leaking coolant pipe, and turned the Apollo 1 capsule into a blazing inferno. The first sign of trouble was heard by Deke Slayton; it was barely a crackle over the faulty communications system that sounded like "fire." Slayton leaped out of his seat, his heart pounding. It couldn't be, he thought. He must have imagined it. But the next voice was clear. It was Roger Chaffee speaking in the tones of a pilot announcing a mayday situation. "We've got a fire in the cockpit." A glance at a television monitor showed a window filled with flame. "We've got a bad fire. We're burning up!" They were Chaffee's last words. Technicians quickly reached the capsule hatch, but it was white-hot and couldn't be touched. When the remains of the astronauts were finally recovered, it was clear they had been desperately, futilely struggling to undo the hatch bolts.

After hearing of White's death, Jan Armstrong's first reaction was anger. She balled her fist in fury and fought back the tears that were welling up. As was so often the case, Neil was flying off somewhere for NASA when she needed him most. The astronaut office sent rookie Bill Anders to help; traditionally it was an astronaut's job to tell a wife that her husband had been killed. Anders was nice enough, but too new to really be a member of the club, which took years.

The Whites were the Armstrongs' next-door neighbors and best friends. And, of course, Ed had leaped over the fence between their houses the night of the fire and helped save her children from being burned to death. Now Pat would no longer be one of them. That was the way it worked; nobody liked it, but when a husband was killed, his wife and children buried his flag-draped coffin and then drifted away. They could no longer empathize; they no longer had anything to fear.

Chapter Thirteen

The era of Apollo moon exploration, 1968 to 1972, was a period of social upheaval in the United States and around the world virtually without precedent in the twentieth century. Assassinations begat riots, massive protests were met with violence, America prosecuted a war vociferously opposed by most everyone, including, in the end, even its architects. A very vocal portion of a generation claimed to want to exit the dominant culture, joining a subculture—or, even more ominously to stewards of the status quo—a counterculture contemptuous of society's strictures against everything from haircuts to sexual mores and drugs.

It was not a propitious moment in history for the astronauts, who were clean-cut straight arrows, unabashed patriots, and mostly military men, to take center stage. Many members of the press had a jaundiced view of the flyers and their small-town, Midwestern ethos. There were numerous skirmishes at press conferences over all manner of issues, from the monumental to the mundane, but the watershed event was when an American flag was placed onstage during a news conference, causing members of the press to erupt in catcalls. Provoked, the astronauts came to their next conference wearing gas masks, emblematic of the routine, violent confrontations between police and protesters of various stripes. The incidents left no doubt where the majority of both groups stood on the pressing controversies of the day. The politics of the space program seemed often to lurk just beneath the surface. Planting an American flag on the moon was seen by some as "imperialist." References to God and prayers said during missions were contentious.

The relationship between the astronauts and the press had become very brittle. But in the weeks and days leading up to the July 15 moon launch, there was open animosity. Most of the national press corps covering the space program were political and social opposites of the flyers: urban versus rural, liberal versus conservative. But the most fundamental difference, and the source of greatest friction, was that the press largely saw the space program as a sideshow designed by the government to take the public's mind off Vietnam, race relations, and other troubling issues of the day. It was seen by the press and much of the public as a slightly circus-like endeavor, akin to shooting someone out of a cannon or old-fashioned daredevil barnstorming, like wing-walking at the Cleveland Air Show in the 1930s. But to Armstrong, the space effort represented the sum of man's collective knowledge. Flying, whether over the cornfields of Wapakoneta or to the moon, was neither magic nor trickery. The necessity of care, planning, and meticulous attention to detail were the lessons he learned from the trauma of having a schoolmate die in his arms.

One of the most grating press questions asked of Armstrong was almost a statement. The reporter archly shouted across the smoky NASA briefing room, "Mr. Armstrong, I know an astronaut who would go to the moon even if he knew he wouldn't come back."

Armstrong spun his head in the direction of the questioner as if he had been slapped in the face. The statement was so fundamentally opposed to his core vision of aviation in general, and spaceflight in particular, that he jumped to swat it away. It was one of the few occasions when more than a weary, slightly annoyed yes-or-no reply was elicited.

"I rule him out. If you knew him, he'd be a boy, not an adult," Armstrong shot back crossly.

Undaunted, the reporter followed up: "Do you mean you don't have a taste for adventure?"

Armstrong replied, "For heaven's sake, I loathe danger, especially if it's useless; danger is the most irritating aspect of our job. How can a perfectly normal technological fact be turned into adventure? And why should steering a spacecraft be risking your life? It would be as illogical as risking your life when you use an electric mixer to make yourself a milkshake."

The whole witches' brew of social bedlam seemed to be headed toward a screeching finale in the summer of 1969. Construction workers and others who were threatened, confused, or just plain annoyed at the messiness of it all wore American flags on their hard hats as a symbol of furious indignation. "America—love it or leave it" was their mantra. College students, hippies, and other rebels turned the flag upside down, wore it on their clothes in defiance, and burned it to outrage the conservative. Skirmishes between the groups were commonplace in cities all over the country. Occasionally, hard-hat types stormed off their worksites to chase and pummel antiwar protesters.

Several signal events occurred within a period of four weeks that summer that will forever define the period: the bacchanal of Woodstock, the horror of the Charlie Manson murders, and the moral sinkhole of Ted Kennedy's Chappaquiddick. Many who felt kinship with none of the cultural combatants longed for escape from the madding crowd.

Under the circumstances, there was a certain Age of Aquarius verisimilitude in the events unfolding in the world's largest building, at Cape Kennedy, Florida. Inside NASA's Vehicle Assembly Plant, which encompasses eight acres (it's big enough to house the Statue of Liberty and the United Nations building), a rocket was being readied for three men who were leaving the planet.

The Apollo 1 tragedy was a pivotal moment for the American space program. It could have ended it entirely, and many hoped it would. After months of intensive investigation, acrimonious debate, and bitter charges and countercharges, it was decided America would land a man on the moon before the end of the 1960s, just as President Kennedy had hoped. The legacy of the lost men of Apollo 1 would be a new, revitalized space program. The men whose lives were going to be on the line would finally have a major say in how the machines they would live or die in were designed. While that doesn't seem a radical concept, it meant changing the basic philosophy of a bureaucratic dinosaur spending hundreds of billions in today's dollars, employing 400,000 people and purchasing from 100,000 contractors. It was going to be a tough beast to turn around.

There were many added safety features, such as hatches that blew outward at the touch of a panic button, the installation of a soundly engineered abort system to blast the astronauts out of harm's way if a rocket exploded under them on the launchpad, as well as hundreds of other features that supplied a margin of safety or just comfort and convenience, something else that had been almost totally ignored.

In Building 9 at the Manned Spacecraft Center in Houston, Armstrong and his Apollo 11 crew members, Edwin "Buzz" Aldrin and Mike Collins, were scrambling to ready themselves for their epochal journey. It was, as Buzz Aldrin's wife, Joan, put it, "normalcy tinged with hysteria."

Learning to fly the lunar module in simulations, Armstrong had to abort many times; once he crashed on the moon's surface, a mistake that would have meant certain death. People in and out of NASA, including many in government and the press, questioned whether the Apollo 11 astronauts could be ready by July 1969. There were still major problems, including an aggravating shortage of training equipment. Until James McDivitt's Apollo 9 completed its mission in early March, Armstrong's group was third in line to use the simulators. The Apollo 9 astronauts needed the lunar-landing module simulator just as much as Armstrong because, even though they were only going into earth orbit, McDivitt's crew was scheduled to fly the LM in space, more than a hundred miles from the mother ship, then redock. Still, Armstrong was frustrated and concerned that he couldn't use the time to strengthen his skills on the simulator, which was the closest engineers could come to duplicating the hazardous trip from the moon-orbiting command capsule to the lunar surface, and with luck hopefully back again.

Armstrong was even more concerned about not being allowed to practice on the weird-looking lunar landing training vehicle (LLTV), which was called the "flying bedstead," since it resembled a bed without a mattress. The wingless jet-propelled device simulated the journey to the moon's surface in a way no computer screen could. It landed and took off on pipelike legs and flew vertically, powered by a single jet engine in the middle of the craft. Reaching an altitude of about two hundred feet, it then hovered and fell to earth at approximately the same speed it would under the moon's gravity, which is one-sixth that of the earth. On descent, sixteen tiny rockets in clusters give the pilot the ability to lower, balance, and raise the craft, much as it would behave on the lunar surface. The ride is short: There's fuel for an eighty-second climb, and eight minutes of maneuvering back to earth.

Unfortunately, the "flying bedstead" had been grounded after it went out of control and crashed, nearly killing Neil in May 1968. The trainer, though diabolically difficult to control, had been piloted safely by astronauts three hundred times, including twenty-seven times by Armstrong prior to the near-fatal mishap. On the day of the crash, he had climbed to two hundred feet without a problem, but on descent a warning light suddenly announced the craft's control rockets were nearly out of helium. Almost immediately, the trainer "began to nose up and roll over." Neil punched the eject button, which hurled him up and away, allowing a powered parachute to open and deposit him back on earth with a bone-rattling thud, while the LLTV erupted in a fireball nearby. After examining films of the accident, it was estimated he had escaped death by two-fifths of a second. He suffered cuts and bruises, but wanted to get back on another trainer right away. NASA ruled that was out of the question until the accident was thoroughly investigated.

Ironically, after completing an accident investigation in November, Joseph S. Algranti, head of Houston's Aircraft Operations Office, bailed out of another crashing trainer the following month. Yet another investigation was undertaken; it rewrote the operating procedures for the craft, but determined there was nothing inherently flawed in its design. Despite that clean evaluation, some of NASA's top officials thought the crew could get sufficient training on the simulator. Chris Kraft in particular was appalled, and asked Armstrong to drop by his office to talk about the future of the LLTV. "It's absolutely essential," the astronaut argued. "It's by far the best training for landing on the moon."

"It's dangerous, damn it," snapped Kraft.

"Yes, it is. I know you're worried, but I have to support it. It's just damn good training."

"So I gave in," recalls Kraft. "Neil was Neil. Calm, quiet, a gentle smile, and absolute confidence."

It was an example of the newfound clout Armstrong and the other astronauts had gained in the wake of the Apollo 1 disaster. The "flying bedstead" training was doubled. In the final weeks before Apollo 2, Neil flew the trainer as often as possible, ending up with more than a dozen successful flights. Altogether, NASA calculated Armstrong and Aldrin spent approximately nine hundred hours in various simulators, practicing how to handle situations such as electrical short circuits and engine misfires during critical phases of the moon flight. Michael

Collins was equally busy; though he had no need to practice the lunar module landing or moonwalk, he was burdened with the task of practicing rendezvous under numerous complicated scenarios. Collins spent four hundred hours rehearsing simulated docking procedures with the lunar module.

Realizing the extreme difficulty of the mission and the odds against its success, Armstrong said, in a weary moment of private candor, "We hope that the public will accept it if we are killed up there." But, publicly, he bristled with confidence when he said, "The three of us have no fear of launching out on this expedition. I'm sure that American ingenuity and American craftsmanship have given us the best equipment that can be made available." Surely, during the course of the long, grueling preparation, and the many setbacks, both emotions alternated in his head.

In the days leading up to launch, the president was briefed repeatedly by NASA officials, as well as by independent scientists, on the odds of the men getting to the moon and back, the chances of them getting stuck up there and slowly dying while the world watched. Nixon was well aware the final decision to go or not go was his, and that he would bask in the success of the mission or see his young administration forever tainted by its ignominious failure.

The government was well aware that the men it was sending on the first lunar mission had a quasi-religious devotion to what they were doing. For the most part they had wanted to go to the moon since boyhood, and almost certainly would risk all at their one shot to see the dream come to fruition. To temper that possibility, NASA administrators promised Armstrong and his crew that if Apollo 11 had to be aborted for whatever reason, they would automatically inherit Apollo 12.

Even with that assurance, Armstrong expressed his concern to Kraft that an overly cautious flight controller would pull the plug on a good descent based on faulty information or misread data. "I'm going to be in a better position to know what's happening than the people back in Houston," was the argument he made repeatedly, according to an exasperated Kraft.

"I'm not going to tolerate any unnecessary risks; that's why we have mission rules." It was an argument Neil could not win. Kraft wasn't about to trust the judgment of an astronaut, not even Armstrong. But Kraft left with the distinct impression he had not succeeded in convincing Neil, and wondered what would happen if there was a serious disagreement at a crucial moment.

NASA Flight Director Gene Kranz, the ironman of the operation with his signature crew cut and red-white-and-blue vest, also wondered what was behind Armstrong's poker face. "As we went through the rules, Neil would generally smile or nod. I knew Armstrong never said much, but I expected him to be vocal on the mission-rule strategy; he wasn't. I believed he had set his own rules for the landing. I just wanted to know what they were. I believed he would press on, accepting any risk as long as there was even a remote chance to land."

But, unlike Kraft, Gene Kranz wasn't concerned and wasn't going to argue with the astronaut. "When you looked at his eyes, you knew he was the commander and had all the pieces assembled in his mind. I don't think he ever raised his voice. He saved his energy for when it was needed. I believed we were well in sync. I would let the crew continue as long as there was a chance."

A student of history, and a hard-nosed realist, Richard Nixon decided during the last hours before the countdown began to do as his mentor, Dwight Eisenhower, had done before launching D-Day. He ordered chief White House speech writer William Safire to draft a brief statement explaining to the American people that the astronauts had been stranded on the moon, that they were going to die there, and that nothing could be done to help them. For Safire, author of the pugilistically alliterative, fire-breathing speeches Vice President Agnew gave blasting "radical/liberals" as "nattering nabobs of negativism," it was chilling and daunting. But the words he wrote showed, in their compassion, the nobler side of Safire's spirit. He had written a speech he hoped would never be read publicly:

> Fate has ordained that the men who went to the moon to explore in peace will stay on the moon to rest in peace.
>
> These brave men, Neil Armstrong and Edwin Aldrin, know that there is no hope for their recovery. But they also know that there is hope for mankind in their sacrifice.
>
> These men are laying down their lives in mankind's most noble goal: the search for truth and understanding. They will be mourned by their families and friends; they will be mourned by their nation; they will be mourned by the people of the world;

they will be mourned by a Mother Earth that dared send two of her sons into the unknown.

In their exploration, they stirred the people of the world to feel as one; in their sacrifice they bind more tightly the brotherhood of man.

In ancient days, men looked at stars and saw their heroes in the constellations. In modern times, we do much the same, but our heroes are epic men of flesh and blood.

Others will follow, and surely find their way home. Man's search will not be denied. But these men were the first, and they will remain the foremost in our hearts.

For every human being who looks up at the moon in the nights to come will know there is some corner of another world that is forever mankind.

One statistic NASA failed to publicize and crow over regarding the Apollo 11 mission involved the results of a full-scale risk assessment run to find the odds of sending a manned mission to the moon and bringing the crew back alive.

According to Haggai Cohen, director of reliability and safety for space transportation systems, the odds were between five and ten to one against it.

At dawn on July 16, 1969, Neil Armstrong and crew member Michael Collins walked with robotic torpor, carrying portable air conditioners that cooled their two-hundred-pound spacesuits, across a narrow footpath leading from an elevator cage to the Apollo 11 craft, perched atop a Saturn V rocket. Thirty-two stories tall, bathed in dazzling white light, impatiently exhaling misty, white steam, its metal body contracting and expanding from the pressure of 960,000 gallons of the supercold fuels it held. The great ship Saturn stood proud. Its five engines boasted 160 million horsepower and 7.6 million pounds of thrust—double the potential hydroelectric power of all North America's rivers. It was the greatest engine ever devised by man.

In Neil's last conversation with his wife, Jan had tersely said, "Go, and good luck."

On July 15, the day before liftoff, a reporter had told her the odds of a successful moon landing were about 80 percent. She had corrected him sharply, "One hundred percent."

"Are you really that confident?"

"Yes, I am."

"Are you a little afraid?"

"No, sir, I'm not."

Neil smiled at the memory as he climbed into spaceship *Columbia*.

Chris Kraft had asked if there was anything else to do, anything they had overlooked. Armstrong had been firm. "No, Chris, we're ready. It's all been done except for the countdown."

Buzz Aldrin wanted one last look at the earth and the spaceship that was about to take him to another world. He later wrote: "While Mike and Neil were going through the complicated business of being strapped in and connected to the spacecraft's life-support system, I waited near the elevator on the floor below, alone for fifteen minutes in a sort of serene limbo. As far as I could see, there were people and cars lining the beaches and highways. The surf was just beginning to rise out of an azure-blue ocean. I could see the massiveness of the Saturn V rocket below and the magnificent precision of Apollo above. I savored the wait and marked the minutes in my mind as something I would always want to remember."

Michael Collins was likewise awed and a bit scared. He wrote: "I am everlastingly thankful that I have flown [a space mission] before, and that this period of waiting atop a rocket is nothing new. I am just as tense this time, but the tenseness comes mostly from an appreciation of the enormity of our undertaking, rather than from the unfamiliarity of the situation. I am far from certain that we will be able to fly the mission as planned. I think we will escape with our skins, or at least I will escape with mine, but I wouldn't give better than even odds on a successful landing and return. There are just too many things that can go wrong.

"I have plenty of time to think, if not daydream. Here I am, a white male, age thirty-eight, height 5 feet 11 inches, weight 165, salary $17,000 per annum, resident of a Texas suburb, with black spot on my roses, state of mind unsettled, about to be shot off to the moon. Yes, to the moon.

"At the moment, the most important control is over on Neil's side, just outboard of his left knee. It is the abort handle. If Neil rotates it counterclockwise, three solid rockets above us will fire and yank the command module free. A large, bulky pocket has been added to Neil's left suit leg and it looks as though, if he moves his leg slightly, it's going to snag on the abort handle. I quickly point this out to Neil; he grabs the pocket and pulls it as far over to the middle of his inside thigh as he can, but it still doesn't look secure to either one of us. Jesus, I can see the headlines now: "MOON SHOT FALLS INTO OCEAN. Mistake by Crew, Program Officials Intimate. Last Transmission From Armstrong Prior to Leaving Pad Reportedly 'Oops.'"

Upon ignition at 6:32 A.M., huge iron talons held the rocket in place for 8.9 seconds, as two-hundred-foot-long plumes of fire thundered in protest. When full power was developed, the temperature just below the command module shot up to1,200 degrees Fahrenheit. The astronauts were sitting atop a seismic event that could be detected a thousand miles away. Suddenly unfettered, it rode a ball of fire, slowly reaching for the sky, finally clearing the scaffolding and appearing like a second sun. Gradually winning the bout with gravity, it raced for the clouds, gracefully rolling over, guzzling fifteen tons of fuel per second, controls set for the unfathomable 24,227 miles per hour necessary to escape Mother Earth and reach the moon.

Neil Armstrong had little to say and nothing to note in his log during countdown, save for instrument readings. In Wapakoneta, Viola fretted on live television, "I hope he opens up a little later in the trip." His outward appearance suggested it was all routine. During liftoff, Armstrong's heartbeat, monitored at Houston, had soared to over 146 beats per minute on Gemini; now it climbed to only 110. Collins was even calmer at 99, compared with 125 on his previous flight; Aldrin was a very cool 88, in contrast to his Gemini blastoff heartbeat of 110.

As the first stage of Saturn made its incandescent separation and the force of gravity rose to four times normal, Mission Control softly intoned the words: "God speed and good luck." Armstrong sounded as calm as his heartbeat indicated, answering, "Thank you very much. We know it will be a successful flight."

Minutes later, the second stage dropped away, momentarily easing the g-forces pressing on the astronauts, and giving earth below another more distant and indistinct pyrotechnics display, followed shortly thereafter by the third stage's firing, which crushed them back into their couches for the final time. The craft was, by then, in a

103–nautical mile orbit, traveling at 17,450 miles per hour, and rapidly gaining speed. It was time to check virtually every system on board so that Houston could determine whether the next stage of the trip—the breakaway from earth—was a go. Armstrong broke the silence that had descended on his relieved crewmen, as well as at command, announcing, "Hey, Houston, Apollo 11. This Saturn gave us a magnificent ride. We have no complaints with any of the stages on that ride. It was beautiful."

After quickly completing the checklist to Houston's satisfaction, they were free to point toward the moon and begin the journey. Collins exalted, "We are climbing like a dingbat now." Aldrin calculated their speed at 35,579 feet per second, or 25,632 miles an hour—more than fast enough to escape earth's clutches. The next job was to prepare their craft for landing on the moon. The astronauts had to separate the 219-cubic-foot command module *Columbia,* their home base for the trip, from Saturn's third stage, then turn it around and connect *Columbia*'s nose to the fragile lunar-landing *Eagle,* which had made the journey safely stored inside the third stage. When that critical task was completed, and the useless remains of the third stage were safely jettisoned to avoid a catastrophic collision, the men were able to remove their spacesuits and lie down for a fitful sleep. The uniform of the day, until *Columbia* reached lunar orbit, was long johns. Apollo 11 was by then fourteen hours into its journey, nearly one hundred thousand miles from earth.

On the second day in space, the crew made a slight midcourse correction and then enjoyed NASA's improved space cuisine. They drank coffee with cream and sugar, which was supplied for the first time in the space program, snacked on brownies, dried apricots, peaches, and pears, and ate sandwiches from four kinds of tubed spread, including ham salad, tuna salad, and chicken salad. At regular mealtimes there were hearty foods, including spaghetti and turkey dinners, albeit dried meals that required rehydration with water and sipping through a straw. Even chewing gum, which had regularly been smuggled aboard flights, was supplied. The reason for the bounty of treats was a realization on the part of NASA doctors that astronauts regularly became so engaged in the flight they simply forgot to eat, a problem that had been apparent since Borman and Lovell's six-hour-long attempt to rendezvous their Gemini 7 craft with Gemini 6.

"The more tension there has been on the flights, the less the crews have eaten," said space nutritionist Dr. Malcolm C. Smith. "We gave each man 2,500 calories per day, but they became so involved with operations they ate nothing at all. The Apollo 9 crew ate nothing for twenty-eight hours."

One of the personal items Neil brought along was a small cassette tape recorder, to provide music, which he hoped would alleviate anxiety over the course of the long trip. Music tapes were donated by a rock-and-roll music producer named Mickey Kapp, who ran Warner Brothers during the sixties. At Armstrong's request, the obscure *Music Out of the Moon* by Dr. Samuel J. Hoffman and Dvořák's *New World Symphony* were included, along with a lot of contemporary pop music and some special-effects noises including loud bells and train whistles. These last were used by the astronauts for some uncharacteristic funny business. When Armstrong grew bored, he held the tape machine to an open microphone to Houston and played a blast or two of bells and whistles. When, on several occasions, startled controllers anxiously asked the astronauts if they had heard the sounds, there were perplexed denials all around. It wasn't until the postflight debriefing that Armstrong and his merry men pleaded guilty, solving the mystery.

As the trip progressed, the astronauts recorded their thoughts, comments, and feelings onto the tapes, gradually erasing the music and the sound effects. Those tapes were handed over to NASA, which eventually transcribed them and included the contemporaneous thoughts of the men in their archives. Much of the material included in this telling of Apollo 11's mission comes from those transcriptions.

Anxious to make sure landing module *Eagle* was undamaged, Aldrin got permission from Houston to crawl through the narrow nose of *Columbia* and into the double-telephone-booth-sized craft to do some housekeeping and check out its complex equipment. To everyone's relief, Buzz came crawling back an hour later, all smiles and thumb up.

All three crew members had their own designated official duties, and took on unofficial jobs as they came along. Collins, who was going to be "housebound" the entire trip, took it upon himself to be the ship's caretaker. "I've been very busy so far," he cheerily told Houston and the astronaut families listening on their squawk boxes. "I'm looking forward to taking the afternoon off. I've been cooking, sweeping, and almost sewing, and you know, the usual little housekeeping things. We are very comfortable up here, though. We do have a happy home. There's plenty of room for the three of us and I think we're all willing to find our favorite little corner to sit in."

As *Columbia* closed in on its target after three long days in space and passed through the shadow of the moon, Armstrong realized that all the magnificent visual images he had been privileged to see in his long career as an aviator were going to pale in comparison. "We were still thousands of miles out but close enough so that the moon almost filled our circular window. It was eclipsing the sun, from our position, and the corona of the sun was visible around the limb of the moon as a gigantic lens-shaped or saucer-shaped light stretching out to several lunar diameters. It was magnificent, but the moon itself was even more so. We were in the shadow, so there was no part of it illuminated by the sun. It was illuminated only by the earth, by earthshine. It made the moon appear blue-gray and the entire scene looked decidedly three-dimensional. It seemed almost as if it was showing us its round- ness, its similarity to our earth, in a sort of welcome. I was sure then that it would be a hospitable host. It had been awaiting its first visitors for a long time."

The content of Neil's first utterances on the moon weighed heavily on him as the hour drew near. During a quiet moment, Buzz gently broached the subject. Neil smiled ironically, indicating the heft of the burden. "Not yet, I'm still thinking it over." He was fully aware of the historic implications of all the details, particularly in light of the fact his movements would be projected via television to the world and endlessly repeated, long after he was no longer alive. After being char- acteristically reticent about the genesis of the "That's one small step . . ." phrase, he came clean six months after the landing, while in the Soviet Union to visit cosmonauts and watch a launch. "Evidently I am guilty of thinking up this phrase while on the moon."

NASA's speechwriters were apparently not asked to contribute, and Neil was certainly not told what to say, so space-agency historians combed the files from time to time, searching for clues. There emerged, in November 1999, a rather compelling theory. While researching a rou- tine query, NASA historian Glen Swanson unearthed a NASA memo- randum dated April 19,1969, just three months before the first moon landing mission, written by Willis H. Shapley, then Associate Deputy Administrator. Shapley had headed up the Symbolic Activities Commit- tee and was concerned that every detail of the moon landing be carefully planned with an eye to how it would play before an audience of friends and foes nearly a billion strong. "The 'accomplishment by the United States' aspect of the landing should be symbolized primarily by placing and leaving a U.S. flag on the moon in such a way as to make it clear that the flag symbolizes the fact that an effort by American people reached the moon, not that the U.S. is 'taking possession' of the moon," he wrote. Shapley went on to describe how the astronauts could avoid giving the wrong impression by also leaving "flags of all nations, one set to be left on the moon . . . and a duplicate set to be returned to earth for possible presentation by the president to foreign chiefs of state." Shapley stated strongly that all symbolic displays should be "simple, in good taste . . . and have no commercial implications or overtones."

Most important, Shapley wrote, all statements and symbols should emphasize "*The forward step of all mankind*" (italics added) aspect of the landing. Armstrong's "That's one small step for a man . . . one giant leap for mankind" certainly caught the spirit of Shapley's rallying cry.

And NASA's history office uncovered yet another example of the phrase back on December 26, 1962, when Dr. Homer E. Newell, then Director of the NASA Office of Space Sciences, addressed the American Association for the Advancement of Science. "The necessary observations and measurements obviously cannot all be made just by man's standing on the moon and looking around," he said. "But a giant step will have been taken. . . ."

Whether Armstrong saw all or none of the history office's examples doesn't much matter. The fact is the thrust of the phrase and elements of it were clearly part of the NASA view and the NASA lexicon. Credit goes to Neil for succinctly stating the leitmotif of the U.S. space program at its crowning moment.

At least once a day during the journey, NASA issued updates to the crew, on sports, world news, national politics, and, most important, what the world was saying about their mission. On the third day, a report from the Soviet newspaper *Pravda* was read with comic gravity. In an uncharacteristically laudatory report on the mission, it referred to Armstrong as "czar" of Apollo 11. Neil rolled his eyes, knowing it would take him a long while to live that moniker down, given the astronaut corps' notoriously prickly sense of humor. As expected, when next the capsule communicator called, he was told "the czar" was busy brushing his teeth and would have to get back to him.

By day three, the tension and confined quarters began exacting a toll. Writing in his diary, Collins noted he had managed to sleep for only seven hours, rather than the requisite nine, and that sleep had been fitful at best. "Despite our concentrated effort to conserve our energy on the way to the moon, the pressure is overtaking us (or at least me), and I feel that all of us are aware that the honeymoon is over, and we are about to lay our little pink bodies on the line. Our first shock comes as we stop our spinning motion [In order to prevent the sun's rays from heating one side of the ship while the other froze, the craft was deliberately made to slowly revolve for most of the flight—this was jocularly referred to as "barbecue mode." Absent gravity, the turning was unnoticeable to the astronauts.] and swing ourselves around so as to bring the moon into view. We have not been able to see the moon for nearly a day now, and the change is electrifying. The moon I have known all my life, that two-dimensional small yellow disk in the sky, has gone away somewhere, to be replaced by the most awesome sphere I have ever seen. It is huge, completely filling our window. And it is three-dimensional. The belly of it bulges out toward us in such a pronounced fashion that I almost feel I can reach out and touch it."

In addition to his awe at the physical sight of the moon, Collins was struck by the accuracy of NASA's computers, which had guided his spaceship to its target through a quarter of a million miles of space, while the target traveled nearly 200,000 miles through forty degrees of its arc. "We are racing through space just ahead of its leading edge," he noted.

As the craft passed within three hundred miles, the moon's gravity reached out and pulled *Columbia* around its dark side and prepared to whip it right back to Mother Earth. To prevent that happening, the astronauts fired their engine for a six-minute burn, putting on the brakes, hard, injecting *Columbia* into lunar orbit.

"When the moment finally arrives, the big engine instantly swings into action and reassuringly plasters us back in our seats," wrote Collins. The men knew they had reached a critical point in the journey, indeed a critical moment in their lives, because an overly long burn would cause *Columbia* to crash on the lunar surface; conversely, if the brakes weren't applied hard enough, they might be hurled irretrievably into space. All three astronauts monitored the dials and gauges intently, praying the onboard computer—less powerful than most year-2004 laptops—would do the job. When the engine went silent, Collins quickly checked the results. "Phenomenal," was his pronouncement. The velocity error was negligible; they were in lunar orbit precisely as planned. "That is one accurate burn, and even Neil acknowledges the fact," he wrote.

There was little to do but somehow try to get a good night's sleep on what would be, for Neil and Buzz, the most exciting night of their lives. Some of the secrets of the eerie, dead sphere they were circling would be theirs come morning—or not, depending on how skillful Armstrong proved at piloting the weird contraption christened *Eagle* by the crew of Apollo 11.

Before covering *Columbia*'s windows to keep out the brilliant earthlight, they carefully prepared their equipment and clothes for the journey; then, when they could think of no other preparation that could be done in advance, they turned out the lights and struggled for several hours before finally drifting into a shallow, restive sleep.

When the NASA wakeup call came, Neil and Buzz were both awake, though still lying in their couches and silent. Mike Collins, who was closest to the microphone, struggled to answer. Following a quick breakfast, the real work of activating *Eagle* began. Cables connecting the two ships were severed, cameras, as well as decidedly old-fashioned tools like shovels, were passed through the narrow tunnel connecting *Columbia* with the landing module. When supplies for the trip were stowed, Buzz took his post in *Eagle* and began a long list of radio checks with Mike in the *Columbia*'s command seat. Armstrong began the work of programming the computer that would, theoretically, guide the landing module to its preselected destination. As the time for *Eagle* to fly came nearer, Houston checked in with the busy astronauts. "How's the czar doing. He's awfully quiet." Neil laughed; he hoped the "czar" thing would be forgotten eventually, but after several days it was still a pretty popular tease. "Just hanging on and punching buttons."

Twenty minutes later, with Buzz and Neil at their positions in *Eagle,* appropriately standing at the controls as they would aboard a seafaring ship, Mike gazed out *Columbia*'s window at the small (it measured twenty-two feet in height and thirty-one in width), ungainly craft, and felt the reality of what was happening sink in quickly. "It was the weirdest-looking contraption ever, floating there with its legs awkwardly jutting out above a body that has neither symmetry nor grace," Collins thought. Aldrin privately agreed. Later he said, "It looks more to me like a praying mantis than it does a first-class flying machine, but it was a beautiful piece of machinery." *Eagle*'s homeliness even struck a chord on Madison Avenue. Volkswagen of America, manufacturers of the enormously popular, utilitarian, and proud-to-be-ugly VW Bug, bought full-page ads that summer with a drawing of *Eagle* captioned IT'S UGLY BUT IT GETS YOU THERE.

He had no intention of telling his crewmates just how unlikely their craft seemed, but couldn't resist a dig. "I think you've got a fine-looking machine there," he joked. "You cats take it easy on the lunar surface." Neil cheerfully called back, "See you later." Mike fought off the dark images that came to him. "I hope so," he thought. "OK, *Eagle*, one minute." When it was time, Collins fired *Columbia*'s thruster, just a red lick in space, enough to separate the craft and give *Eagle* a little room to maneuver. Slowly, the landing module separated from the mother ship and arched into its own orbit, gradually drifting down. Sixty miles above the surface, Neil took control, firing his thrusters to slow *Eagle*, beginning a powered descent. Looking out a triangular window etched with a grid pattern, the pilgrims plunged feet-first toward their goal, a small red flame flickering in *Eagle*'s nether region, controlling the fall. Then, gradually, *Eagle* rolled over until its crew was facedown, parallel to the surface, watching the dead, silent craters and canyons grow larger and clearer. Disconcertingly, the landing craft, with its finely milled aluminum-foil walls, creaked and groaned as though threatening to come apart. *Eagle* had a fragility that made the astronauts careful not to touch its walls, let alone lean against them. Buzz mused at the less-than-comforting thought that he could have probably made a hole in the craft's wall with a screwdriver. Adding to the sense of impermanency and hurried design were the bundles of exposed wires and plumbing.

On cue from the computer, the engine blasted to full throttle and *Eagle* began a twelve-minute powered drop to just six thousand feet above the tortured lunar surface. As they descended, Buzz rattled off numbers from the computer guidance system, while Neil kept his eyes glued to the window grid, making sure the information melded with the reality before him. Mount Marilyn (named by Jim Lovell after his wife) passed reassuringly beneath *Eagle*, meaning they were on course, and that the crystal-clear pictures Tom Stafford had taken a few months earlier on Apollo 10 were serving as accurate mental maps. The system seemed to be working splendidly—until a yellow caution alarm flashed on. Neil's trained eye saw it immediately. "Program alarm. Twelve-O-Two." The onboard computer was overloading, telling them it couldn't cope with all the requests for data. Houston immediately overruled the alarm, reassuring the crew that it had been expected. Everyone involved was aware the computers were woefully inadequate. That was a given.

As the descent continued through five thousand feet, the craggy surface of the moon began to come into sharp focus. Then another alarm sounded, a more urgent cry; the computer was inadequately dealing with data and was shutting down. But again Houston gave an immediate "Go" order, overriding the warning. Confident flight controller Steve Bales knew virtually all there was to know about the computer system, including its flaws, and calculated that the computer would help, but the success or failure of the landing would ultimately have to depend on the skills of the astronauts.

Armstrong continued a fast, sure approach to the flat tableland NASA computers had chosen for a landing site, after analyzing hundreds of thousands of photos taken by unmanned craft as well as previous Apollo flights that had circled the orb. But the maddening alarms were exacting a price—despite Houston's lack of concern, the astronauts were no longer visually double-checking decisions being made by the computer; instead they were concentrating on the instruments.

One minute later, at 4:15 P.M. Houston time, *Eagle* passed through four hundred feet. The sun was to their backs, so the landing site was out of the shadows and could be seen in sharp contrast. Straight ahead, and looming toward them fast, was geography bearing no likeness to a smooth plain—it was a six-hundred-foot-deep crater, a razor-sharp escarpment that would tear *Eagle* to shreds.

"I was surprised by the size of the boulders," Armstrong said later, "some were as big as motor cars. And it seemed like we were coming up on them pretty fast; of course, the clock runs at about triple speed in such a situation." Neil said nothing; he just reacted: disconnecting the computer and taking manual control, cutting hard to the downrange side, skimming just over top of the boulder field. Aldrin remained impassive; from his position he could see only straight ahead or to the right, while the boulder field, which appeared as big as a "football stadium" to Armstrong, was to the left and out of his sight line. ("He couldn't see it! He couldn't appreciate that at all!" Armstrong recalled during debriefing. "We were coming right into the northeast slopes of it. And there were a lot of big boulders on that slope. Geologically interesting, but not a good place to land.") A radar warning light flashed, uselessly late. The sudden acceleration blast against the ghost-like lunar surface, previously undisturbed for a billion years, raised a massive cloud of moondust that encircled them and severely decreased visibility.

Controllers in Houston had been listening intently to Aldrin's calm voice reading off *Eagle*'s rapidly declining altitude and slowing forward motion; everything seemed to be going smoothly. Suddenly that reverie was dashed. Aldrin's figures indicated that *Eagle,* apparently coming in for a landing at a dead-slow eight miles per hour, had accelerated to fifty-five miles per hour. One of the steely controllers recalled mouthing the words, "Dear God." Nothing in the years of planning had predicted this. Something bizarre was happening; Armstrong was silent as a sphinx, and every time Houston tried to get a message to *Eagle* it came out sounding like chicken scratching, and cut out altogether due to problems with the ship's steerable antenna.

Armstrong had no interest at that moment in chatting with Houston; there was nothing they could have told him, anyway. The situation resembled Armstrong's ordeal nearly twenty years earlier, fighting a futile battle to keep his ravaged Panther airborne over North Korea, all the while listening to the clockwork tones of a traffic controller—likely sipping coffee and smoking a Lucky Strike—vectoring him to an airstrip over a hundred miles distant that may as well have been a ten thousand miles away.

But on that July day, when Armstrong was desperately searching a desolate alien planet for a safe spot to alight, succor from Houston was not an option. In addition to all the other failures and problems, communication between *Eagle* and Houston was flickering in and out, with increasingly long dead spots. Dependent on a tedious relay of information through Collins in *Columbia* to *Eagle,* Houston would have been unable to effectively take charge of the landing. Finally, out of the duststorm *Eagle* had created, Aldrin continued reading the all-important speed and rate of descent while Armstrong's eyes swept the lunar surface, which alternated between brilliant, blinding radiance and murky shadow.

Another warning light bathed the tiny cabin with its ominous red glow, signaling that *Eagle* had just ninety-four seconds' worth of fuel left. Without the cushion of its retro-engine, a drop of just ten feet would mean damage to *Eagle* sufficient to sentence both men to death on the moon. Aldrin later wrote in his memoirs, "Even after years as a fighter pilot and astronaut, I felt that first hot edge of panic."

Their altitude was one hundred fifty feet. At that moment, 4:16 P.M., Armstrong spoke for the first time since the crisis had begun. "I got a good spot." ("I changed my mind a couple of times again. I was absolutely adamant about my right to be wishy-washy about where I was going to land. Finally we found an area ringed on one side by fairly good-sized craters, and on the other by a boulder field. It was not a particularly big area, only a couple of hundred square feet, about the size of a big house lot. But it looked satisfactory. And I was quite concerned about the fuel level. We had to get on the surface very soon or fire the ascent engine and abort.") Aldrin continued to carefully monitor the descent rate and speed, calling out the figures like a watch aboard a Mississippi River steamer. "Ease her down," he said. At forty feet, *Eagle* was again kicking up a blinding duststorm of sparkling grainy dust—a full minute had elapsed since the warning. Thirty feet from the surface, *Eagle* began drifting backward, which set off an alarm in Armstrong's brain. The spot was good, not great; it was impossible to tell if there were boulders hiding in the gloom just behind them. He gunned forward a tad. The dust was so thick they were virtually flying blind. Houston crackled a terse fuel reminder: "Thirty seconds." There were more moments of interminable waiting, then four lights on the big control board in Houston flashed, indicating the four landing struts had made contact—though whether soft contact or hard remained to be learned.

Eagle was at rest. The blinding dust suddenly, inexplicably, was gone, affording the visitors a crystal-clear view of the moonscape. Armstrong later marveled, "The dust didn't settle. It *disappeared* immediately after engine shutdown." Conscious that the world was waiting, Armstrong announced in a famously calm voice that men had survived and a nation had collectively made history. The words were loud and clear: "Houston, Tranquillity Base here. The *Eagle* has landed." Armstrong's heartbeat at that moment registered 155 beats per minute, slightly more than double normal for him.

While the Apollo commander's first words on laying human footsteps upon the planet six hours later would prove the stuff of myths, Armstrong's stark announcement of safe landing after the tense drama *Eagle* had narrowly survived seemed more stirring for many. Newspaper editions published early Sunday evening, before the moonwalk, typically declared it the phrase that would be remembered. "There is a magic about such words—uttered by a man discovering a new land or testing a new invention—that has almost rivaled the event itself," marveled *The New York Times*. It was compared to Christopher Columbus's lookout shouting *"Tierra, Tierra,"* in sight of San Salvador on October 11, 1492, to Samuel Morse tapping out the scriptural quote, "What hath God wrought!" on May 24, 1844, in the first telegram ever, sent from Washington, D.C. to Baltimore, Maryland, and to Charles Lindbergh's droll comment upon completing his solo Atlantic voyage in 1927: "Well, I made it."

Chapter Fourteen

There was a collective sigh all over the world. At Mission Control in Houston, astronaut Charles Duke, the designated Capsule Communicator for Apollo 11, exulted: "Roger Tranquillity. We copy you on the ground. You've got a bunch of guys about to turn blue. We're breathing again. Thanks a lot."

Gene Kranz remembers: "I experienced a chill unlike any in my life. I am totally unprepared for the flood of emotion. I am choked up, speechless, and I have to get going with the stay/no stay, and I just cannot speak."

NASA had no idea Armstrong had picked out a name in advance for *Eagle*'s temporary lunar base, but "Tranquillity" struck most everyone as appropriate, particularly given the harrowing nature of the flight from orbit to surface.

Neil quickly filled Houston in on just how nerve-racking the last minutes had been, explaining the gaps of silence while he corrected the computer's course toward doom and searched for a safe landing site. But there was no time to relax. The book on lunar landing, which was largely written by Buzz, called for immediate preparation for liftoff and return to *Columbia*. The routine safety precaution was made all the more urgent by the computer problems and resultant alarms on the way down. If the alarms had actually been symptoms of more serious malfunctions, they might actually have to immediately abort the visit and return to the mother ship. The two windows of opportunity for rendezvous were three minutes and twelve minutes after touchdown; otherwise the *Eagle* and its passengers would have to stay at Tranquillity Base until *Columbia* completed a full lunar orbit, which took about two hours. It was one more potential life-or-death situation. Man's first minutes on an alien sphere, as represented by Neil's presence, were spent in deep concentration, running through all of *Eagle*'s systems, including life support and propulsion.

In Houston, Gene Kranz was polling his flight controllers on the stay/no stay decision. At eight minutes there was a stay, which was promptly relayed to *Eagle*. Minutes later was a second stay, and a tense wait for the final order to continue the mission. Suddenly Kranz received the "jolt" he had most feared. Landing-module control-systems engineer Bob Carlton reported: "Flight, the descent engine helium tank pressure is rising rapidly. The back room expects the burst disc to rupture. We want the crew to vent the system."

Immediately, venting began. Carlton eyed his telemetry display, anxiously watching the response. After a long pause, he was able to exhale, "Flight, we're now okay, the pressure has dropped and the system is stable."

When the frenzied burst of activity was finished and Houston and the astronauts were satisfied everything checked out, there was finally time to gaze with wonder at the lunar surface.

One of the first startling discoveries was that in the airless void of the moon, color, normally refracted through the atmosphere, was almost nonexistent. "There doesn't appear to be too much of a general color at all," Aldrin said.

"It's pretty much without color," Armstrong agreed. "It's gray and very white chalky gray." But the overall first impression of the moon as seen through the triangular window of *Eagle* was a sportsfield at night under the lights. "The sky is black, it's a very dark sky. But it still seemed more like daylight than darkness as we looked out the window," Armstrong later recalled. "It's a peculiar thing, because the surface looked very warm and inviting. It looked as if it would be a nice place to take a sunbath. It was the sort of situation in which you felt like going out there in nothing but a bathing suit to get a little sun." (Of course, he was well aware an unprotected human would lose consciousness in about ten seconds and his blood would boil in about three minutes on the lunar surface.)

Preparing to leave the relative safety of landing module *Eagle*, the astronauts certainly reflected on the cautionary opinions that had been offered them by some of the world's top scientists over the months of mission planing. Edinburgh University Professor Richard L. Gregory, a specialist on the brain and perception in strange environments, consulted by NASA, gave a grim prognosis. "So utterly alien is the lunar environment, there will be a dearth of reliable clues to interpret precisely what the eyes record. Optical illusions will abound—many quite capable of resulting in fatal errors of judgment. The threat to the human mind will be no less than the physical dangers." Another scientist warned the astronauts that their "muscular control on the moon may be no better than a child's."

Cornell University astrophysicist Thomas Gold felt the explorers should be roped together like mountain climbers, because in his opinion the moon's surface was "a deep and treacherous dust layer" that would swallow the astronauts. He also warned of crustlike layers that might cloak deep caverns. And there were concerns about solar flares, eruptions of hot gases raining down that could incinerate the men and their ship. But because astronomers said the occurrence happened only once every two years, it was considered a reasonable risk. Chemists posited that minerals on the moon deprived of air for millions of years might react to the introduction of oxygen by exploding. All the warnings had been presented to the astronauts, whose judgment was: We're grateful for the heads-up, and we're still willing to take the risks.

Buzz Aldrin decided to put his fate in the hands of a higher authority. In the small personal preference kit each man was allowed, he had brought a small wine chalice, a tiny container of wine, and some favorite Scripture jotted on paper. Without a word, he brought the items out and prepared to perform a Presbyterian communion service. "As I prepared, I asked for a moment of radio silence. I could see Neil looking at me like, 'Now what is he up to?' But he often looked at me that way. I felt it was the right thing to do and was determined to see it through." Doubtless, the "disdain" Aldrin would remember in Armstrong's stare—even four decades later—was more like chagrin. Jim Lovell and Bill Anders had stirred a mountain of controversy, much of it negative toward NASA, the previous year when they had read Scripture from Genesis on Christmas Day while in lunar orbit. What had seemed an innocent gesture of faith to them was criticized as slighting other religions and a way of claiming the space program and even the moon for Christians.

But to Buzz, his lunar Communion on Sunday evening, July 20,

1969, was an important private testimony, withering glances be damned. Having thought long in advance what prayers would be appropriate, Aldrin avoided what he thought would be a selfish prayer for his family, or a grandiose benediction for all mankind, instead asking for the lunar mission and its spirit of exploration "for all mankind" to be blessed. "I am the wine and you are the branches. Whosoever remains in me and I in him will bear much fruit, for you can do nothing without me." He then poured a tiny amount of wine, which touched the chalice and curled up right into his mouth. When Buzz finished the ritual, he turned the microphone back on and addressed the world: "This is the landing module copilot. I'd like to take this opportunity to ask every person listening in, whoever and wherever they maybe, to pause for a moment and contemplate the events of the past few hours, and to give thanks in his or her own way."

The original plan called for the astronauts to sleep four hours while standing in the cramped *Eagle*. But neither man had ever imagined they would actually be capable of sleep, or even rest, with the moon awaiting its first living visitors. With Houston's assent, they began suiting up as soon as *Eagle* was fully prepared for the return trip to *Columbia*, and they were satisfied no damage had occurred during the trip down. Donning the spacesuits, which weighed 190 pounds on earth, though just 33 pounds on the moon, was a daunting task that Neil compared to a woman dressing for a prom in a telephone booth with no one to help get the zipper up.

The suits were masterful pieces of engineering. They were capable of stopping a micrometeorite traveling 64,000 miles an hour, which is 300 times faster than the speed of a high-powered rifle bullet. The portable life-support system pumped water throughout the suit, ensuring a constant temperature, despite the moon's drastic fluctuations, which can range from 243 degrees Fahrenheit at the zenith of the fourteen-hour lunar day to 279 below zero at the nadir of the lunar night. Naturally, NASA planned the moon voyages to avoid the extremes. The coldest surface temperature during the visit was around zero; the hottest, as *Eagle* began its ascent, was below one hundred. The spacesuits also provided electric power, four hours of oxygen, and radio communications. The famously reflective facemask—which captured the only still image of Armstrong on the moon, mirrored in Buzz' face, because Neil took all but one of the pictures—was coated with gold, the only substance NASA found that effectively blocked the sun's ultraviolet radiation. Adding to the difficulty of suiting up was the constant fear that a clumsy move would damage the craft, break a switch, or smash a dial. In simulation this had happened several times.

When the suits were operational, six and a half hours after landing, air was vented from *Eagle,* which was necessary before opening the hatch. But even with the air pressure down considerably, they discovered it wouldn't budge. Like a couple trying to twist the lid off a stuck jar of jam, first Neil then Buzz gingerly tried pulling the handle without success. They pushed and pulled, ever so gently, fearing damage to the ship; they coaxed, cursed and prayed, but with no luck. Armstrong's message, "Houston, we can't seem to get the hatch to open," brought confused silence. Frustration mounting over a conundrum that later would seem comical, Buzz desperately pried at a corner of the hatch, straining to just apply slow steady pressure. Finally, it gave just a fraction of an inch, allowing the last of *Eagle*'s air to jet out into space, and the hatch was open.

At 9:51 P.M. Houston time, the "Greatest Show Off Earth," as the *Chicago Sun-Times* billed it, began with Armstrong cautiously, clumsily, backing out of *Eagle,* aided by Aldrin. "Relax a little bit," coaxed Buzz. "How am I doing?" Neil asked. "You're doing fine," Aldrin reassured him. By 9:55, he was finally outside, standing erect on the narrow ledge of *Eagle,* which the astronauts called "the porch." There was a nine-rung ladder attached to the porch, then a three-and-a-half-foot drop from the last rung to the surface, which seemed a long distance to a man enveloped in a miniature spaceship. In fact it seemed such a leap that both men feared that climbing back up to *Eagle* might prove difficult and dangerous. While the world waited anxiously for the first televised images of the moonwalk, Armstrong practiced pulling himself up the ladder a few times. Satisfied the climb was doable, he opened a pod in the side of the ship activating a tiny (by the standards of 1969) black-and-white television camera. At that moment, a hazy, flickering image—at first comically upside-down—flashed onto the screens of hundreds of millions of people: a billion, by some accounts, most of whom would never forget where they were, who they were with, and the thoughts that went through their heads. In New York's Central Park, J.F.K. International Airport, London's Trafalgar Square, and Seoul, Korea, giant screens were set up where tens of thousands of earthlings could watch humanity's first steps on the moon. Several

African nations issued transistor radios so that even remote tribes could join in history's great accomplishment.

> **Houston:** OK, Neil. We can see you coming down the ladder now.
> **Armstrong:** OK. I just checked getting back up to that first step. It didn't collapse too far. But it's adequate to get back up.
> **Houston:** Roger. We copy.
> **Armstrong:** It's a pretty good little jump. . . . I'm at the foot of the ladder. The *Eagle*'s foot pads are only depressed in the surface about one or two inches, although the surface appears to be very, very fine-grained as you get close to it. It's almost like a powder. I'm going to step off *Eagle* now.

The thirty-eight-year-old explorer seemed to hesitate, gathering his thoughts, then tentatively placed a boot on the lunar surface. Finding it solid and supportive, he rested more of his weight on it, then, finally convinced it would support him, placed both feet on the moon and stood, a ghostly-white figure, all alone.

Buzz, waiting for Armstrong to deliver whatever pithy words he might have prepared—he still had no idea what Neil was going to say—thought the pause "seemed like a small eternity." Finally, the commander of Apollo 11 spoke to the people of earth a quarter of a million miles away. "One small step for a man, one giant leap for mankind."

Fifteen minutes later, Buzz was backing ever so carefully out of *Eagle,* "buoyant and full of goose pimples." As excited as he was, Aldrin was able to get off a wry jest that reflected on the gravity of the moment: "Now I want to partially close the hatch, making sure not to lock it on the way out." Neil responded, "A good thought." It was indeed a good thought; the danger was that a leaky valve might repressurize *Eagle* while they were gone. It would have made a near-perfect seal and they would never have gotten back in.

As Buzz made his way down the ladder, Neil stood by to offer assistance, if needed, his custom Hasselblad out and ready to shoot. "Neil, in the tradition of all tourists, had his camera ready to photograph my arrival." Armstrong's first shot was a sharp picture of Aldrin backing down the spindly ladder—which looked as though it would snap under his weight—with the weird orange-foiled craft in the background set against a pitch-black sky.

Buzz's first impression was of the peculiar calculus of a planet without atmosphere. When he kicked some of the "very, very fine-grained sand," each particle scattered in the exact same pattern and landed almost precisely the same distance away—far different from the untidy randomness of earth, where everything is affected by the sundry gases that constantly swirl about, making the planet habitable for naked beasts. "Magnificent desolation" was the thought that kept going through Aldrin's head.

Struggling with all the discipline they possessed, the astronauts quit gazing at the "brilliant oasis" that was their home planet, glistening green-and-blue in the far, far distance, the unnaturally brilliant, almost eerie whiteness of their spacesuits and the stark harshness of the colorless lunar surface, instead turning to the urgent chores they were charged with accomplishing in just under two hours. First in order of importance was the gathering of soil samples in case, for any reason, they should have to cut the mission short. Geologists and other scientists the world over were holding their collective breath waiting for Neil and Buzz to break out their shovels and get at least one scoop of whatever the moon was made of in the soil sample pockets stitched into the legs of their spacesuits.

Neil pushed his shovel into the surface and found it slid easily six or eight inches below the surface. "I'm sure I could push it farther, but it's so hard for me to bend down farther," he said, struggling to work in the bulky suit. Then, finally, with the sample safely stowed, he straightened up and said, "The sample is in the pocket, Houston." Across the miles, the small triumph was acknowledged. Capsule Communicator Bruce McCandless crackled back, "This is Houston, roger, Neil." Astronaut/geologist Don Lind, listening over a monitor at the space center, breathed easier at once. "He is certainly going to get back to the spacecraft with his pants on, so we will have this sample for sure."

Next they uncovered a stainless-steel plaque that had been attached to the *Eagle* and removed it. Aldrin focused the television camera on Armstrong as he held it up for the world to see. The inscription read: HERE MEN FROM THE PLANET EARTH FIRST SET FOOT UPON THE MOON, JULY 1969, A.D. WE CAME IN PEACE FOR ALL MANKIND. After what seemed a suitable number of seconds, the plaque was leaned against the leg of *Eagle,* and the amateur, unchoreographed "space opera," as one newspaper account put it, continued with the unfurling of a three-by-five-foot American flag. It was an aspect of the show that had caused a minor flap, including charges it smacked of symbolic imperialism—not a particularly surprising imbroglio, given the tenor of the times. The preference of the Apollo 11 crew was to carry the blue-and-white flag of the United Nations, a proposal that was given a wary look at NASA, then passed on to Congress, where it was soundly rejected. ("The provider of the money for the program would not go along with this," Armstrong recalled years later.)

Minutes after the Stars and Stripes "fluttered" on the moon, the man who would become emblematic of sixties strife, Richard Milhous Nixon, made history by placing the first transplanetary telephone call. Nixon had been avidly following Apollo 11, losing sleep staying up to watch television broadcasts. And while the canny old politician certainly saw great political hay in the space program, he was also genuinely enthused. H. R. Haldeman watched the landing in the Oval Office with Nixon. "When Neil hit the surface, P [the president] clapped and said 'Hooray.' He's very much excited by the whole thing. Was fascinated with watching the moonwalk. He had Frank Borman [the Apollo 8 astronaut who had become the President's advisor on the space program and liaison with NASA] in to describe what was happening." Talking to the press the following day, Nixon described talking to Borman about what Armstrong was doing as the equivalent of "asking Christopher Columbus what he thought of Magellan's chances."

Armstrong and Aldrin were giddily "kangaroo-hopping" in the diminished gravity when the call came from NASA to get in place for the presidential phone call. As perfectly designed by White House and space-agency public relations maestros, the new president, having been inaugurated just six months prior, was shown on a split screen sitting in the Oval Office, talking to the astronauts. Nixon had been given numerous drafts for a brief speech, but had thrown them all away, instead penning his own words. At NASA's direction, Aldrin and Armstrong had stopped hopping about and were standing at attention on either side of the flag, the mounted television camera square on them.

"Hello, Neil and Buzz. I'm talking to you from the Oval Room in the White House. This certainly has to be the most historic phone call made from the White House," he said, speaking just a bit too fast. "Because of what you've done, the heavens have become a part of man's world. And as you talk to us from the Sea of Tranquillity, it inspires our efforts to bring peace and tranquillity to earth. I just can't tell you how proud we all are of what you have done. With every American this has to be the proudest day of our lives. For one priceless moment in the whole history of man, all the people on this earth are truly one—one in their pride of what you have done, and one in our prayers that you will return safely to earth."

The astronauts looked as though they were struggling to keep from bouncing, but their excitement and the strangeness of suddenly having shed all but a fraction of their weight made them look like they couldn't quite stay still. Because it took several seconds for the president's voice to reach them, and several seconds for a response to get back to earth, there were awkward silences between the exchanges. Finally, Armstrong's response was heard, his voice cracking with emotion. "Thank you, Mr. President, it's a great honor and privilege for us to be here representing not only the United States, but men of peace of all nations, men with interest and curiosity and men with the vision for the future."

Nixon ended the conversation by thanking the astronauts and promising he would be there to greet them aboard the U.S.S. *Hornet* when they splashed down in the Pacific the following Thursday. The president was going to be very involved from that moment on, elaborately celebrating the success of the mission and shaping the way the space program would have an impact politically.

The speechifying over, the astronauts set back to the task at hand, which included gathering about thirty pounds of soil samples, twenty pounds of rocks, and activating two experiments that would stay behind providing a stream of scientific data for some time to come. These included a device to measure seismic activity, continually transmitting the results back to earth, and a so-called "Laser Ranging Retro-Reflector," consisting simply of a hundred circular reflecting surfaces. Laser beams projected from earth would bounce back, providing a precise measurement of the distances from earth to the moon at any given moment. A third experiment was to return to earth. Consisting simply of a large piece of aluminum foil, it was unfurled, attached to a pole, and hung facing the sun. The idea was to catch samples of the gases, or charged particles, contained in the mysterious winds that swirl through the solar system, which some scientists surmise might someday be surfed by spaceships with sails.

In addition to serious experiments, Buzz and Neil brought up and left on the lunar surface sentimental remembrances honoring astronauts and cosmonauts who had perished in the line of duty. One was the patch of Apollo 1, the planned voyage of their close friends Ed White, Gus Grissom, and Roger Chaffee. The other was a medal struck for the occasion honoring Soviet cosmonauts Yuri Gagarin and Vladimir Komarov. Gagarin, the first man in space, was the star of the Soviet space program and a national hero. He was killed in a freak accident while piloting a MiG near Moscow. Komarov, as commander of Soyuz 1, experienced a problem similar to Neil's Gemini 8 malfunction and was forced to abort. After surviving a far-too-hot reentry, his parachutes tangled, and he watched helplessly as his craft hurtled through the sky and slammed into the earth at more than four hundred miles per hour.

Both explorers also brought small tokens their wives had asked them to take to the moon, as well as one from Mike Collins's wife. They have never revealed what they were, though it's probably safe to say they were very personal items that must come to mind whenever they gaze upon the moon.

Working hard on complex experiments under exotic conditions, including diminished gravity, light that ranged from harsh, angular glares to deep shadows, requiring frequent pauses for the eyes to adapt, and wearing spacesuits, was difficult and a challenge; but all in all they found the working conditions pleasant. "There were a lot of things to do, and we had a hard time getting them finished," Armstrong recalled in post-flight debriefing. "But we had little trouble, much less trouble than expected on the surface. Temperatures weren't high; they were comfortable. The primary difficulty was just far too little time to do the variety of things we would have liked. We had the problem of a five-year-old boy in a candy store."

Nervous NASA scientists and doctors had wanted a short leash on the first moonwalkers, particularly fearing the effects of the alien environment on their bodies, and partially out of a generalized fear of what might be out there. Armstrong and Aldrin were told to range no farther than fifty to one hundred feet from *Eagle,* and on no account to venture into the lunar hills or canyons, out of radio range. Within those parameters, and in the short time remaining, the astronauts did the kangaroo hop, which consisted of leaning toward the direction you want to go, pushing off, and bouncing ahead. They had quickly learned, by trial and error, that getting around was effortless and easy, nothing like the dangerous, daunting task scientists had predicted. The biggest hindrances proved to be the incredibly bumpy terrain and steep lunar curvature. "It seemed to me . . . like swimming in the ocean with six- or eight-foot swells and waves. In that condition, you never can see very far from where you are. This is exaggerated by the fact that the lunar curvature is so pronounced," recalled Buzz. Another problem was determining the true horizon. "There is a decrease in the clues a person has as to which way is up, which way up really is." Clearly, it was no place to stray too far from the landing module and get lost.

The fine-grained surface was "slippery," and the effect of the one-sixth normal gravity combined to make the unwary moonwalker appear inebriated. In just two hours on the surface the men became nimble kangaroo hoppers; and would spend lifetimes yearning to exercise the skill again.

Bouncing around the moon, Aldrin had his first chance since landing to "zing off out of sight" of the camera that had been trained on the explorers since they arrived and contemplate the enormity of what they had accomplished as well as the work and the dangers that lay ahead. "My God . . . what will it be like if we really carry this off and return to earth in one piece, with our boxes full of rocks and our heads full of new perspectives for our planet?"

A little less than two hours after Neil's first step, the "consumables" in their spacesuits—the oxygen and other life-sustaining substances—were dwindling. It was time to begin stowing the invaluable booty stashed in the fishing tackle–like boxes.

A very low-tech pulley system had been devised for the purpose. Leaking dust, tangling in the lines, nearly losing a box of what was undoubtedly the most valuable film stock in the universe when it crashed to the ground, and taking far longer than planned, the chore was finally accomplished. The astronauts also inadvertently fouled the interior of *Eagle* with dust and fine grains of moon rock, ensuring a less-than-comfortable return trip. And dust wasn't the only thing fouling the cabin of *Eagle*. Empty food containers, filled urine bags, and sundry other detritus was strewn about the tiny ship. The lot was tossed out the door, where it would bear mute witness that man had become an interstellar litterbug.

Having been on the go for twenty-two hours straight, Neil and Buzz were exhausted; even adrenaline was in low supply. There was no question about attempting liftoff and rendezvous with *Columbia* in their depleted state—particularly in view of the heart-stopping problems experienced on descent. *Eagle* was repressurized, but Aldrin and Armstrong decided to attempt to sleep with their helmets, gloves, and suits on anyway because of the choking dust, and in case a rent developed in *Eagle* or the oxygen system failed. And there was another prosaic reason: *Eagle's* cockpit was a very noisy place, even at rest on Tranquillity Base. The life-support systems, powertrain, and computers whirred, clanged, hissed, and banged. It was not a ship designed for comfort, but for efficiency and lightness. To their relief, the astronauts discovered that with their helmets on the only sound was steady white noise. The other impediment to sleep was the bright light. Even with shades drawn, the lunar surface, still lit as brightly as a sports arena at night, reflected into *Eagle*. In addition, there was no provision to dim the myriad switches, dials, warning lights, and displays that glowed brightly.

Nevertheless, the men knew they were desperately sleep-deprived and had to rest. Aldrin lay on *Eagle's* floor and Armstrong on the ascent-engine cover. They were incongruous places to secure a good night's rest, but all that was available. "I'll have to say that I had the better sleeping place," Aldrin said in post-flight debriefing. "I found that it was relatively comfortable on the floor, either on my back with feet up against the side, or with my knees bent. Also, I could roll over on one side or the other. There was ample room on the floor for one. But there wasn't room for two."

Sleeping in a spacesuit was not nearly as uncomfortable as it sounds. "I don't feel that having the suit on in one-sixth gravity is that much of a bother. It's fairly comfortable. You have your own snug little sleeping bag, unless you have a pressure point somewhere. Your head in the helmet assumes a very comfortable position. I don't see any need for taking the helmets off."

Neil also made the best of his situation, and improvised to provide a measure of added comfort. "I didn't mind sleeping on the engine cover. I didn't find it that bad. I made a hammock out of a waist tether—which I attached to some structure handholds—to hold my feet up in the air and in the middle of the cockpit. This kept my feet up about level with or a little higher than my torso." Once again, their years of training and ardent discipline served well; soon both managed a "state of drowsiness" that would serve as something close to sleep. But even that was interrupted well before the prescribed three hours. "After a while, I started to get awfully cold," Armstrong recalled, "so I reached in front of the fan and turned the water temperature [the water was flowing through tubes in his suit] to full up—max increase. It still got colder and colder. There was a never-ending battle to obtain a minimum level of sleeping conditions, and we never did. Even if we could have, I'm not sure I would have gone to sleep."

Noon Houston time on Monday morning was the window for *Eagle* to rise off the lunar surface, orbit the sphere five times, and dock with *Columbia*. Virtually every system on Saturn V, *Columbia*, and even *Eagle* had been built with multiple redundancies, which engineers knew was the only way to reduce risks inherent in the mission. The one exception was *Eagle*'s ascent engine, because of weight constraints that were, at the time, pretty much immutable. Accepting that quandary, the ships designers had shifted to another risk-reducing scheme: simplicity. The propellants were "hypergolic," or self-igniting; there was no throttle, just an on-and-off switch. The brilliantly engineered machine had few moving parts beyond some electrical equipment, including an arming switch, circuit breakers, and a ball valve that released the fuel, causing liftoff. It had to work; there was no other way home.

One last chore on the moon was dumping more gear to lighten the ascent weight load, including the portable life-support backpacks that had served the astronauts so well during their two-hour, twenty-minute romp. *Eagle* was depressurized one last time, and the hatch pried open, a task the men were getting good at, the way one gets used to a sticking screen door. Through the open portal, they bade the moon farewell, wondering if they would ever return, and chucked two backpacks.

Perhaps the accident was caused by the lack of sleep, or just luck catching up with men who had worked a long, complex "daisy chain" with nothing going wrong.

The huge television audience watched it happen. The second of the backpacks flew out the narrow hatch, seemed to catch momentarily on the door, and, in slow-motion, cleanly sheared off what looked to be a switch of some sort. It was in fact the circuit breaker through which power was to flow to the ascent engine. The backpack hit it just at the right angle to snap off the switch, possibly rendering it unusable and severing the connection between the power source and the power-train. Due to weight constraints, all safety covers had been eliminated on *Eagle*. It was one of the calculated risks inherent in the project. Immediately, both astronauts made their clumsy way to the broken switch, bumping into each other and indelicately bouncing backward. Tenderly, like touching a baby, Armstrong felt to see if the shattered switch could be jury-rigged well enough to get them home. Amazingly, when he pushed the pin in, it stuck in the "on" position. Both men backed away, as though speaking or even breathing might cause it to spring back out. With great relief, they returned to the task of lifting off. Of course, if the switch hadn't been fixable, there were ways to build an alternate route around it, and the men had trained how to make such emergency repairs. But neither relished the idea of doing experimental surgery on *Eagle*'s electronics at that stage of the game.

On the return trip *Eagle* grew even smaller, because the no-longer-needed descent engine would be shed, left on the moon with the rest of the multimillion-dollar pile of throwaways. Only the four-and-a-half-foot-high, 172-pound ascent engine would be under *Eagle* to propel it home to *Columbia*. The spiderlegs, fuel tanks, and engine of the descent pod would all stay where they landed at Tranquillity Base.

Now, the part of *Eagle* that would fly home to *Columbia* was no longer the improbable, homely spider that had descended from lunar orbit, but a legless extraterrestrial bug, odd-shaped and metallic on top, bristling with appendages below. It, in fact, looked a bit like the flying saucer of celluloid imagination.

While Houston and *Eagle* prepared for liftoff, feeding coordinates into the computer that would, with luck, achieve a smooth rendezvous with *Columbia* on its twenty-fifth lunar orbit, there were two nagging worries. One was a slightly embarrassing technical failure: Houston wasn't precisely sure where Tranquillity Base was located on the lunar surface. Ever since touchdown, NASA's geological survey team had been scrambling to unravel just how far away from the planned landing site Neil had gone while scrambling to avoid the deadly escarpment.

The United States Geological Survey in Houston and the Center for Astrogeology in Flagstaff, Arizona, desperately studying maps and analyzing all the information available, had finally come to a consensus. But it was just an educated guess. There had been no provision for an aborted site and a zig-zag, last-second dash to find a safe landing zone. The one hope for a completely accurate fix was the laser retroreflector experiment Aldrin and Armstrong had assembled a few hours prior. But, thus far, Houston hadn't been able to locate the reflector with the laser.

Less than an hour prior to scheduled liftoff, Capsule Communicator Ron Evans apologetically briefed the astronauts on the situation: "We have a fairly high confidence that we know the position of *Eagle*. However, it is possible that we may have a change of plans. But in the worst case it could be up to thirty feet per second, and of course we don't expect that at all." Meaning: If they were far off on *Eagle*'s location, a successful rendezvous would require some quick and accurate throttling up or down to thread the needle properly—tricky work at five thousand miles per hour. Of course, it was for such contingencies that Buzz Aldrin, a man with a genius for astrophysics, who held a Ph.D. in space rendezvous from the Massachusetts Institute of Technology, and Neil Armstrong, one of the coolest hands in the history of aviation, were chosen for the job. NASA believed the Apollo 11 team could do it, and so did they. In the end, NASA's failure to ascertain the exact location of Tranquillity Base had no great impact on the docking of *Columbia* and *Eagle*, which was fortunate, because it wasn't until five days after splashdown on July 29, when film taken by the astronauts was processed and studied, that an official determination was reached.

The second nagging concern as *Eagle* prepared its ascent was the elephant in the living room the world knew about but was trying hard to ignore. In a colossal act of mendacity, the Soviet Union had launched Luna 15, a relatively unsophisticated, unmanned "sample-return" mission, which raced past Apollo 11 and was in lunar orbit at the same time as *Columbia*. Soviet officials gave assurances that Luna would not "interfere" with Apollo. But the mere fact they would raise the issue was deeply troubling. In the end, the outrageous attempt to steal Apollo's thunder ended in another international humiliation for the Soviets, when Luna suddenly spun out of control and slammed into the moon, fortunately far from Tranquillity. The first test of the U.S. seismic measuring device was to duly record its jarring thud. TASS, the official Soviet news agency, announced the disaster with typical artifice, saying Luna's work "had ended."

Monday afternoon, at 12:50 Houston time, twenty-one hours after landing on the moon, Neil lit the candle under *Eagle,* sending the first of five thousand pounds of propellant through the craft's four jets (and blasting the American flag, so carefully planted, right out of its mooring). The machine touted as "the best-tested engine in the universe" had worked despite moondust, hyper-cold temperatures, the almost complete vacuum of space, and the general vicissitudes of visiting an alien world. *Eagle* lifted off in the airless atmosphere with an almost eerie ease, accelerating from zero to 3,000 miles per hour in two minutes, settling into a cruising speed of 4,137 miles per hour, while vertically rising at more than eighty feet per second. "Very smooth, very quiet," Armstrong said wonderingly. Again, the moondust that coated the craft as well as the men behaved in an unexpected way. The concern was that it would spread everywhere on liftoff, coating the port and infiltrating the delicate analog instruments. Instead, it formed into tight clumps, acting once again almost as if it was organic, swarming like millions of tiny creatures.

For slightly less than six minutes, the diminished *Eagle* powered toward lunar orbit, wallowing like an overburdened beast, right and left, as the remaining fuel in its tanks sloshed back and forth. Once in orbit, it raced round the moon, catching up with *Columbia* after a chase of about five hours. Aligning the circular orbits and eventually docking the two craft was a process of immensely complex calculation—an exercise Aldrin reveled in carrying out, having spent a chunk of his life studying the problem. Both men had docked in space before, and both had succeeded despite near-catastrophic malfunctions. A stuck thruster had turned Armstrong's Gemini 8 rendezvous into a whirling blender ride, and was the closest to an airborne disaster up to that point for the space program. On Aldrin's Gemini 12 mission, the rendezvous radar had completely malfunctioned, denying him the information necessary to synchronize orbits. But, gleefully, Buzz did the computations himself, using charts he had devised while a graduate student at M.I.T., and successfully docked, earning the enmity and scorn of some and the unreserved admiration of many others. Experience had taught both astronauts that the next chore was one of the last extremely delicate maneuvers of the journey—a great challenge, rife with danger.

Michael Collins was perched in the forward window of *Columbia,* scanning the skies, waiting anxiously for his crewmates. "It was a nice, clear, crisp lunar day," he recalled. "The moon didn't look sinister or forbidding, as it can at very low angles. But that day, with a high sun angle, it was a happy place." Collins was as cheered and relieved as any wife or child or dear friend of a fisherman watching his ship, at long last, crown the horizon, when suddenly *Eagle* appeared, at first its beacon light a tiny speck in the distance, then growing "larger and larger, brighter and shinier, and right smack dab where it should have been."

Columbia and *Eagle* were bare-bones craft, pared down to 30,000 and 5,000 pounds respectively, but the potential for a slight miscalculation causing the machines to clamp together, then buckle, tearing the guts out of one or another was a possibility not to be dismissed lightly. When Armstrong maneuvered to within a few feet of *Columbia*, *Eagle*'s drogue slid easily into *Columbia*'s probe, which was the tentative initial coupling snapped into place by three small latches. It was the handshake preceding the hug—just enough of a connection to keep both more or less in place, but not so tight as to cause a cataclysm if it suddenly jerked loose. From then on it was up to Collins. With one eye to the computer screen that registered all green lights on the operation and another on what he could plainly see through the window, Collins made the almost irreversible decision to activate the hydraulic, gas-driven system that would begin clamping twelve capture latches firmly in place. Armstrong "put the plus thrust" to bring the *Eagle* home in a hard lock; then, suddenly, there was a swaying motion felt in both vehicles followed by a violent trembling and shaking. "All hell broke loose," Collins remembers. Armstrong and Collins realized simultaneously that if they didn't quickly move to a correct lineup there would be no choice but to abort the rendezvous completely, separate, and begin the dance all over again. After about ten seconds of violent oscillations, which seemed to last forever, the ships were properly lined up; with a loud bang that rocked both crafts, all twelve bolts slammed into place. It was a rocky but successful reunion.

Soon, Collins opened the hatch that separated the two ships and floated down the tunnel into *Eagle* for a victory greeting. "Thank God, all the claptrap works on this—its final workout," Mike Collins thought at the time. "The first one through is Buzz, with a big smile on his face. I grab his head, a hand on each temple, and am about to give him a smooch on the forehead, as a parent might greet an errant child;

but then, embarrassed, I think better of it and grab his hand, and then Neil's. We cavort about a little bit, all smiles and giggles over our success, and then it's back to work as usual."

Within an hour, their treasure trove of invaluable moon jewels had been transferred to the mother ship, and it was time to bid the good ship *Eagle* good-bye, committing her to a fate she did not deserve—a cold, lonely orbit of the moon, and finally, as she ran out of steam, a lazy drift down to a violent crash-landing. The sixty-hour journey home started at 12:55 P.M., Houston time, with a trans-earth injection—a blast of *Columbia*'s maneuver engines to break free of the moon's gravity and begin the long coast home.

Drained from the tension and labor of the previous five days, sleep came easily for all three men as the moon glowed bright in their port window, and earth was still a distant warm green-blue orb in the far distance. *Columbia* was headed home at slightly less than five thousand miles per hour, a speed that would increase as the moon's gravity slackened and the earth's far greater pull increased. As the three men drifted into deep sleep, a familiar, slightly annoying phenomenon occurred, one they hadn't discussed—perhaps symptomatic of the less-than-warm personal relationships among the three men.

Buzz had noticed it first: tiny bright white flecks traveling through his vision, not from the outside, from inside, as though through his brain. "I saw them the first night out. They were very small and very rapid. If you weren't looking right, you couldn't move your eyes fast enough to see it." Cautious about what he perceived as Neil's skeptical, occasionally almost condescending attitude toward his enthusiasms, Buzz kept the phenomenon to himself all the way to the moon. But when it started again on the journey home, he felt compelled to mention it. "I hate to impose on you," Aldrin remembers saying, "but would you look out for these things? I think I'm going out of my mind." Neil's response was a bemused silence. It wasn't until after splashdown that he confessed to have experienced the same thing throughout the flight. "It was a pinpoint of light, instantaneous," Neil said. "If you tried to look real hard, they'd come about one a minute." Armstrong had it right. Deep-space cosmic rays pulse at a rate of about one per minute. In the years to follow, the white flashes became a familiar annoyance to star voyagers, the result of space radiation bombarding spacecraft and passing through astronauts' brains. Doctors surmise the radiation might become a danger on long flights, like a year-long journey to Mars. "It's possible the particles could destroy a small number of brain cells on prolonged exposures," said NASA radiologist Dr. Charles Barnes at the time. Astronauts in earth orbit aboard a shuttle or space station are protected by the 25,000-mile-deep Van Allen radiation belt that shields earth from most cosmic rays. But the flashes of radiation the Apollo 11 astronauts discovered in their darkened space capsule will have to be addressed if deep-space travel ever returns to our agenda.

By Wednesday, July 23, NASA scheduled a prime-time television appearance at eight in the evening, Houston time, for the astronauts to prepare the world for Apollo 11's fiery triumphal return, and to show off the booty they were ferrying home. As the broadcast was being set up, Mission Control was again bedeviled by a cacophony of weird sirens, bells, and whistles over the radio, which, incredibly, left NASA's top scientists flummoxed and scratching their crew cuts in wonder, while the astronauts cackled like schoolboys. "Your sure you don't have somebody else in there with you?" asked controller Charlie Duke. "Still no explanation of the weird noises emanating from Apollo 11, if indeed [they are] from Apollo 11," commented another perplexed flight controller.

Armstrong held up vacuum-sealed bags of the mysterious moon-dust; Collins demonstrated how water clings to a spoon in a weightless environment; Aldrin prepared a ham sandwich. Aldrin then read from Scriptures: "Personally, in reflecting the events of the past several days, a verse from Psalms comes to mind: 'When I consider the heavens, the work of Thy fingers, the moon and the stars which Thou hast ordained. What is man that Thou are mindful of him?' "

In signing off, Neil wanted to thank the nation for making his dream come true.

"A hundred years ago, Jules Verne wrote a book about a voyage to the moon. His spaceship, *Columbia,* took off from Florida and landed in the Pacific Ocean after completing a trip to the moon. It seems appropriate for us to share with you some of the reflections from the crew as the modern-day *Columbia* completes its rendezvous with the planet earth in the same Pacific Ocean tomorrow.

"The responsibility for this flight lies first with history and with the giants of science who preceded this effort. Next, the American people who have, through their will, indicated their desire. Next, the four administrations and their Congresses, for implementing their work. And then to the agency and industry team who built our space-craft, the Saturn, the *Columbia,* the *Eagle,* and the little EMU ("extra vehicular mobility unit"), the spacesuit, and the backpack that was our small spacecraft out on the lunar surface.

"We'd like to give special thanks to all those Americans who built those spacecraft, who did the construction, designs, and the tests and put their hearts and all their abilities into those craft. To those people tonight we give a special thank-you, and to all the other people listening and watching tonight, God Bless You. Good night from Apollo 11."

A few hours after Apollo 11's last television variety show, Neil cued one of the tapes Hollywood producer Mickey Kapp had made for him to *Music Out of the Moon,* by Dr. Samuel J. Hoffman. It was a strange piece of music, featuring Dr. Hoffman's "virtuoso" work on the theremin. Léon Thérémin, the eponymous inventor of the instrument, experimented with electronic musical in the 1920s Soviet Union, eventually developing a device requiring the player to move his hands between two electrified antennas, producing ethereal sounds similar to a wind instrument but really quite unique. At the height of Hoffman's popularity in the 1940s and early 1950s, his theremin music was included on the soundtracks of Hitchcock's *Spellbound,* as well as *The Lost Weekend* and *The Day the Earth Stood Still.* At Purdue, Neil had wooed Jan playing a 78 record of the dreamy *Music Out of the Moon,* featuring a chorus whose oohs and ahhs impressed some, including the Apollo 11 crew, as so over-the-top to be just plain silly. But it was their song, and he had made up his mind to bring Dr. Hoffman to the moon. From over 125,000 miles in space, through NASA's control room to a special squawk box set up in the Armstrong house in El Lago, he wooed his wife all over again, playing their old favorites, including "Lunar Rhapsody," "Celestial Nocturne," and "Moon Moods."

Neil explained only that it's "an old favorite of mine." Capsule Communicator Charlie Duke thought the strange music sounded "a little scratchy, either that or your tape was a little slow." Mike Collins laughed. "It sounds a little scratchy to us, too, but the czar likes it."

The astronauts were up in the early hours of Thursday morning, aching with excitement. The great, green home planet loomed huge in the porthole; just hours remained until splashdown at a site 950 miles southwest of Honolulu. Angle being everything upon reentering earth's unforgiving mantle, calculations were checked and double-checked, by computer and by hand.

One of the last problems in the long daisy chain was weather above the splashdown site. There were violent thunderstorms all through the corridor Columbia would travel following reentry. The ship was well designed for most contingencies, but lightning wasn't one of them. The crew could be lost just as they approached the safety of Mother Earth. In addition, the area had heavy cloud cover, five- to seven-foot swells, fifteen- to twenty-five-knot winds, and occasional cloudbursts. The landing site had to be switched and the aircraft carrier *Hornet* ordered to steam at flank speed to reach the closest safe location, nearly 250 miles south. The new site was far from ideal, with equally stormy seas and strong winds. But there was far less chance of the electrical storms and severe turbulence that could literally shake *Columbia* apart.

At ten thousand miles in space, the astronauts could make out huge roiling storms, resembling monstrous whirligigs preying upon sections of the vast Pacific Ocean. *Columbia* was feeling Mother Earth's powerful call home; the craft's speed had exceeded fourteen thousand miles per hour and was steadily building.

As they streaked through the rapidly darkening sky, there was one more part of the shrunken spaceship to discard: the service module that had contained their supplies, electrical power, and other "consumables." At about two thousand miles from earth, the service module was released; it clung to *Columbia* for a split-second, then shrieked away. It would reenter the earth on its own, unprotected by a heat shield, quickly flaming to a white-hot five thousand degrees Fahrenheit, then disintegrate into ash and scatter to the winds. Houston acknowledged separation at approximately 10:00 A.M.

Columbia, now just a ten-by-twelve-foot cone-shaped sliver of the mighty 363-foot Saturn-Apollo rocket launched eight days prior, was cleared for landing. But unlike trains, planes, cars—virtually any other form of transport—*Columbia* was not slowing in preparation for landing, but rapidly picking up speed. Collins determined the ship was exceeding 23,000 statute miles per hour. *Columbia's* only brakes were the earth's gaseous shroud. Collins double-checked that the ship's automatic thrusters were set to keep *Columbia's* heat-absorbing shield, which covered its blunt end, facing the direction where atmospheric contact would occur. All three men made last-minute checks that everything had been carefully stowed, all systems on their spacesuits were functioning, and the straps tethering them to their couches were taut.

With the Coral Sea visible in their porthole, the men of Apollo 11 experienced the first shock of reentry. Three days of space reverie, as if sailing on a smooth summer lake, was shattered by a bone-crunching collision with the thinnest layer of earth's outer mantle—the exosphere. The ship groaned under the strain, suddenly enveloped in a nimbus of flame. *Columbia*, at that moment, had attained its maximum speed of the entire voyage: 24,677 miles per hour. The astronauts were plastered to their seats, struggling to cope with crushing gravity, six times normal, making the men feel as though they weighed nearly a thousand pounds.

Houston, monitoring the rapid buildup of heat under *Columbia*, warned the astronauts the heat lock would soon shut down radio communication, just as certain as if they were on the back side of the moon. Capsule Communicator Ron Evans announced, "You're going around the hill there shortly, but you're looking good." Armstrong responded, "See you later."

The temperature under and around *Columbia* was a searing five thousand degrees as it streaked northeastward across the Pacific Ocean, passing the Gilbert Islands, briefly straddling the International Time Zone, and mercifully slowing.

As the astronauts gritted their teeth and prayed the very worst part of their voyage would soon end, President Richard Nixon was steaming toward their splashdown site aboard the communications ship U.S.S. *Arlington*. Nixon had enjoyed a pleasant night sleeping in the captain's quarters after an excellent meal washed down with martinis and French wine. Life was less sanguine for his deputy, H. R. Haldeman, whose cabin was next to a radio shack overwhelmed with messages for the president and his staff and an iron door that clanged loudly open and shut throughout the night. When he was summoned at 4 A.M. for the helicopter ride to the aircraft carrier *Hornet* to watch splashdown with the president, it was a relief. "It was beautiful on the flight deck, absolutely dark, millions of stars, plus the antenna lights on the ship," he wrote in his diary. "[Astronaut Frank] Borman said it looked more like the sky on the back side of the moon than any he had ever seen on earth. The helicopter left in the dark and flew over the ocean to the

Hornet. Landed and went through quick briefings on the decontamination setup and the recovery plan. Then waited on the bridge for the capsule to appear. It did, in spectacular fashion. We saw the fireball (like a meteor with a tail) rise from the horizon and arch through the sky, turning into a red ball, then disappearing. Waited on the bridge an hour or so until we could see the helicopters over the capsule and the raft in the sea. We were steaming toward them. Watched the pickup through binoculars, then with the naked eye. [President Nixon] was exuberant, really cranked up, like a little kid."

A single drogue chute was deployed at 23,000 feet to stabilize the craft's attitude, then at ten thousand feet, three drogue chutes opened, catching and violently slowing the ship down to about a hundred miles per hour, gradually moving its direction from horizontal to downward. (Six months later, Armstrong said "awaiting the opening of the parachutes" was, for him, the most stressful part of the entire voyage.) Four thousand feet above the Pacific, three huge red-white-and-blue chutes fluttered up into the sky, quickly became tumescent, and jerked *Columbia*'s speed down to a sensible, survivable twelve miles per hour. Five minutes later, the charred, blackened capsule—paint and markings completely burned away—was plopped into the stormy Pacific, just two miles from its target, unfortunately upside down. Hanging from the ceiling, Collins groped for the switches that filled several flotation bags with gas, gradually righting the ship and enabling the astronauts to climb out of their spacesuits, which were extremely heavy and cumbersome in earth's gravity. A rescue helicopter was quickly hovering overhead, and divers wearing biological suits reached the bobbing ship, greeting the men with isolation suits for them to don. As soon as they crawled out of *Columbia* and onto the rescue raft, the astronauts began a weird sort of mutual grooming, dousing and scrubbing one another with a powerful disinfectant, sodium hypochloride. That accomplished, they were lifted to the helicopter in baskets and ferried to the U.S.S. *Hornet,* where a cheering deck of sailors and the President of the United States waited to greet them.

When the astronauts stepped out of the helicopter, they were covered in biological isolation garments and breathing through gas masks, which it was hoped was protection enough to prevent the spread of any alien biocontaminant to the thousands of sailors they were among. While the astronauts were enjoying the adulation of the crowd, the two boxes of material they had brought home were already on the way to Houston. Aboard two separate helicopters, they were sent to nearby Johnson Island, placed aboard a C-141 cargo plane, and flown direct to Houston's Ellington Air Force Base. NASA's Lunar Receiving Laboratory was in possession of the long-awaited material by 9:00 A.M. CDT on July 25.

Nixon ordered the military band to play "Columbia, Gem of the Ocean," then followed the astronauts down to the Mobile Quarantine Facility (MQF)—actually a customized recreational vehicle—where they would stay until flown home to Houston for the remainder of twenty-one days in isolation. Air- and water-tight, the MQF was composed of three compact areas: a lounge, a galley, and a sleeping/bathing area, where the astronauts would enjoy their first showers in eight days. It was designed to house up to six people for ten days; mercifully, the Apollo 11 crew were just three and would be confined far less than ten days.

Speaking on a telephone while viewing Armstrong, Aldrin, and Collins through a thick glass window, looking rather uncomfortably more like lab specimens than returning heroes, Nixon offered congratulations. Ironically, he had been unable to have dinner with them before the journey because of fears he would pass a flu bug or cold to the astronauts; on their return, he could only view them through glass out of fear they would infect him with a space virus. But despite being treated as though they were harboring alien life forms, the astronauts were beaming with joy and triumph unfettered by their prison-like temporary habitat.

The scripture of engineering, the foundation of their belief system had not failed them. Indeed, they had come back as prophets of technology, prepared to recite the mantra: that linear, Aristotelean logic was the key to the universe. The world was not about spells and shamans and magic; it was about the power of the zero, the transistor, and the silicon chip. And our machines had the power to set man free from drudgery, disease, and even from the earth. Whether the participants knew it or not, it was a defining moment. The future wasn't going to be about returning to nature or rejecting the values and systems of intuiting reality that had built the modern world; it was going to be about computers, cell phones, Nasdaq, digital imaging, and CAT scans.

Richard Nixon was, as H. R. Haldeman had described, as "excited as a little kid;" when he approached the astronauts in their pen, he had a secret he was bubbling to share. At the beginning of June, Haldeman had sent a detailed memo to presidential aide Dwight Chapin planning Nixon's part in the splashdown ceremony and a party that would be held when they were freed from quarantine. "The President is intrigued with the idea of a very big dinner after the Apollo 11 group come back from the moon. He envisions this as at first something in the State Dining Room, with a good musical afterwards. The more he got to thinking about it, the more he thought it ought to be bigger and perhaps at the Waldorf-Astoria in the Grand Ballroom. Then he didn't like the idea of New York and was thinking about Chicago, and ended up being primarily intrigued with the possibility of Los Angeles, doing it at the Century Plaza."

By the time Nixon welcomed the astronauts home, plans were set in stone. It was to be the biggest state dinner in the history of the nation, set not in Washington, D.C., but in the president's native California, at "space-age" Century City, a 180-acre complex of stark, brushed aluminum skyscrapers—a soulless-looking, new city many would come to see as representing the worst instincts of the space age. All the president had to do was convince the guests of honor to attend.

"Neil, Buzz, and Mike, I want you to know that I think I am the luckiest man in the world, and I say this not because I am the President of the United States, but particularly because I have the privilege of welcoming you back to earth." Then, as the astronauts watched incredulously, the thirty-seventh president of the United States, overcome with joy, suddenly got happy feet and danced a jig. Aldrin later reflected it was the moment the momentousness of their deed sunk in.

The design of the small window the astronauts could peer out of to see their guests was not one of NASA's finer achievements. The three men had to crouch down, their faces absurdly close together, to get a view of their visitors, unless they also bent down. Speaking to a captive audience, the president opened with an inane joke about having made his call to the moon collect, then assured them their wives were "three of the greatest ladies and most courageous ladies in the whole world today." He suggested there was no choice but to accept his offer, because their "courageous" wives already had. "I will let you in on a little secret," he said feigning sotto voce, with signature mawkishness. "I made a date with them. I invited them to dinner on the thirteenth of August, right after you come out of quarantine. It will be a state dinner held in Los Angeles. The governors of all the fifty states will be there, the ambassadors, others from around the world and in America. They told me that you would come, too. All I want to know is: Will you come? We want to honor you there."

Smiling at the sudden absurdness of it all, Neil spoke for his crew. "We will do anything you say, Mr. President."

But Nixon waved him away as if to say a reply hadn't really been necessary. "One question that I think all of us would like to ask: As we saw you bouncing around in that float out there, I wonder if that wasn't the hardest part of the journey? Did any of you get seasick?"

Neil said: "No, we didn't, and it was one of the hardest parts, but it was one of the most pleasant, we can assure you."

Characteristically, Nixon switched the topic to sports. "Did you know about the All-Star game?"

> **Buzz:** Yes sir, the capsule communicators have been giving us reports.
>
> **The President:** Were you American League or National League?
>
> **Buzz:** National League.
>
> **Neil** (almost correcting Buzz): Neither one.
>
> **The President:** There is the politician in the group.
>
> **Neil:** We are sorry you missed that. (Proving that he was indeed.)
>
> **The President:** You knew that, too?
>
> **Neil:** We heard about the rain. We haven't been able to control the weather yet, but that is something we can look forward to.
>
> **The President:** You look great. Do you feel as good as you look?
>
> **Neil:** We feel great.
>
> **The President:** Frank Borman feels you are a little younger by going into space. Do you feel a little bit younger?
>
> **Neil:** We *are* younger than Frank Borman.
>
> **The President:** He is over there. Come on over, Frank, so they can see you. Are you going to take that lying down?
>
> **Borman** (bending over to peer through the little window, taking in his caged colleagues): They look a little heavy.
>
> **The President:** Let me close off with this one thing . . . this is the greatest week in the history of the world since creation, because as a result of what happened in this

week . . . the world has never been closer together before.
I only hope that all of us in America, as a result of what
you have done, can do our own job a little better.

   We don't want to hold you any longer. Anybody have a
last—how about promotions? Do you think we can
arrange something?

Neil: We are just pleased to be back and very honored that
you were so kind as to come out here and welcome us
back. We look forward to getting out of quarantine and
talking without having the glass between us.

The President: Incidentally, the speeches that you have to
make at this party can be very short. If you want to say
"fantastic" or "beautiful," that is all right with us. Don't
try to think of new adjectives. They've all been said.

When the presidential party was gone and the televison cameras
turned off, the men were left in the cramped holding cell to relax and
perhaps to ponder what was next, and what would happen to them if
they were contaminated with an unknown, predatory virus.

During the summer of 1969, a first novel by Harvard Medical
School student Michael Crichton called *The Andromeda Strain*
climbed the bestseller lists and made prime beach reading. It was a
harrowing story of a satellite sent into earth orbit to collect upper-
atmosphere bacteria for use in a biological warfare experiment. When
the satellite crashed to earth, an incurable virus, unlike any ever seen
on earth, was loosed on a desert town, wiping out the populace,
instantly turning human blood to a fine powder—not entirely unlike
the powder Aldrin and Armstrong discovered on the moon.

The cautionary tale was the talk in bars, at water coolers, and
around dining-room tables, rousing fears. Even NASA scientists were
concerned, many arguing that three weeks in quarantine might not be
long enough for a space virus to incubate. Buzz later wrote in his book
Men from Earth, "If strange microbes were in this soil, Neil and I
would be the first guinea pigs to test their effects." But all three astronauts had been fully aware of the hazards a trip to the moon held.
Indeed, as test pilots, fighter pilots, and astronauts their every day was
fraught with risk; they courted danger and most often found it.

Columbia was flushed with many gallons of hypochloride, sealed,
brought aboard the carrier, and placed next to the astronauts. Two

days later, *Hornet* steamed into harbor at Ford Island, Hawaii, as crowds of thousands cheered. Having returned from a trip to a foreign land, and importing cargo, the astronauts were required to file a General Declaration for Agriculture, Customs, Immigration and Public Health. The form, dated July 24, 1969, listed "place of departure" as "moon," and "cargo" as "moon rock and moon dust samples." Under the section asking "Person on board known to be suffering from illness other than airsickness?" was typed "none." But under the heading "Any condition on board which may lead to the spread of disease?" it was noted, ominously: "TO BE DETERMINED." The form was passed through a biocontainment "transfer lock" and signed by all three astronauts.

With that less-than-clean immigration report on file, the astronauts peered out the little window of their Mobile Quarantine Facility as it was loaded onto a flatbed truck and backed up to a giant C-141 Navy cargo carrier for the flight home to Houston, where they were housed in the former crew reception area, which had been transformed into an isolation facility with reasonably comfortable private rooms and baths for the astronauts, their doctors, and attendants. And finally they could see their families again—if only through glass.

Chapter Fifteen

"When we opened that first box of moon rocks, the hushed expectant atmosphere in the Lunar Receiving Laboratory was, I imagine, like that in a medieval monastery as the monks awaited the arrival of the True Cross," recalled NASA geologist Dr. Robin Brett. The scientists charged with examining Apollo 11's treasure trove from the moon were protected by gas masks, standing beside a stainless-steel chamber operating thick black rubber gloves built into a glass portal on the front of the case. Tests had proved the rocks to be about three billion years old and, while composed of ingredients known to man, including titanium, oxygen, aluminum, and magnesium, the proportions were different from any rocks found on earth. Exposed to polarized light, the drab gray rocks flared with color: yellow, purple, orange, blue, and a profusion of reds, indicating a large array of minerals. Most intriguing was evidence of minute traces of organic material. It was what many scientists were most hoping to find; what others most feared they would find. The most scientists who examined the evidence could conclude was that "the synthesis of organic compounds, similar to that which takes place in living organisms, has occurred on the moon . . . which in more favorable circumstances, lead to the spontaneous appearance of life." Still, even a trace of organic life meant the moon wasn't just a pile of dirt; it had, at least at one time, contained life, perhaps the one-celled animals scientists expected, if anything, to find. Anything was possible.

Ronald Buffum was a twenty-seven-year-old technician at NASA's newly instituted Lunar Receiving Lab when the Apollo 11 mission delivered its extraordinary forty-eight-pound cache of unidentified alien material found on the lunar surface. When friends learned he was going to be "playing with moon rocks," he was teased both that he should bring one home and that he was going to turn into a little green man, or worse, if he touched them. When the day came that he finally saw a tiny nugget of moon material looking more like a piece of used charcoal than the Holy Grail, Buffum was underwhelmed, but impressed enough with the strangeness of the ancient rocks to follow the rules for avoiding exposure to them very carefully. Whatever secrets the rocks held, Buffum was going to be cautious around them.

As with everything else associated with the first moon mission, the press and public had a voracious appetite for news about the moon material. In the dog days of early August, Washington was rife with rumors, and the papers were hunting the next big space-related headline. To keep the stories under control, NASA officials ordered the Receiving Lab to work twenty-four-hour shifts, conducting thousands of tests. In one experiment considered both urgent and crucial, moon dust was carefully ground up, mixed with sterile water, and injected into twenty-four mice, which had been bred under germ-free conditions. Twenty-four others were injected with ordinary earth dust. A team of doctors including NASA veterinarian Dr. Norman D. Jones sat up all night in the laboratory, observing the mice.

Buffum had drawn the early shift on the morning of August 1, and at 3:30 A.M. was wearily but deliberately shaving scrapings for microscopic examination of meteorite material. They were peculiar even for moon rocks, with a Swiss-cheese texture, filled with tiny gas bubbles called "vesicles." His arms thrust all the way into the vacuum chamber, performing the tedious job, Buffum noticed the vacuum pressure seemed to be tugging at his gloves quite a bit stronger than usual. He called over his shoulder to George Williams, a forty-two-year-old backup glove operator and lab technician, asking for help. As Williams approached, Buffum called out loudly that the pull was so strong he couldn't remove his arms. Panicked, the young lab technician screamed just as the glove's thumb blew off, exposing his hand. Air rushed into the vacuum chamber, yanking Buffum deeper inside, scraping the flesh off his right arm. Williams looked at the scene in horror, grabbed Buffum around the waist, and pulled him back with all his strength. While the men struggled, trace amounts of moon dust seeped through the rent glove and swirled into the air. Terrified workers scrambled for their gas masks as lab supervisor Richard S. Johnson directed the resealing of the chamber, which he later said took "less than a minute," exposing just the three or four rocks in the chamber to earth air. The rest of the rocks under examination had been separately sealed.

Buffum and Williams were immediately taken to the lab's isolation section, where Buffum was treated by Dr. William R. Carpentier, who was himself in quarantine with the astronauts and thirteen others, including public relations men, stewards, and several technicians who had also been accidentally exposed to the astronauts or other contaminated items. When Buffum was sufficiently recovered, he was welcomed to the strange purgatory. And, to his amazement, he was greeted and welcomed by probably the most famous man in the world at that moment in history, spaceman Neil Armstrong, who also led a tour of the battered and burned *Columbia* spacecraft, which had joined them in isolation.

The astronauts tried to set an upbeat, jubilant tone in their hermetically sealed world, trying to define the experience as merely a pause in the great adventure. But it was proving to be a daunting and torturous experience for all. Neil's thirty-ninth birthday on August 5 was celebrated with as cheery a mien as possible. Cakes with birthday candles thoughtfully baked by his fellow inmates, copious quantities of Scotch consumed with his space mates, and long phone conversations with Jan and the boys, tinted with melancholy, were a poor substitute for home. After successfully completing a journey to another world, which had taken a lifetime, he was trapped in limbo, whiling away the hours strumming a ukulele and playing Ping-Pong.

And there were nagging worries. Buzz had been running a low-grade fever since splashdown, which he stubbornly refused to admit to anyone, especially NASA doctors Chuck Berry and Bill Capentier. Each time the seal of their prison was opened and another unlucky accidental contaminee tossed into the petri dish, there was an unavoidable, chilling tinge that they had infected yet another innocent earthling, and that muddled success would be their legacy rather than triumph.

As well as being a possible personal disaster for Buffum and Williams and others, the accidents were a setback for NASA's dictate to quickly rule on the danger level of the moon materials, identify any virus or toxins, and, with luck, identify an antidote.

Repairs and sterilization to the only vacuum chamber available were going to take as much as sixty hours, so the contents of the second box had to be examined in a separate area, inside a cabinet filled with dry nitrogen, an inert gas that appeared to have little effect on lunar rocks and dirt when tested on the first sample.

The following morning, groggy but relieved, the scientists pronounced the mice injected with moon dust perfectly fit; the same good news didn't hold for the mice exposed to earth dust—they perished. Many more toxicity and viral tests remained to be done as quickly as practicable. But there was a sense of growing confidence that the worst fears would not be realized. The bulk of scientific opinion held there was no danger whatever in the moon samples. Dr. Chuck Berry, chief physician of the astronauts, and three other NASA health officials flew to Atlanta to address the Inter Agency Committee on Back Contamination, the group of scientists responsible for initiating the quarantine, and the only ones who could lift it, to present their findings. After some debate, the men met in closed session and pronounced the quarantined group free of "abnormal health conditions," but prescribed regular, thorough checkups over the next two years for all who were contaminated, meaning it would be a long time before any of the twenty-three who wound up in quarantine were completely worry-free.

By Sunday, August 10, after the prescribed twenty-one days in quarantine, the astronauts and their companions attended a ten-minute church service conducted by Jesse Stewart, a cook who also happened to be a Baptist church deacon, and prepared to go home to their loved ones.

Before an audience of the world's press and more than three hundred NASA workers, Dr. Berry produced a razor and with a flourish sliced open the plastic cover sealing the isolation area from the world. After pushing on the gray steel door several times and failing to dislodge it, he threw his shoulder into it, springing the entrance wide open. The anxious detainees surged forward, past the astronauts, who were last to get out. While the newly mustachioed Collins and Aldrin stopped to gladhand the throng of NASA employees, who had come to see them freed, only Neil stopped at the microphones to speak to the public and the press.

"I'd like to take this opportunity to thank all my gracious hosts here in the Lunar Receiving Laboratory," he said. "I can't say that I would choose to spend a couple of weeks like that, but I'm very glad we got the chance to complete the mission."

Cars were able to whisk Collins and Aldrin away fairly quickly, but Armstrong was swamped by press and well-wishers who blocked his getting home, just the sort of annoyance he was going to find increasingly infuriating and increasingly unavoidable. For the first time in five weeks, the astronauts were home, but not for long. The following Wednesday, the frantic schedule NASA and the Nixon administration had set for them to tout America's conquest of space was to start with a vengeance.

Monday morning, Buzz's wife, Joan, convinced him he didn't own a suit that would pass muster at palaces and in the company of presidents, kings, and queens. So he set out for a shopping mall, assuming it would be an easy chore. It was that morning he realized what life was like for the Beatles. The astronauts had all gained a measure of fame during the Gemini program, but this was an entirely different level. He was followed by a motorcade of paparazzi, who weaved in and out of traffic, oblivious to their own safety, his safety, or that of anyone else. Desperately, Buzz and Joan cut through Ellington Air Force Base, but found since it was a public facility the photographers continued the pursuit. In desperation, he stopped at the base exit guard station, entreating the military police to at least delay them so he could make a getaway. Fortunately, for a space hero, they complied, and he managed to buy a suit in relative peace. For Neil, life had taken a similarly bizarre turn. "Neil went out to sit by his pool and relax and play with his kids for the first time in months," Buzz recalls. "And suddenly three Japanese photographers scaled his fence, furiously snapping pictures. He was so outraged, he was speechless. They kept asking him to pose and practically followed him into his bedroom. That day we knew life would never be the same."

Neil echoed the feeling. "This is certainly the part we're least prepared to handle," he said that week.

Later in the day, Neil's venture to work and later for a haircut and tuxedo fitting was similarly dogged. In addition to the buzzing swarm of photographers, the czar of Apollo was trailed by a large throng of reporters, vociferously representing the world's press. Warned of his often glib retorts and laconic ways, they determined to take up the challenge. At the entrance to the astronaut office, when Jan dropped him off, Armstrong, wearing the astronauts mufti, dark sunglasses, white short-sleeve shirt, and tie, responded to a cacophony of shouted questions saying only that he intended to spend the day doing, "work, work, work," and disappeared. Surrounded by press at the barbershop as his buzz cut was renewed, Armstrong cheerily insisted, "It's just another day." Neil was learning how maddening being the object of press attention was going to be, and, from their point of view, vice versa.

At 5:30 in the morning of Wednesday, August 13, the three men, their wives, and their eight children arrived on the tarmac at Ellington Air Force Base in a convoy of government station wagons. In the already blistering heat, baggage was loaded aboard Air Force Two, a fifty-four-seat jet that normally served as backup to the president's plane. A half-hour later the clowning, giggling children and excited adults were settling into their plush yellow-and-green chairs and sofas in the forward, presidential quarters of the plane, somewhat nervously aware that the larger aft cabin was filled to overflowing with newsmen and photographers, who would follow the astronauts and their families all over the United States and the world during feverish months of parades, adulation, and speechmaking. Just how closely they would monitor the lives of the astronauts became painfully obvious the following day, when news of Joan Aldrin's sewing a button on the sleeve of Buzz's aqua-colored suit and of Mike Collins shaving off his mustache became international news items.

Once airborne, the kids excitedly explored the plane. Mischievous twelve-year-old Rick Armstrong came perilously close to putting a curious hand on the red "hotline" phone before Neil barked, "Don't you dare touch that!" in the nick of time. Rick smiled back at his dad with a "just kidding" look. Air Force stewards served scrambled eggs, bacon, freshly squeezed orange juice, and Cream of Wheat, as NASA public-affairs man Julian Scheer briefed astronauts and their wives on the protocol for addressing the mayors, United Nations' officials, diplomats, and other dignitaries they would be meeting. In the final hour of the trip, Neil played chess with his six-year-old son Mark, who was fast becoming a skilled player.

First stop was New York City's La Guardia Airport, where they were met by Mayor John Lindsay, quickly ushered onto a helicopter, and flown high over New York Harbor. The city was expecting them. Parading down the East River, fireboats formed a phalanx in the harbor and saluted with high, arching funnels of water aimed at the sky, dozens of foghorns moaning a greeting. The party landed at the foot of Wall Street and climbed into convertibles for a parade up Broadway— temporarily named Apollo Way—during which hundreds of thousands of computer data cards joined two and a half tons of ticker tape to flutter down from skyscrapers. The turnout was the "biggest ever in the history of New York," according to the city's Public Events Commissioner, John Palmer. It eclipsed the prior largest gatherings, including John Glenn's parade in February 1962, when he became the first American to orbit the earth aboard Friendship 7; Charles Lindbergh's celebration in 1927, when 15,000 soldiers marched; and General Douglas MacArthur's parade in 1951, after he was relieved of his Korean command. Four million people lined the city's canyons, waved from open windows, hoisted children upon their shoulders, and cheered the historic event enthusiastically. The confetti resulted in a blizzard-like whiteout that, at times, prevented the astronauts from seeing the crowd or being seen, and the roar of the crowds, reverberated through the concrete gulches of Manhattan, made conversation impossible on the street or even in offices with sealed windows. Nevertheless, the day was flawed by a scheduling error that had the parade running forty-nine minutes ahead of schedule, with thousands taking their places to cheer, only to learn the parade had passed them by.

At the United Nations, the atmosphere was tense over a new outbreak of Arab-Israeli violence and a planned emergency session of the General Assembly. But time was made to politely listen to Armstrong and Aldrin speak briefly about having left "footprints on the moon . . . that belong to all mankind." Secretary General U. Thant surprised and slightly irritated the visitors when he said the Apollo 11 mission fulfilled mankind's vicarious longing "to get away from it all," reducing the Apollo project to the level of a weekend in Las Vegas. Though it was easy to see how a man with the secretary's intractable problems might want to get away from it all.

The families helicoptered back to Air Force Two for the flight to Chicago, where in place of their New York host, the dapper, urbane John Lindsay, they were corralled by the blustery, pugilistic Richard Daley. "How could the mayor of a major city have such rough mannerisms?" Buzz wondered of Daley, who the year before had inspired unprecedented chaos and violence at the Democratic National Convention, termed a "police riot" by the Walker Report to the National Commission on the Causes and Prevention of Violence. During the chaotic convention week, undeniably fractious demonstrators, as well as newsmen, delegates, passersby, and even nurses and doctors who attempted to treat them were savagely beaten, while Daley cursed the victims on national television and goaded the out-of-control police on. Like the moonwalk, the riot was televised; horrified viewers the world over saw police chant "kill, kill, kill" as they clubbed, punched, and kicked anyone unfortunate enough to be in their way.

At Daley's City Hall office, when the astronauts didn't move fast enough to pose for a photograph, Daley angrily waved at them: "Yo! Yous, OVER HERE." After the astronauts dutifully lined up and smiled for their picture with Daley, he rewarded them with huge sterling-silver punchbowls, engraved with each astronaut's name, gifts from the mayor and the citizens of Chicago. The bowls were passed around to be admired, then quickly taken away. They would be packed up and shipped. Months and months went by and they never arrived. Daley's office finally admitted to NASA they had vanished.

The Chicago parade also attracted upward of two million even more enthusiastic revelers, whose fervor and warmth drove Jan Armstrong to say, "It makes me want to cry." In New York and Chicago, there were languid attempts to mount a protest against the astronauts. But neither attracted passionate enmity toward the astronauts; that would come later, in Los Angeles.

In lower Manhattan's Union Square, a rallying point for antiwar activity, a handful of protestors carried signs saying BILLIONS FOR SPACE, PENNIES FOR SLUMS and RACE FOR PEACE, NOT SPACE. In Chicago, five hundred young black gang members, wearing colored berets, assembled military style in front of City Hall, some carrying lengths of pipe, bricks, and other weapons. Bitterly complaining that an $80 million construction project designed to train and employ young blacks had been shut down, they were demanding to talk to the mayor and the astronauts. "They left a million dollars' worth of equipment on the moon and we're still hungry," a leader of the group told reporters. "We're talking about the right to work to get off welfare."

In Chicago's lakeside Lincoln Park, scene of many violent clashes during the Democratic Convention, consecrated ground to many who bled there, NASA learned there was a fairly large gathering of young people: an amalgam of students, hippies, street people, inner-city black youths, and gang members milling and remonstrating over the astronauts' visit. With confidence bordering on hubris, space-agency officials, convinced the astronauts' charisma was all powerful, suggested an impromptu, face-to-face meeting. The three agreed, despite objections from their own security people, and walked into the park to meet the students.

Entering the crowded park off Michigan Avenue, across from the Conrad Hilton Hotel, which had been headquarters of the Eugene McCarthy campaign, viewed by many young people the previous summer as a last-best-hope movement, Armstrong and his crew waded into the crowd, ignoring the heavy aroma of marijuana wafting through the hot, still August air, and the surprised stares of hirsute, jean-clad young people. Cautious but determined, the men removed their jackets and made their way through the crowd toward a podium where speakers had apparently been warming up the crowd. As the mob melted away, falling back to gape at the astronauts, it became obvious to Neil and the others that this crowd was no different than any other; they were awed, shocked, star-struck, and beaming with glee at being in the presence of men with outer space mojo. Armstrong was immediately shown to the microphone and began to speak, thanking his audience for coming, explaining how humble and gratified he felt to have been, by happenstance, chosen to be first on the moon, and then launched into the standard NASA stump speech, the same words he would have delivered to the Rotary Club, extolling the great benefits that would flow for medicine, education, and industry, benefitting all God's children. But he added a few lines of his own, injecting words that caught the Zeitgeist of the moment: "This is the beginning of a new era—the beginning of an era when man understands the universe around him and the beginning of an era when man understands himself." It was a hit. The kids actually applauded. They probably didn't hear much of what he said with the rumble of traffic down Michigan Avenue, police sirens, rock music blaring, and the general carnival atmosphere, but it was magic. This crazy astronaut guy with a crew cut, dressed in a suit and tie, out there in Lincoln Park, on the hottest day of the year, talking to a rag-tag band of kids, and he had just come back from walking on the moon. Wow!

Buzz Aldrin, who also delivered words he had been furiously scribbling on the back of an envelope, later wrote, "The students were receptive and polite"; he felt that the dire warnings of hostility had been merely a "false alarm." On the heels of their triumphal encounter with the counterculture, Armstrong and company rejoined their families and jetted toward daylight, to the terminus of their day's 4,808-mile journey, the City of Angels.

Nixon had not lied when he told the astronauts, trapped in their Mobile Quarantine Facility, that the "biggest formal state dinner in American history" would lure a galaxy of stars, if only the astronauts would agree to be fêted. Fourteen hundred and forty members of the power elite class of 1969 attended, including: forty-four United States governors, the president's cabinet, the Supreme Court, many members of Congress, and foreign diplomats from ninety countries. Actors of all sort, from Fred MacMurray to James Stewart; cowboy actors Gene Autry and Andy Devine; politician actors Ronald Reagan and George Murphy; comedians Jack Benny, Red Skelton, Bob Hope, and Jonathan Winters (who called the party "one of the biggest nights of my life"); singers Tony Martin, Connie Francis, and Pat Boone; evangelist Billy Graham; captains of industry, fifty astronauts, World War II heroes, General of the Army Omar Bradley, and Air Force General Jimmy Doolittle; plus Mrs. Jack Drown, who once taught elementary school with Pat Nixon, and said she was "startled" to be there. There were notable no-shows; Jackie Onassis sent regrets, as did Howard Hughes, Harry Truman, and Charles Lindbergh. Senator Ted Kennedy was still keeping a low profile in wake of the drowning death of campaign aide Mary Jo Kopechne at Chappaquiddick Bridge in Massachusetts, an accident that happened the day Aldrin and Armstrong walked on the moon.

Appropriately, the extravaganza took place on what had been part of the back lot of 20th Century Fox movie studios. The hotel was on the Avenue of the Stars, which intersected with Constellation Boulevard, Galaxy Way, and Empyrean Way.

The astronaut families arrived at 7:30 P.M. Pacific Time in a United States Marine Corps helicopter, which landed on the hotel's back parking lot, nearly sixteen hours after their day began in Houston. Despite elaborate security—which included hundreds of Los Angeles police officers, aided by Secret Service squads, who sealed off the hotel hours before the arrival of the honored guests, shut down the pools, defoliated surrounding vacant lots, and halted all deliveries—the astronaut families couldn't help but see and hear the three thousand noisy demonstrators laying siege. Organized by the Student Mobilization Committee to End the War, many carried signs protesting Vietnam, chanting "Ho, Ho, Ho Chi Minh." Some carried estimates of the war's daily death toll, reading AUGUST 13: 1,450 VIETNAMESE AND 200 AMERICANS DEAD. Other signs read BRING THE TROOPS HOME NOW. Pot was openly smoked, despite the presence of hundreds of law-enforcement officers, and the Century Plaza Hotel's huge formal fountains were turned into a communal bath. Some protestors interviewed by journalists said they weren't necessarily opposed to the space program; they merely sought to take the opportunity to get the president's attention and media coverage. Others clearly did take issue with the costly project, waving hand-lettered banners with messages like BILLIONS FOR DEFENSE, BILLIONS FOR SPACE, NOT ONE PENNY FOR PEACE.

Ushered up to a nineteenth-floor two-bedroom suite, just around the corner from Nixon's Presidential Suite and the vice president's Royal Suite, the Armstrongs had a view from their balcony of the Fox lot and the set of the then-popular television series *Peyton Place*. The bars were stocked with beer, whiskey, California wines, and gourmet treats; spun-sugar confections in the shape of the moon with globes full of candy adorned the dining-room tables. After less than an hour spent relaxing and freshening up, the couples were escorted down to the 24,000-square-foot California Ballroom, where the Marine Band played, and tables for ten were set with gold-rimmed china, gold table cloths, gold napkins, and gold candelabras that seemed to sprout roses, chrysanthemums, and daisies. Flags of the fifty states and the territories and the American, Presidential, and United Nations colors hung from the ceiling of the three-story ballroom. Hors d'oeuvres tables, groaning under the weight of huge carved-ice eagles whose talons seemed to be holding great trays of prawn and lobster, greeted the guests, who milled about slightly stunned at the enormity of the extravagant celebration.

When the president, vice president, and astronaut families entered the room and filed toward their tables, the Army Carols trumpeted a fanfare, followed by the Marine Band's rendition of "Ruffles and Flourishes" and a rousingly imperial "Hail to the Chief." During dinner, the Marine Band, the Air Force Strolling Strings, and the Army Drum and Bugle Corps alternated, playing a combination of patriotic songs and moon tunes, from "Moon Over Miami" to "Moon River" and pop songs of the day like "Up, Up, and Away." In the midst of the incessant euphony, guests were served supreme of salmon Commodore, filets of beef Perigourdine, artichokes Colombia, petits carrottes, limestone lettuce, fromages de Brie, Bel Paese, Roqueford, and claire de lune for dessert, all washed down with California wines. Crabs had been flown in from Washington State, blackberries from Oregon, limestone lettuce from Kentucky, prawns from Louisiana, and lobsters from Boston.

Nixon was too excited by the party he was throwing to remain seated for long, at one point comparing himself to "a proud Jewish father at his son's bar mitzvah." Halfway through the first course, the president took Neil by the arm from table to table, constantly patting his back, answering questions for him, while introducing the top rung of guests. "Are you tired?" asked a sympathetic matron. "You bet he's tired," Nixon replied. "But he looks great," the woman said. "Well, he's very young," the president answered. Wernher von Braun thought the astronauts looked better than at any time since they plunged into the space race. "For the last nine years under pressure of the moon program, I don't think I've ever seen them so relaxed."

Back on the dais, Nixon introduced the star voyagers to the room and a vast international television audience, then presented them with the nation's highest civilian honor, the Medal of Freedom. "I want to say very simply to our three astronauts, we thank you for your courage. We thank you for raising our sights, the sights of men and women throughout the world to a new dimension. The sky is no longer the limit. This is the highest privilege I could have to propose a toast to America's astronauts. Let's raise our glasses to America's astronauts."

Buzz Aldrin said, "The honor you have given us goes not just to us as a crew, but to . . . all Americans, who believed, who persevered with us. What Apollo has begun we hope will spread out in many directions, not just in space, but underneath the seas, and in the cities, to tell us unforgettably what we will and must do. There are footprints on the moon. Those footprints belong to each and every one of you, to all of mankind. They are there because of the blood, sweat, and tears of millions of people. Those footprints are a symbol of the true human spirit."

Armstrong was given the final word. "We were privileged to leave on the moon a plaque saying 'For all mankind.' Perhaps in the third millennium a wayward stranger will read that plaque at Tranquillity Base and let history mark that this was the age in which that became a fact. We hope and think that this is the beginning of a new era. I was struck this morning by a proudly waved, but uncarefully scribbled sign. It said, 'Through you we touched the moon.' It was our privilege today across the country to touch America."

The forty-five-member Army Chorus took center stage to sing the "Star Spangled Banner," which was immediately followed by the Marine Band's reprise of "Hail to the Chief," a piece of music Richard Nixon couldn't hear often enough.

All three U.S. networks and various foreign television news organizations carried the event live and in color. Commentators sat high above the ballroom floor in booths specially built for the occasion, intoning breathless, bite-by-bite descriptions of the extravaganza. The television arrangements, camera angles, and overall look of the event, including the tenor of the coverage, was methodically orchestrated by a young protégé of California Governor Ronald Reagan, Roger Ailes, who would go on to create the "Morning in America" ads and other slick television imagery that helped get Reagan elected, reelected, and lionized. Ailes later had a hand in the founding and building of the fourth American TV network, Fox.

At 2:30 in the morning Houston time, the astronauts and their wives finally retreated to their suites, having gotten through the ordeal "subsisting on adrenaline and Scotch" in Aldrin's words.

Back in Houston the following day, the three men taped a *Meet the Press* session, then road in a parade through downtown Houston and were honored guests at the Astrodome Bonanza Show, hosted by Frank Sinatra. Afterward, Sinatra gave a private dinner party for the astronauts and their wives, who admitted to being star-struck for the first time.

Finally there was a break, and two weeks to travel anywhere the families desired at government expense. The Armstrongs had long talked about visiting a dude ranch out west, where they could ride horses, hike the trails, photograph wildlife, fish, play with Rick and Mark, and renew their marriage, which had been sorely tested in the course of nearly eight years utterly devoted to leaving footsteps on the moon. NASA called the governor of Colorado to see if he had any suggestions. By chance he was staying at the 6,000-acre Rocky Mountain ranch of bombastic Learjet mogul Harry Combs, who was a fan of Armstrong, though the two had never met.

"They were asking to find a dude ranch where Neil Armstrong can hibernate after coming out of quarantine from being on the moon," Combs recalls. "I said, 'You put the man on the moon on a dude ranch and there's gonna be thousands of people coming to look at him and not the horses. So I tell the governor we'll just put him up at my place. Well, Armstrong calls me up and says: 'Harry Combs. I've heard of you—the president of Gates Learjet.' And I say 'Yeah, well I've heard of you, too.'"

The Armstrong family spent the following two weeks blissfully unmolested with miles separating them from fans and press, living the lives of gentlemen ranchers and preparing for the next round of madness. Some time later, Neil gifted Combs with a copy of the Wright Brothers' handwritten notebooks, and the two became friends and business partners.

On September 6, vacations over, the astronauts attended functions related to their profession separately for the first time in a great while; Mike Collins to New Orleans and a homecoming celebration in his adopted hometown, Buzz Aldrin to Montclair, New Jersey, where he was honored, and Neil back to Wapakoneta, Ohio, for a parade and jubilee that would eclipse the great gathering the town and region had put on three years earlier, in wake of the arguably failed Gemini 8 flight. As in 1966, the town still had no methods of crowd counting, but the *Chicago Tribune* pegged attendance at "maybe 100,000" in a town with only 7,000 full-time citizens. Bob Hope came along for the visit, adding to the excitement, and the crowds stood eight and ten deep along the two-and-a-half-mile route.

The jubilation, however, was tempered by a report in the West German magazine *Stern,* a newsweekly roughly equivalent to *Time* or *Newsweek,* claiming that Neil was a militant atheist. It was a charge Armstrong could have brusquely dismissed; NASA's public-relations sensibilities could not. It was a mortifying, scurrilous charge hurled at the emblem of America's space program and could not go unanswered.

Wapakoneta, of course, was the ideal place to refute the story. Surrounded by his mother, father, and grandmother Korspeter, Neil joined in spirited renditions of religious anthems with the All-Ohio Youth Choir. Then, speaking to a seventeen-and-younger-only youth conference at the Wapakoneta Redskins football field, attended by three thousand, he reiterated his point: "The peace and beauty of outer space made me even more aware of the power of the Supreme Being."

Neil's aged Sunday-school teacher, Oscar J. Weiker, was even called upon to reassure the world. Toward the end of his talk with the ebullient youth (none of whom would have thought to question their local/celestial hero's faith in the Almighty), Neil pitched toward a more contemporary exposition of faith, saying that he was convinced man was coming very close to solving the mysteries of the universe. "We are entering the age of Aquarius. I believe that the age of Aquarius will come. The stars of Aquarius told me the rendezvous point of Apollo 11." What had worked with inner-city kids in Lincoln Park worked equally well with fresh-faced Midwestern farmboys, giving Armstrong a dose of hope that would rather quickly be dashed.

Chapter Sixteen

On September 16, 1969, the three astronauts and their families were in Washington for the unveiling of a stamp commemorating the moon landing, to be followed the next day by a historic speech before a joint session of Congress. None of the astronauts had been consulted about the stamp, nor were they given an opportunity to preview the design prior to the ceremony. So it came as a surprise, if not a shock, that the stamp portrayed a likeness of Neil, alone, walking on the moon, and was captioned FIRST MAN ON THE MOON.

Armstrong was embarrassed, Aldrin "hurt," and Collins angry. It was a thoughtless slight that soured the day. Nevertheless, the men soldiered on, signing sheet after sheet of the stamps, which would generate a great deal of income for the U.S. Postal Service, but benefit the astronauts and NASA not at all.

The following day was to be the grand honor that would salve the slights and humiliations they had endured. Coming fifty-seven days after *Eagle* landed, the event had been delayed by Congress's summer break, and again by the death of Senator Everett Dirksen. A joint session of Congress in which members of the Senate and the House, along with the Supreme Court, cabinet officers, diplomatic corps, the president, and the vice president all come together to honor and hear a speech by an individual is a rare moment. It was done when General Douglas MacArthur was relieved of his Korean command for overstepping the limits set by Harry Truman, and seldom since.

Like MacArthur's occasion, the Apollo 11 astronauts' appearance before Congress had a deep subtext of controversy. On the day the

mission was launched, Vice President Spiro Agnew, the Nixon administration's thrust-and-parry front man, had suggested a manned voyage to Mars was next and would be accomplished as soon as the early
eighties. There were immediate howls of outrage from Congress as
well as civil-rights and antipoverty groups, who saw billions being
diverted from their constituencies to a crash program to reach yet
another dead planet.

Senator Ted Kennedy, speaking from the moderate corner of the
space program's critics, felt Apollo should be allowed to continue, but
that once "lunar landing and exploration are complete, a substantial
portion of the space budget can be diverted to pressing problems such
as hunger, poverty, pollution, and housing here on earth." NASA and
the astronauts had to tread lightly, avoiding drawing any lines in the
sand, but encouraging the program's supporters and assuaging its critics. All three amateur politicians did a remarkably good job under the
circumstances.

Armstrong took the podium first to give thanks to the Congress
for supporting the program so far and to introduce Buzz Aldrin. "It
was here in these halls that our venture really began," he said.

Aldrin ended his statement acknowledging that the future of
United States space exploration was going to be determined by the
politicians' interpretation of the lessons learned by the crash program
that had put men on the moon. "Our steps in space have been a symbol . . . that this nation can produce equipment of the highest quality
and dependability. This should give all of us hope and inspiration to
overcome some of the more difficult problems here on earth. The
Apollo lesson is that national goals can be met where there is a strong
enough will to do so. 'A small step for a man' was a statement of fact; 'a
giant leap for mankind' is a hope for the future. What this country
does with the lessons of Apollo . . . will determine just how giant a
step we have taken."

Armstrong, who had composed much of his speech while vacationing with his family in the Rockies, allowed himself to be slightly
less grounded, evoking the great mysteries space exploration seeks to
answer, and how the answers apply to the governance of the republic.
"In the next twenty centuries, the thousand generations the earth's axis
requires to describe a giant circle in the heavens, the Age of Aquarius,
humanity may begin to understand its most baffling mystery. Where
are we going? The earth is, in fact, traveling many thousands of miles

per hour in the direction of the constellation Hercules—to some unknown destination in the cosmos. Man must understand his universe in order to understand his destiny. . . . Several weeks ago, I enjoyed the warmth of reflection on the true meaning of the spirit of Apollo. I stood in the highlands of this nation, near the continental divide, introducing to my sons the wonders of nature and pleasures of looking for deer and elk. In their enthusiasm for the view, they frequently stumbled on the rocky trails, but when they looked only to their footing, they did not see the elk.

"To those of you [who] have advocated looking high, we owe our sincere gratitude, for you have granted us the opportunity to see some of the grandest views of the Creator. To those of you who have been our honest critics, we also thank, for you have reminded us that we dare not forget to watch the trail."

So well had the astronauts hewn the fine line they were meant to straddle that several often harsh critics were swayed, at least slightly. The *Washington Post* editorial page chose to reprint the latter part of Armstrong's speech under the headline A SPACEMAN'S SENSE OF BALANCE, as part of their call for a continued "orderly" manned space program, eschewing any "crash effort" to put a man on Mars. But even as the din of the last standing ovation from the government leaders faded, the death knell was chiming at the other end of Pennsylvania Avenue for U.S. manned exploration of other worlds.

A week later, the October 6 issue of *Newsweek* magazine carried a poll of 1,321 Americans with incomes ranging from $5,000 to $15,000, roughly 61 percent of the white population. Of that group, 56 percent thought the government should be spending less money on space, while only 10 percent thought more was warranted. That was Nixon's "silent majority," the mainstream, working-class heroes, who had put him in office to stop the crazy "radical/liberal" ideas and profligate spending they had come to associate with Washington. Apparently they liked watching live space exploration on TV and cheering at parades, but didn't like paying the piper. Alarmed presidential aide Peter Flanigan sent a memo to the president citing the poll and warning "obviously this is the heart of your constituency."

Another senior White House advisor, John R. Brown III, wrote a memo on December 6 to domestic policy chief John Ehrlichman in high dudgeon over the new government-funded National Educational Television network's (the forerunner of the Public Broadcasting System, or PBS) first special of the week, devoted to a recent conference on hunger. It "did little good for the administration unless the viewer was to offer praise for providing a forum where the hunger militants could voice their numerous complaints. [George] McGovern and Jesse Jackson dominated a panel discussion . . . constant references were made to space as an example of spending that could have been far better spent on hunger."

Brown followed up with a New Year's Eve memo to the administration's hardball spin doctor, Lyn Nofziger, railing at Ted Kennedy for apparently only supporting NASA programs in his state. "Senator Kennedy has called for cuts in the budget for NASA, urging the funds be used for alleviating poverty and rebuilding slums. However, when told that the administration had decided to close the Space Agency Research Center in Cambridge, Massachusetts, Kennedy said he was shocked. He said the closing of the NASA center in Cambridge was only 'false economy.' The president requests you have one of our space enthusiasts in the Senate attack Kennedy for his hypocrisy on this issue."

Nofziger went to work with relish, dispatching a return action memo the following week. "I have gathered material for an attack on Senator Kennedy. However, I think this is the wrong time to do it, what with the inquest going on at Chappaquiddick. Let's wait until the repercussions of that are over, so it doesn't look like we are kicking a drowning man."

In the end neither the soaring entreaties of Armstrong and Aldrin to search for man's destiny by learning to understand the cosmos nor rabbit punches from the president's lieutenants could save the space program from the will of the people who were paying the bills. With the polls on the table, Nixon's July enthusiasm shriveled and died in December's chill.

The space program was growing to vast proportions, encompassing a space shuttle program, a space station project, the Viking program to photograph and map Mars, as well as an enormously expensive manned mission to Mars. NASA was going to have to be hacked down in scale just at the moment of its greatest triumph, with the Apollo 11 crew set to embark on a round-the-world victory lap that would see international adulation for the United States' achievements, unparalleled since the end of World War II.

Special Assistant to the President Clay Whitehead was given the task of sorting out the various projects, deciding which were in the national interest and which were simply too costly for the nation to afford. "Nixon wasn't hostile to the space program. But he wanted to make sure it served the nation's military and industrial needs. He liked the pomp and show of it, and the publicity of dealing with the astronauts. But he never displayed any strong feelings for the space program while the author was responsible for NASA at the White House. Mostly he was saying: How much can we cut back? The president came to believe it did nothing for him politically.

"There was no question the rest of the Apollo moon landings were going forward. The money was already in the pipelines for six more trips. The debate was: Do we build a space shuttle—a big one or a little one? Do we build a space station? Do we send the Viking craft to photograph and map Mars? Do we send men to Mars? NASA and the National Space Council, chaired by Vice President Agnew, were mutually enthused proponents of doing everything. But, from a national policy viewpoint, it was clear that it was unrealistic and unaffordable. The manned mission to Mars was outrageously expensive as well as very risky. That went off the table quickly. That left the shuttle and space station, which NASA had very cleverly packaged as a symbiotic pair; you couldn't have one without the other. The budget bureau took the position we shouldn't do any of it. I disagreed, taking the position we should do a full-sized shuttle and a scaled-back space station. After a period of squabbling, the president took my recommendation."

Whitehead and the president felt the notion of sending men into space was pointless, other than for "romantic" reasons. "From a military and economic point of view, there was no way you could make the case." But strong support for the nation continuing to have the capacity to project men into space came from another quarter. "I got very intensive briefings from the Central Intelligence Agency and the Department of Defense about the Soviet Union's space program. I came to the conclusion we didn't know enough about what the Soviets were doing. If they were to embark on a major program to put men into space, it could have had a negative political impact, and it could have jeopardized national security."

Whitehead came away from the C.I.A. briefings convinced the space shuttle had to have a "meaningful payload capacity," and to allow NASA's pleas for a space station, named Skylab, which weighed 80 tons and was over 100 feet long. It's successor Skylab B was cancelled to save money.

Just as NASA thought it could lick its wounds and limp on, another ax fell, ending the Viking Mars unmanned-exploration project. "About half of the money had already been spent," recalls Whitehead. "The rocket was built and nearly ready for launch." NASA head Jim Fletcher objected strenuously, shocked at the magnitude of the wasted effort and money precipitous cancellation would cause. "He was told to go fly a kite."

Whitehead asked the president if NASA could cut its budget in other ways to find funding for Viking's completion, and was given the go-ahead. "It was one of my few jobs of outright pandering. I told Nixon the first pictures of Mars would come back just as he was finishing his second term. He could see the possibilities right away. Unfortunately, as it turned out, he was no longer president then.

"I called Fletcher and said, 'Jim, I think we can get it restored, but you and I will have to find substantial budget cuts. I told him to come over to the White House, alone, without an entourage of staff. We sat down in a conference room for two days going through NASA's budget. We cut and cut. He hated it. It was like killing the man's children. Finally we came up with cuts equal to the cost of Viking and the program was able to continue."

Chapter Seventeen

Five years after the moon landing, Armstrong shared a laugh with Buzz Aldrin, recalling how they had privately agreed at the time they had about a fifty-fifty chance of landing *Eagle,* walking on the moon, and safely returning to earth. "I thought a project of that complexity had about as much chance as a blind hen in a foxes' den," Neil said, and he compared stepping onto the surface of the moon to playing "Russian roulette with a twenty-chamber revolver and only one shell. I remember the elation of finding we weren't going to sink into the surface."

Michael Collins said, "I wasn't sure we'd pull this thing off until we were on our way home." But amidst the excitement of the moment, they never admitted the slim odds, which they were positive were about accurate. That it was not worth mentioning at the time and funny years later says much about the difference between test pilots and regular people.

The aftermath of the 1969 moonwalk was a tsunami of attention that left Armstrong, Aldrin, and Collins dazed, exhausted, and on the verge of meltdown. Buzz would later marvel at how "we all got through so much liquor with so few consequences."

Neil flew to Los Angeles on Saturday, September 28, for the annual banquet held by the Society of Experimental Test Pilots and dinner with Charles Lindbergh, talking with the "Lone Eagle" for the first time since Apollo 11. The two met only a few times before Lindbergh's death in 1974 at the age of seventy-two. But the friendship inspired Armstrong to create a lasting memorial in Lindbergh's name. Soon after his death, Neil and retired General James Doolittle, famed for his audacious, confidence-inspiring "raid" on Tokyo in the grim early months of World War II, created the Charles Lindbergh Memorial Fund to support the work of young scientists, explorers, and conservationists.

The Armstrongs returned to Houston late on Saturday night to prepare for their trip. The week started early on Sunday, September 29, with a surprise wake-up call from the White House. The president asked after Jan and the kids, then launched into an off-the-cuff and unexpected briefing. He wanted Neil to tell each of the foreign leaders he met that the United States was looking for "partners in space," to share the expense, the glory, and to reap the commercial rewards that would eventually follow from orbiting satellites and other advances. The president said he hoped they would not be too overwhelmed by the trip, and invited Neil and Jan to the White House for dinner immediately upon their return. It was a hint that some sort of reward or challenge was in the offing, something that Armstrong would certainly have to be prepared to deal with. There was no question he had no future as an astronaut in the remainder of the Apollo program—that was certain. There were too many men waiting for the few assignments remaining and the first man on the moon had already gotten the ultimate prize. His main plan involved finishing the master's-degree program in aeronautics he had started at the University of Southern California during the Edwards Air Force Base years, and beginning a new career as a university professor. Government and politics held no allure whatever. Unfortunately, there was going to be precious little time to think and reflect on the future for some time to come.

The twenty-five-nation journey, named the "Giant Leap" tour—as though they were a rock band—included a dozen ticker-tape parades and dinners with presidents, kings, and movie stars. Even as NASA was being massively downsized (or, indeed, because the agency's glory days were fast fading), the government was insistent the astronauts make as much as possible of their international renown. At a time when U.S. prestige around the world was at a low ebb over the Vietnam war, the administration was intent on using the goodwill tour to burnish the nation's image. Being cast in such a role was a less-than-comfortable fit for any of the men, particularly Armstrong.

"As the traveling and speaking wore on," Aldrin recalled, "Neil became more and more withdrawn." The persistence of the various hucksters, both from private business and his own government, drove Armstrong to utter distraction. Even fellow astronaut Frank Borman, known as Father Borman, the astronauts' adviser, had thrown them a hard curveball, saying on the eve of the tour that "all material things" would be theirs if they played their cards right. "It was one of those awful moments one encounters in life," said Aldrin, who came to feel no two Americans had been as exploited as he and Armstrong since Robert E. Lee and Ulysses S. Grant. "Cold, tight-lipped rage" was how a *Life* magazine reporter following the tour described Armstrong's annoyance.

The arduous journey began for the astronauts and their wives on Monday with a familiar early-morning flight aboard Air Force Two from Ellington Air Force Base. First stop was Mexico City, where they were nearly crushed when an enormous and overly friendly crowd surged forward during a City Hall ceremony in their honor. When the situation was under control, Neil took the podium and delivered a brief speech in well-practiced Spanish. Local papers billed the astronauts "conquistadores of space."

Bogota, Colombia, was also turned into a nightmarish mob scene when an excited crowd broke through police lines to paw and yank the astronauts' clothes. The following day they landed in Buenos Aires for another motorcade and reception, then on to Rio. At each stop they were required to shake hundreds of hands, wear glued-on smiles, and pose for pictures until nearly blinded by flashbulbs.

On October 3 the Giant Leap tour and its exhausted band left South America for the Canary Islands, off the coast of North Africa, to finally rest for a few days, swim, and recharge. Unfortunately, knots of people, which quickly grew into crowds, gathered wherever they were spotted. On the beach, tourists asked for pictures and autographs. The rest stop, such as it was, ended quickly and the tour resumed with a visit to strongman Generalissimo Francisco Franco's Spain. The astronauts were singularly unimpressed, noting his "weak handshake." But

Juan Carlos de Borbón, who would take over the reins of Spain as king when Franco died, and his wife, Sophia, charmed the visitors. The handsome, dashing Juan Carlos, a pilot himself who had visited Cape Kennedy and was keenly interested in the space program, struck a warm friendship with Armstrong during the visit. "He is a young leader who has what we felt was great potential for bringing our countries together. Both he and his wife, Sophia, received us informally in their palace, and impressed us with the sincerity of their warm greeting," Armstrong wrote later in his official report on the trip to then National Security Advisor Henry Kissinger.

The astronauts' visit to France was more formal; their meeting with the imperious president, Georges Pompidou, was televised, and watched by a record audience of many millions. The night was marred first by Pompidou's long, out-of-kilter speech extolling the glories of France, and then by an unemployed actor with mental problems, who leaped onto the stage and ran menacingly toward Neil, wielding a pencil. Armstrong's reaction was thankfully fast, catching the disturbed man's wrist with the pencil not six inches from his eyes. He held on until police rushed the stage and dragged the attacker away.

In London on October 14, nerves were beginning to fray. News that a second and third press conference before the notoriously inquisitory British press had been scheduled annoyed both Buzz and Mike. But Neil was, in Aldrin's words, "*really* pissed off."

They rode in motorcade after motorcade, waving to crowds, dining and drinking their way across Europe, visiting the Netherlands, Norway, and Rome, where Pope Paul VI gifted them with statues of the Three Wise Men, and Gina Lollobrigida threw a party in their honor that lasted all night. Lollobrigida also became a lifelong friend. He would later pose for portraits for her series, "The World's Most Interesting Men," the sort of thing Neil would only do for a trusted friend. A few years later, the actress spoke revealing words about the toll fame had taken: "When I first met Neil, he was not so naive as he is now. Much more daring. I threw a party for him and his Apollo 11 friends at my house in Rome. Neil and I have been good friends ever since; he is a warm gentle man. It is really marvelous that he didn't lose his head—that he should want to be completely unknown as if he hadn't done anything. Remarkable."

In Berlin, a strikingly attractive young woman burst out of the crowd, running toward Armstrong until police restrained her. Seeing the incident, he walked over, led her away from the police, and spoke to her. She literally swooned. In Yugoslavia, the astronauts lunched with an "extremely cordial" Marshal Tito and went on a duck-hunting expedition he arranged for them.

In Africa, President Joseph Mobutu of the Congo presented the men with the nation's highest honor, the National Order of the Leopard, and their wives with the National Order of the Zaire. The three couples were lodged in private villas, a bit more rustic than they were used to, with outdoor, three-nozzle showers meant to be used in groups, and surrounded by unfettered lions—the cabinet minister assigned full-time to their care assured the visitors they were quite tame. There was a full-scale native dance ceremony led by Miss Congo, which Buzz decided to join, leaping from the dais and cutting in on Miss Congo's dance partner. The other dancers fell back and the drumbeat quickened as the astronaut and the African beauty danced an impromptu tango, simultaneously delighting President Mobutu, who stood and cheered, and utterly unnerving Armstrong, who sat and frowned. "Neil didn't think it was appropriate because we were representing the president of the United States," said Aldrin. "But later on he came around."

Armstrong and company helped celebrate the Shah of Iran's birthday party; stopped off in East Pakistan; enjoyed a "small private dinner" with Prime Minister Sato of Japan and "a number of important members of the Japanese Foreign Ministry"; met Emperor Hirohito; rode in parades honoring their achievement in Seoul, South Korea; and made several stops in Australia. Then they jetted back to Washington via Anchorage, Alaska, where the wives had a snowball fight while Air Force Two was refueled.

The tour ended November 6 on the White House lawn, with the Marine Band playing. President and Mrs. Nixon welcomed the six travelers home and insisted they spend the night. Following cocktails and dinner with just the astronauts and their wives, Nixon got down to business, thanking them for the years of risky, hard work and for willingly taking on their exhausting tour. Waving away their response dismissively, he leaned close and said, "Now, what can I do for you?" Neil and Buzz were both interested in aeronautics research, but hadn't worked out specifics in their minds. Nixon recommended they think hard about it over the next few weeks. Mike Collins had already told the president he was enjoying his role as goodwill ambassador and wanted a State Department job. Nixon called Secretary of State William Rogers and the deal was done. Nixon went off to work on a speech and the astronauts retired to their quarters to toast the future with the bottle of Scotch they found waiting with glasses and ice. Their prospects seemed bright indeed. Judging from the president's resolute handling of Mike's request, they had only to ask and their dream job would materialize. But the air of weary euphoria over their triumphal world tour obscured some basic facts—for instance, the astronauts were not as universally beloved at home as they appeared to be abroad. There was an increasingly bitter political struggle churning over the war in Southeast Asia, and a raft of domestic issues, including poverty, drugs, law enforcement, censorship, skirt length, and men's hairstyles. Stepping out of their spacesuits and into high-profile government jobs would make them political lightning rods.

The nomination several weeks later of Collins for the post of assistant secretary of state for public affairs was said to have been Secretary Rogers's idea to reach out to youth disaffected by the Vietnam War. "The Bureau of Public Affairs will place increased emphasis on . . . its contacts with the youth of this country in recognition of the unprecedented attention young people have directed to the nation's foreign policy," read the State Department's official announcement. In other words, Collins was going to explain the war to young people. The trouble was that Nixon and Rogers saw the astronauts as youths, because relative to them they were, but teenage college students who marched against the war saw them as forty-year-old militarists.

Collins quickly waded into the quagmire, saying antiwar dissidents were "poorly equipped with the facts," and "they have oversimplified to where Hanoi is good and Saigon is bad."

Meanwhile, Armstrong was appointed chairman of the Peace Corps Advisory Council and head of NASA's aeronautics programs. Aldrin took what appeared the safer path, deciding to stay in the Air Force, with his sights set on following in his father's footsteps and earning a general's star.

The reaction in newspapers and on Capitol Hill to Collins and Armstrong's new jobs was swift and savage. Speaking of Collins's nomination, Ohio Democratic Congressman Wayne Hayes thundered: "He is about as qualified to hold that job as a pig is to be a figure skater. When one of them gets into a capsule, apparently it qualifies them to do anything."

The *Washington Star*, a relatively conservative paper, normally sympathetic to the Nixon administration and to the space program, also questioned Collins's qualifications, suggesting he had no idea what the job entailed. "The young man may have been overwhelmed when Messrs. Nixon and Rogers dangled under his nose a plum paying nearly double his Air Force salary." The paper fretted that "in the bottomless federal piggy bank, the waste of Collins's million-dollar training may be small, but the crippling of an essential public information program is beyond price, as is the tarnishing of a space hero."

The *Washington Post* was certain that Armstrong and the space program were way out of sync and largely irrelevant to concerns of the day. "Mr. Armstrong may find that potential Peace Corpsmen have their minds more on the draft than the moon; his lunar experience will make it no easier for volunteers to talk about My Lai with the people they serve overseas. . . . they have little or no constituency among those young people they have been assigned to reach, and they are unlikely to convince dissenters to go easier on foreign policy."

NASA administrators felt buffeted by the fallout and determined to step back from the fray, disassociating the space program from the war in Southeast Asia that was growing more loathsome and egregious in all respects to an increasingly clamorous portion of the public, a sentiment that was being driven by media with a clear antiwar agenda.

By Thanksgiving 1969, NASA was determined to draw a line in the sand. The White House had proposed sending Neil Armstrong and Frank Borman to join Bob Hope's perennial U.S.O. pilgrimage to entertain the troops that Christmas. NASA chief Thomas O. Paine objected strenuously. Having Armstrong pictured cheering on the troops, just as the grisly details of the massacre of civilian women and children in a Vietnamese village called My Lai led the news was unacceptable. They feared it would link the moonwalker with the war and could wound the agency just when it was most vulnerable. Nixon's reaction was predictable and violent. In a desk-slamming fury, he ordered Haldeman to fire anyone who dared defy him. The president was as aware of My Lai as anyone. His concern was to emphasize it was "totally contrary to national policy" and "it happened under the other administration at a time when the war was escalating." The political posturing would be his tilt, not NASA's. My Lai was to be portrayed as the Lyndon Johnson administration's shame; Neil Armstrong and Apollo 11 the Nixon legacy.

Bob Haldeman's confidential memo, dated November 25, 1969, was, as White House counselor Tom Whitehead said thirty years later when he perused it, "pure Bob." Blunt as a stroke from a poleaxe, it read: "This is to confirm that the President firmly orders that whatever objections have been raised regarding Borman and Armstrong going to Vietnam are to be over-ruled. He was shocked to learn that there have been some questions raised as to whether it is desirable from our viewpoint to have such a visit made by Borman in December as the President had instructed, and also a question as to whether Armstrong should go over to be with Bob Hope on Christmas Day. The President would like to be sure that Director Paine knows that he is shocked at any thought within NASA that this would be contrary to national policy, and that if there is any appearance in the public press of any objection to this decision to send these men over, by any staff member in NASA, that person is to be fired immediately."

The response from a chastened but still feisty NASA was to cave on Borman, and attempt nimble bureaucratic foot-dragging on Armstrong, the trophy astronaut. "Borman's trip to Vietnam is set for this month. With regard to Armstrong, Paine did have some question as to whether a trip with Bob Hope is the right context for Armstrong. He is not the forceful type of fellow that Borman is, but rather more thoughtful and careful. Armstrong will, of course, go with Hope if the President desires. If not, it may be well to see if a more suitable context for the trip could be devised. May I have your opinion, please?"

On December 20, Neil Armstrong flew to Bangkok, Thailand, on an Air Force flight to meet with Peace Corps officials as President Nixon's special representative. The following day, he joined Bob Hope, actress Connie Stevens, and a "bevy of show girls" to rehearse for the comedian's sixth consecutive Christmas visit to American soldiers stationed in Vietnam.

TV's *Hawaiian Eye* star Stevens had, earlier in 1969, won notoriety for her well-publicized divorce from Eddie Fisher—the proximity of the perky, blonde beauty and the astronaut would cause *Los Angeles Times* gossip columnist Joyce Haber to pen a "blind item" linking the two romantically—a bit of mischief that would have a long life. TV gossip Rona Barrett chimed in, claiming Armstrong was "gazing with baleful eyes" at Connie Stevens in Las Vegas on January 18, 1970, a few weeks after the Hope tour. A year later, the story was still buzzing: In *Parade* magazine, Walter Scott's widely read "Personality Parade" column responded to a query about the "rumor of a romance between astronaut Neil Armstrong and Connie Stevens" with a confirmation/ denial: "They have been seen infrequently in restaurants of late, which always gives rise to rumor of romance no matter how unfounded. Armstrong is married and the father of two sons." Over thirty years later, a photocopy of the column and a handwritten note about the Rona Barrett item lingered in NASA's clipping file.

Following a day of rehearsal, during which Armstrong practiced his role as Hope's straight man, the troupe moved by Chinook helicopter to the forward base of the U.S. First Infantry Division at Laikhe, where more than 10,000 soldiers waited in the stifling jungle heat.

Hope's trademark laconic jokes reflected the characters who peopled the public stage, as well as the horrors and minutiae of the day: Timothy Leary and LSD, Tiny Tim, airplane hijackers, *Mad* magazine, and the cantankerousness of Vice President Spiro Agnew. Hope turned to Armstrong and said, "Your step on the moon was the second most dangerous of the year." Armstrong replied, "Who took the most dangerous?" Hope quipped, "The girl that married Tiny Tim." That comic duo was followed by Connie Stevens, who minced onto the stage to a cacophony of wild catcalls in a skin-tight red micro miniskirt, then astounded and silenced the testosterone-charged audience by singing "Silent Night" a capella, in a clear, strong mellifluous voice.

Shows were given at numerous frontline bases, including the Marine fortification at Da Nang, which had been under near-continuous siege, and Camp Eagle, twenty-five miles north of Saigon, where sixteen thousand paratroopers waited from 3:00 A.M. for the show to start the following afternoon. At all stops, Nixon's political acumen proved sage; Armstrong's simple statement when he took the stage each night, "I want to thank you for what you are doing here," drew thunderous standing ovations lasting for minutes.

Basking in the warmth of affection for Armstrong, Hope said he had been asked by President Nixon to "tell the boys that he had solid plans for ending the war." The seemingly innocuous words had an incendiary effect, reversing the mood and eliciting angry jeers and booing. Nixon's army had had its fill of solid plans for ending the war.

In the six months since returning from the moon, Armstrong worked hard politicking for the space program, NASA, and the United States. Contrary to NASA's assessment of him as not "forceful" enough to represent the agency in Vietnam, Neil exhibited a great deal of skill and charisma, as well as a comfort level with crowds and foreign leaders. He had a megawatt smile, quick turn of phrase, and was developing into a pretty good speech giver. All of which led the press to wonder if he was going to join John Glenn, giving Ohio two former astronaut senators. On his first public appearance in 1970, at Purdue to receive an honorary doctorate of engineering on January 9, reporters peppered him with political questions. The answer was less than Shermanesque, but he assured both students and clamoring newsmen he had no political ambitions, though he didn't want to seem to be criticizing other astronauts who did, particularly Glenn. "After all, politics should have something more than lawyers representing the people."

Accepting an honorary degree before ten thousand people in the university's basketball arena, Neil presented Purdue President Dr. Frederick Hovde with a surprise—a 1969 Purdue centennial flag that had been to the moon aboard Apollo 11.

Later in the month, he visited another university to accept a real degree. For years while flying at Edwards, Armstrong worked toward a master's degree in aeronautics at the University of Southern California, a necessary step toward his real ambition—to be a teacher, completing the second of his lifelong goals. The final requirement for the degree was to deliver a lecture on a topic he was uniquely qualified to discuss: moon-landing techniques and procedures. As always, a large caravan of press trailed in his wake, recording the occasion.

The rest of the winter was spent fulfilling the tedious duty of accepting endless awards, posing for pictures with firemen, presidents, and professors, eating bad food at overlong banquets, and smiling when he likely felt more like screaming.

Then, in April, the accident everybody feared happened. Apollo 13, the third moon shot, with its crew of Jim Lovell, Fred Haise, and command-module pilot Jack Swigert, launched at thirteen minutes after 1:00 P.M.—13:13 in military time. In addition to all the unlucky 13s involved, the mission had been filled with bad portents. The prime command pilot, Ken Mattingly, was exposed to measles, forcing his replacement with Swigert—a devastating blow to Mattingly and the crew that had trained with him for so long. Then there was a delay of two days due to the discovery of a poorly insulated helium tank and a defective oxygen tank that had been rejected by the crew of Apollo 10, sent back to the factory, and supposedly fixed, though still behaving suspiciously. Anxious to get under way, Commander Lovell decided to take his chances.

Five minutes after liftoff, the ship began to vibrate suspiciously, and instruments indicated the center engine of the second stage had shut down prematurely. One more worrisome omen.

Then the ride smoothed out and the crew settled into a "boring" flight. Fifty-five hours after launch, 200,000 miles in space, Apollo 13 was suddenly rocked by a sharp bang, followed by violent vibrations. The rogue oxygen tank had exploded, knocking out two of three fuel cells, and oxygen from the one remaining tank was rapidly venting into space. The astronauts were in a dying ship, streaking deeper and deeper into space. Jim Lovell's famously sober SOS—"Houston, we have a problem"—became an international catchphrase. A hundred daunting problems had to quickly be solved if the men were to return home alive. New procedures had to be devised and tested in NASA simulators before they could be implemented on board the stricken craft. Neil and all the other astronauts on public-relations duty were immediately called to Houston to pitch in and do everything possible to avert the disaster looming for the three men, the space program, and the nation.

Reflecting on the crew's reaction to the crisis, Lovell said, "We could have bounced off the walls for a while. But afterward we'd have faced the same problems. Instead we went right to work."

With less than fifteen minutes of oxygen left, the command module had to be evacuated. The crew crowded into the landing module, planning to use it as a life raft spinning around the moon, which was looming ominously in their portal, and limp back home using the very minimum amounts of energy. It was going be a long, dark ride through space, with the temperature hovering around a bone-chilling thirty-eight degrees Fahrenheit.

But, even in the relative safety of the undamaged LM, there was trouble. Carbon dioxide was gradually building, turning the atmosphere lethal. Lithium hydride scrubbers would help, but the LM had less than a quarter of what was needed for the four-day journey home, and the square command-module canisters were incompatible with the LM environmental system, which had round openings.

Working furiously, astronauts in Houston pieced together a desperate, but finally brilliant, makeshift solution. A fan was removed from one of the spacesuits, taped to a canister from the command module using cardboard and plastic bags. The suit's fan drew carbon dioxide from the cabin, forced it through the canister, and fixed it. It worked, and gave the crew enough breathable air to make it home.

An estimated billion people watched the drama on television or listened to radios—nearly a third of the world's population at the time. They breathed a sigh of relief with the astronauts when it looked like the mission would return home.

Against the odds, Apollo 13 returned to earth and splashed down safely, but NASA and the nation had suffered a severe shock. Future flights were canceled until further notice; all of NASA's procedures and equipment was reexamined. A board of inquiry was appointed, with Armstrong representing the interests of the astronauts. In the weeks that followed, he guided the members through a simulation re-creating the explosion, taking them step by step through Apollo 13's near disastrous trip.

The harsh conclusion was that NASA engineers had made several drastically careless mistakes, including raising the voltage to the command module's oxygen tank heaters without modifying the affected switches. The result made a catastrophe almost inevitable. Temperatures inside the heaters reached a thousand degrees while still on the launchpad, damaging the Teflon insulation and welding the switches in the "on" position. Thus the Apollo 13 crew were launched with a ticking bomb that exploded 200,000 miles in space.

While sharply critical, the board's report strongly emphasized the unanimous conclusion of all eight members, including some of America's top rocketmen, that manned space flights could be made safe and should continue.

On July 1, approaching his fortieth birthday and the anniversary of Apollo 11, Armstrong was scheduled to begin his new desk job as Deputy Assistant Administrator for Aeronautics at NASA headquarters. The family had reluctantly sold their house in El Lago and bought a large split-level at 12 English Way in Bethesda, Maryland, a leafy suburban cul de sac half an hour to forty-five minutes from NASA headquarters during the rush-hour commute.

A measure of Neil's fame and the warm feelings he generated was the *Houston Post*'s lead editorial of May 27, 1970, headlined: ADIOS, GOOD LUCK, NEIL. "Neil Armstrong is a warm and unpretentious human being. He has been a good neighbor and a good citizen. Houston wishes him the best in his new endeavor and hopes that, in time, he will return to live among us."

But before he could settle in at 12 English Way or at his new NASA headquaters, there was one more Apollo 11–related goodwill trip to undertake—an eleven-day whirlwind trip to the Soviet Union as a guest of the U.S.S.R. Academy of Sciences, on the occasion of the thirteenth meeting of the International Committee on Space Research. But far more exciting to Neil was the opportunity to visit Star City, the Soviet space program's version of a combined Houston, El Lago, and Cape Kennedy, and to watch—albeit only on live television—the launch of the Soyuz 9 on an eighteen-day orbital mission. He became one of a handful of Westerners to have seen the inside of the ultra-secret space complex, presumably a tribute to the high regard the Soviets had for him. In fact, a report in *Izvestia* published the day Neil left the country contained high praise, comparing him to the U.S.S.R's most revered postwar hero, Yuri Gargarin. "He has an open strong face. His movements reveal restraint and modesty. He somewhat resembles Gargarin."

Unfortunately, in the time it took to fly from Washington to Moscow, the U.S. Army initiated a "military incursion" across the Laotian border. The only fallout—despite the fact Neil was representing the president of the United States—was that his visit was downplayed in the state-controlled press, which, as far as Armstrong was concerned, was doubtless a plus.

He arrived in Leningrad on May 24 aboard an Air Force plane and was greeted by two of his Soviet counterparts who had toured the U.S. space facilities the previous summer, cosmonauts Georgi Beregovoi and Konstantin Feoktistov. The trip started off on a collegial note, with a dinner in Neil's honor that night at the apartment of Beregovoi, attended by a number of cosmonauts and Soviet space-program officials. The toast and talk of the dinner concerned the near-disastrous journey of Apollo 13, which the cosmonauts had followed with the same high anxiety and desperate hope as the Americans.

Despite the Cold War that raged between their governments, the astronauts felt they were members of a fraternity with a bond beyond politics. With a great deal to talk about, the party went on until 3:00 A.M., with the men toasting one another, sharing their experiences, and watching films of Soviet launches, many of which had never been seen by Westerners. A question on the minds of the spacemen was: Could the two nations put their differences aside and cooperate in space, particularly on building a space platform? Unfortunately,

Armstrong had been categorically forbidden to "make any specific proposals and likewise they made none to me." Clearly, the Cold War would
have to ratchet down considerably before cooperation could begin.

Armstrong was eager to participate in the space-research meeting,
which was attended by 800 Soviet delegates and 420 others, representing thirty nations. He intended just to listen and learn; then the next
day he would give the standard lecture on the moon landing. But when
he strode into the classic columned hall of the Tauride Palace, where
the czar's parliament once sat, it was immediately obvious that his
presence at the erudite gathering was going to have far more disrup-
tive effect than expected. Once he was recognized, the speaker at the
podium was drowned out by a clamor that swelled to an excited roar.
Much of the audience leaped to its feet and swept around him, clutching programs, pleading for autographs. After fruitlessly banging on
the gavel and many shouts for order, the meeting's chairman gave up
and walked away to wait for the tumult to die down. Stunned, Neil
dutifully signed hundreds of autographs until he was finally allowed to
take his seat.

His Soviet minders attempted to prevent a repeat of the chaos at the
next session, entering the hall by a less conspicuous back entrance. But
the attempt was futile; as soon as he was recognized, the scientists again
surged forward, this time overwhelming guards, nearly knocking Armstrong down. Quickly dispatched police waded into the crowd, attempting a rescue, shouting in outrage at unauthorized cameras. "No
pictures, no pictures," they bellowed in Russian. One overexcited del-
egate was injured when he attempted to scramble over a railing and
fell. Finally extricated from the mob, Neil took the podium and delivered a thirty-minute address, accompanied by the same color slides of
the moon voyage he had shown all over the world. The applause at
the end was thunderous, and when he was joined and congratulated
by cosmonauts Beregovoi and Feoktistov, there was another long
ovation.

Next day, Neil and the cosmonauts left for the Siberian town of
Akademgorodok, or "Science Town," where many of the Soviet Union's
scientific community and their families were housed, largely isolated
from the prying eyes of the West, as well as free of the harsh deprivation
that was the lot of the vast majority of their countrymen. The three
made the journey in a Soviet Ilyushin-18, which Armstrong flew for
part of the trip.

Despite the requisite trappings of a formal state visit, the cosmonauts tried their best to show Armstrong some of the special pleasures reserved for Soviet space heroes. During the Siberian leg of the journey, there was a short cruise with a group of writers, artists, and scientists aboard the state-owned yacht *Fakel* down the Ob reservoir. Unfortunately, in keeping with the jagged pattern of the visit, a tempest kicked up, tossing the luxury ship violently, smashing fine china set out for the planned luncheon and causing some of the honored guests, though not Neil, to suffer severe seasickness.

After nearly two hours of stormy seas, the *Fakel* was steered into a safe cove and finally moored. Neil echoed the general sentiment yelling, "Abandon ship" and leading the weary passengers, who mostly staggered unsurely down the gangplank, seeking the comfort of dry land. For the strong of stomach, a picnic of traditional Russian fish soup and black bread was served.

On the return to Moscow, Armstrong met Soviet Premier Alexei Kosygin and presented him with moon rocks and the tiny Soviet flag he had carried to the lunar surface.

On behalf of the American astronaut corps, Armstrong placed flowers at the urns in the Kremlin wall containing the ashes of cosmonauts Yuri Gagarin and Vladimir Komarov, and presented their widows with the memorial plaques, which had also gone to the moon.

A few years later, in his new life as a college professor, Neil took advantage of the proximity of Russian classes to study and gain a fair mastery of the language, which served him well on numerous visits over the years.

On July 1, Armstrong took over NASA's aeronautics office and officially ceased being an astronaut. But in a brief press conference he admitted to having his eye still on another spaceflight. "I don't see it as a permanent parting. I foresee that space and aeronautics will not always be so far apart."

The office had jurisdiction over a range of aeronautics projects he had been intimately involved with at NASA throughout his career, and in that sense, wasn't at all the make-work job the critics in the press had suggested. He was responsible for conducting research into airport safety, both civilian and military, new aircraft applications, including short-take-off-and-landing craft, and supersonic and hyper-sonic planes, like the controversial Super Sonic Transport (SST) that was to be America's challenge to the Concorde then being developed by the French and British governments. A great lure of the job for Armstrong was that it required him to be on top of the latest aeronau-tical technology, meaning he would be able to fly all the new birds as they came off the assembly line—a very agreeable duty.

Just a few months into the job, the former test pilot visited the Boeing aircraft plant in Seattle, Washington, and took a lumbering new 747 jumbo jet, with a seating capacity of 362, for a ninety-minute spin over the Olympic peninsula. Not surprisingly, he found the behe-moth "slow."

But even as he was placing pictures of Jan and the boys on his desk, the reality of the daunting ceremonial duties Nixon had in mind for Armstrong in Washington grew apparent.

Prince Charles, the twenty-one-year-old heir to the British throne, and his sister, Princess Anne, were making their first visit to America, and Armstrong was expected to be on hand to show the young royals space exhibits at the Smithsonian, and to attend a buffet and rock-music dance on the White House lawn hosted by Julie and Trisha Nixon.

Charles turned out to be a knowledgeable afficionado of the space program as well as a flyer and parachutist. The prince had recently completed a course at the Royal Air Force College and was training on the newest generation of jet fighters. The two struck up a friendship immediately, and Charles invited Neil to visit the royal family on his next trip abroad and take the controls of one of the latest RAF jets.

Then there was the first anniversary of Apollo 11 and its raft of knotty obligations. All three crew members were to reunite for a trip to Jefferson City, Missouri, the unlikely site of the official celebration, chosen because it was the district of powerful Congressional Space Committee member James Symington, a strong NASA partisan. Then they would fly to New York City to present United Nations Secretary General U Thant with a U.N. flag that had been to the moon, as well as a lunar sample.

On the first anniversary, Armstrong appeared to many uncharac-teristically subdued and pessimistic. He said he fervently wished just twelve months prior that the moon landings would have had a galva-nizing, even spiritually uplifting influence on the world, causing mankind to "look a little further into the future with an aim toward solving problems before they become problems. We seem to be tied up with today's problems. This is a very inefficient way to solve problems, from the rear, always catching up. Attacking problems from the front side—it's a great deal easier to provide a viable solution and a meaningful one."

One of the problems facing the world that summer was helping the people of Peru dig out from under an earthquake of appalling proportions that struck without warning on May 31, killing seventy thousand people and leaving a million homeless. Armstrong felt that constant monitoring of the earth's surface changes from space could have given advanced warning of such a cataclysmic event. It was a program he hoped to get under way during his time as a NASA administrator. "Maybe ten years from now there won't be any more Perus. We can't prevent the earthquake from happening, but we ought to be able to see it coming and move people out." A visceral engineer, Neil was apparently losing patience with the then in vogue pop-sociology approach to mankind's ills. "The technological goals have now been replaced by the sociological. Lord knows that every day, every country is faced with difficult problems. But if it *is* a difficult problem and you are challenged to get into it, you have a better chance of solving it."

His confidence in the developing technologies was such that predictions of control over the earth's elements seemed reasonable. "I'm going out on a limb, but I'll predict that within this century we will abolish natural calamities. That is calamities of a meteorological variety: hurricanes will be reined, tornadoes tamed, cyclones slowed to a carousel's pace, and droughts ended."

He even held hope that the world's nations would become so enthralled with space in the wake of the moon landing that war would quickly become obsolete. "Perhaps as the space age club of nations expands, we can also see nonviolence expanding."

Despite the severe cuts space exploration had suffered under the new budget, Neil remained convinced, correctly as it turned out, that the program would never wither and die. "I suspect the space program is now inevitable. That is, it's a thing that now exists and will continue to exist for the rest of man's existence."

Most upsetting and truly hard to fathom, a year after Apollo 11's successful landing, followed by Apollo 12's in November 1969, were newspaper reports quoting large numbers of people at home and abroad who believed the moon landings were a hoax. Sadly, he admitted it was a hard thing to simply prove. "I think that one would find that in order to perpetuate such a hoax, without a few leaks around the agency, would be a much more difficult job than actually going to the moon."

The three Apollo 11 astronauts dutifully performed the anniversary tasks required of them, but the pique felt by Armstrong over the pat recycling of pointless, clichéd questions was already showing on the first annual marking of the flight. To a journalist who noted he looked "slightly heavier" than a year earlier, and wondered about other changes, Armstrong snapped, "The principal change in my life has been that people now keep asking me how my life has changed." Each anniversary would inevitably be an opportunity for the world to compare the man he presently was to the man he had been that glorious July of 1969.

Chapter Eighteen

In the late summer of 1970, Armstrong attended the fiftieth anniversary of the German Sport Gliding Association fair at Wasserkuppe, and joined that nation's leading female pilot, Hanna Reitsch, in glider flights across the Roehn Mountains.

Back in Washington, the NASA Administrator for Organization and Management determined that Armstrong would require two full-time assistants and $10,000 per year in travel expenses. He was clearly expected to get around quite a bit, administering his far-flung division, with 2,500 employees and an overall budget of $160 million.

The first charge was to use the political capital of an astronaut hero to help with the annual budget battle, which NASA Deputy Administrator George Low characterized as a "buzz saw" for the agency. The high command of NASA and the Department of Transportation "specifically asked that you should be personally involved in this effort," Low informed Armstrong in a memo. "I understand there are meetings next week. I had previously heard you were already participating in this work, but thought I had better send this note to make sure," Low wrote, a trace of panic evident between the lines.

Armstrong weighed in the next month, duly touting NASA's aggressive aeronautics agenda. "The frontiers of flight have not all been explored," he argued. "The applications of NASA's advanced research in aeronautics will continue to keep the United States in first place in commercial aviation in the years ahead." And he dropped the headline-grabbing bombshell that plans were on the boards to build a commercial craft that would eventually allow "casual travel" at six

thousand miles an hour, more than three times the speed of the proposed Super Sonic Transport planes that were stirring waves of controversy but would in fact never make it off the drawing board in the
United States. Armstrong's broad vision for the future was contained
in his first NASA publication, titled *Aeronautics,* released to the press
that September.

Letters and memos generated by Neil's division show he was
involved in a plethora of projects ranging from gearing up an ambitious "regenerative life support system" to maintaining a space-station
crew for months without resupply, including more prosaic projects,
such as applying techniques for airplane ground control on "taxiways,
aprons, and runways" garnered at NASA research facilities for use at
commercial airports. Also under his jurisdiction was the NASA
Research and Technology Advisory Subcommittee on Aircraft Operating Problems. The group of eighteen appointees from the aircraft
industry and government had a mandate to advise the agency on
problems including turbulence, clear-air turbulence, runway slipperi-
ness, noise, cosmic radiation, fog modification, and pollution.

In November, the former astronaut was in England to receive the
gold medal of the Royal Geographical Society from the Duchess of
Kent, and to speak out on the subject of the environment—a popular
subject that fall—before the World Wildlife Fund.

"The earth today is an oasis of life in space," he told the group's second international congress. "It is the only island we know is a suitable
home for man. I have a deep sense of the finite significance of our
fragility. We are a fragile planet, physically so interdependent. If you
could touch this planet with your thumb it would feel soft as toothpaste.
We must continue to find ways to protect it. The importance of protect-
ing and saving that home has never been felt more strongly. Protection
seems most required, however, not from foreign aggressors or natural
calamity, but from its own population."

Other speakers at the conference offered Malthusian scenarios of a
dystopian future with "galloping degradation" of the planet and an
unsustainable population of six billion in thirty years—interestingly, a
census estimate that was right on the money. "The human race is
doomed to extinction," thundered Dr. Luc Hoffman, vice president of
the fund.

Armstrong disagreed, but was clearly concerned about and committed to campaigning for environmental conservation. He said he

refused to believe the majority of the business community was deliberately destructive of the environment, but they were clearly apathetic and that had to change immediately. As mild as the statements now seem, they caused a stir, coming from an establishment figure, an icon of the power elite, and a man famous for riding the greatest gas-guzzlers ever built. Perhaps as a result of being part of such profligate use of fuel, he was well ahead of the curve regarding the need for a national energy policy. "Any public transportation system must be designed to be converted to some other kind of fuel within thirty years."

From England, Neil flew east to India, joining Apollo 12 commander Pete Conrad to attend the Fédération Aeronautique International conference, meeting with the nation's president and prime minister, and speaking before the Indian parliament, Lok Sabha. The latter gave the men an unprecedented—for foreigners—standing ovation.

The Indians, though receptive and admiring of America's spacemen, had been like much of the Third World, relentlessly and successfully infused with Soviet misinformation and propaganda regarding space exploration. Even well over a year after the first moon landing, and with a second flawless trip complete, the average Indian's impression was that the Soviets were, in fact, well ahead in space technology, though they believed America had fooled the world into thinking the opposite was true through a cunning public-relations effort. *The Hindu,* India's national newspaper, stated the view flatly on November 24, 1970: "Though they have been well ahead in the space race, the Russians have been rather slow in the public-relations race." While it can't be said Armstrong and Conrad were able to set the record straight in a two-day visit, they obviously did make a very strong impression without attempting to overtly enter the propaganda fray.

"As emissaries of goodwill—and with peace on earth as their main theme—they made no attempt at all to introduce an element of cold war into the space race," wrote *The Hindu* after the astronauts' visit. "On the contrary, they spoke of the imperative need for understanding with such fervor—and from such a high pedestal—that all wars and revolutions, whether in Vietnam, West Asia or elsewhere seemed totally out of place in the heartwarming atmosphere of goodwill and peace exuded by them."

Most of all, Armstrong impressed the skeptical Indians on a human level. "And in this galaxy of space heroes, Neil Armstrong looked every bit a hero's hero—a man of great composure and equanimity with an almost computerized mind, who had all the answers on his fingertips about the intricacies of his historic moon-landing mission, and the many challenges ahead before man can master space technology. And looking at his shy and sensitive face, one could hardly believe that one was face to face with a man whose name will remain enshrined forever in the history of man."

One of the most contentious aeronautics-related issues before the new Congress during the winter of 1971 was the question of subsidizing and building a supersonic passenger plane. The British-French Concorde project was going ahead, and the Soviets had the supersonic TU-144 already in use. In fact, Neil had flown the plane during his last Russian visit and thought it a fine flying machine. Hearings on the planned U.S. version were scheduled before the Senate Appropriations Committee in early March and he was to be the star witness for the pro side of the issue.

Democratic committee chairman Allen Ellender of Louisiana spelled out what was expected of Armstrong in a February 23 letter. "Neil, this is extremely important because last year the Senate voted against the SST (Super Sonic Transport). This year we need *dramatic* evidence in order to reverse the current majority existing in the Senate." The letter said the committee had "obtained a Russian 'sales film' on the TU-144 that is very, very good. I would like you to present this film to the Senate Appropriations Committee and describe your personal impressions of the Russian supersonic transport."

Clearly, Neil was not expected to share any environmental concerns, noise-pollution problems, or economic practicalities, issues on which he was knowledgeable. Instead the committee wanted a cheerleader, not a role that came naturally to an engineer with an innately skeptical mindset.

In the end, the project was discontinued for a dozen reasons, ranging from clamorous environmental concerns, including rather unlikely fears the plane would virtually destroy earth's upper atmosphere, to the extremely *likely* worry that the noisy craft would make life even more miserable for people living on airport flight paths. But the death knell for the project was in the math: It was a multibillion-dollar project being proposed merely because our neighbors had one, and it would likely never turn a profit.

As the second anniversary of Apollo 11 approached, there were endless, almost nightly functions Neil and Jan were expected to attend, award ceremonies, official dinners at the White House, and State Department receptions. An endless stream of awards were offered, nearly all of which NASA pushed hard for their star astronaut to accept. They ranged in value from the genuinely prestigious Sylvanus Thayer Award—named for the fifth superintendent of the United States Military Academy, dubbed the "father of technology in America" for establishing the first modern engineering curriculum—to an ormolu water bucket from the Arlington, Virginia, Fire Department.

But an advantage to his position was access to NASA's fleet of jets, something Neil often took advantage of, whether just for the old thrill of soaring through the clouds or to visit old friends for a quick weekend. As a result, Neil had a way of showing up most anywhere in the country unexpectedly. His old Navy buddy Ken Danneberg was "surprised but certainly not shocked" to see Neil bounding down from a T-38 jet at the corporate airstrip near his oil-exploration business in central Colorado. "Neil just wanted to get away for the weekend and surprise us. We had been in the habit of getting together often, for golfing weekends, hunting or fishing. But since the buildup for Apollo 11, his life really wasn't his anymore in a number of ways. During those years Neil worked around the clock, and even when he was with you he was off in another world."

Neil spent a rare relaxed weekend at the Danneberg family home in Cherry Hills Village south of Denver, golfing and confiding that he was growing increasingly weary with Washington and the pressures of public life. There was no way he was going to accede to entreaties that he follow John Glenn's move into politics. In fact he was heading in quite the opposite direction, toward a private life far from the crowds, photo opportunities, and congressional hearings.

When Neil left to fly back to Washington, Danneberg's wife was surprised to find the guest room bed had been stripped. Later in the day, the Dannebergs discovered their two teenage daughters had shredded the sheets into little pieces. "They had set up a stand, like a lemonade stand, and had a good business going, selling souvenirs of Neil's visit," laughs Danneberg. "It was a great success. Eventually they sold out. I was afraid they were going to start cutting up the mattress."

Another Navy buddy, John Moore, the man who taught Neil to fly jets, paid a surprise visit shortly after his return from Colorado. "Neil was in a White House office, just around the corner from the president, working on a speech, when I came in," recalls Moore, who had retired from NASA and was well on his way to becoming a millionaire in the waterbed business. "I expected to find him bubbling with happiness at the regal surroundings, but it was immediately clear he had soured quite a bit on his life in Washington. He told me he was fed up with being Nixon's poster boy, wheeled out like a prize trophy when they wanted to impress a visiting dignitary. He felt as though he had signed on to be a greeter at a Las Vegas casino, like some punch-drunk fighter propped up to lure the heavy rollers. He told me he felt he had more than given NASA and the United States government its pound of flesh. He was at the end of his tether. That was the end of his Washington days."

Another visitor, University of Cincinnati administrator Richard Huston, feared the pressures of the job in Washington were causing Armstrong health problems. "He had a corner office overlooking the Capitol dome, and he mentioned something about watching pedestrians down the street and having trouble focusing on them. He said there was something wrong with his eyes. Then he joked that he wouldn't be able to pass the astronaut test if NASA found out."

The second anniversary of the moon landing passed in relative quietude. A congressional move to rename Washington's National Airport after Neil was stopped at his request, though several elementary schools quietly appropriated his name. In Wapakoneta, Ohio, no parades or ceremonies were planned, save a luncheon for Neil's mother and father. Ground had been broken for the million-dollar Neil Armstrong Air and Space Museum on the edge of town, just off Interstate 75. Built with funds raised by the Ohio Historical Society, the museum's heart was a spherical Astrotheater designed to show a twenty-minute film about manned space travel. And while the goal of the exhibitions celebrated all air and space pioneers from Ohio, including the Wright Brothers, John Glenn, and others, plainly the focus of the Neil Armstrong Museum was going to be Neil Armstrong. NASA, quite naturally, contributed substantially, donating moon rocks, the Gemini 8 capsule, whose malfunctioning thrusters nearly cost the lives of Neil and Dave Scott, a Dyna-Soar X-20A, spacesuits, and other hardware associated with the astronaut's career. Eventually, Russian friends donated artifacts of the Soviet space program, including a model of Sputnik, several Russian spacesuits, and items from the Mir space station.

The Armstrong family donated personal effects: his Schwinn

bicycle; report cards; the Aeronica Champion plane in which he received his first flying lessons; favorite books on the subject of aviation; and photo albums.

Neil was out of the country as the day of the anniversary passed, in Japan on Mount Fuji, attending an International Boy Scout Jamboree. As sponsor of his old outfit, the Upper Sandusky troop, that year, he was determined to be with the boys regardless of planned ceremonies, which he was coming to see as redundant and pointless. But since the subject was clearly on the minds of many of the scouts, he touched on it with an irreverent quip: "The purpose of all those space walks was to take out the garbage. What do you do with all those Tang wrappers?" He camped out with the boys despite heavy rains and minor mudslides, happily participated in musical numbers, and was carried in a parade on the shoulders of scouts proud to claim him as one of their own.

A year spent at NASA headquarters, punctuated with stints glad-handing for a White House that seemed increasingly besieged by a furious army of dissenters, and enraptured by skullduggery behind its heavily enameled doors, was more than enough.

He accomplished some important things at the agency in the field of aviation safety and instituted useful air-safety projects. Contacts with the Soviet cosmonauts and space officials seemed to have pushed both countries in the right direction, toward pooling their assets and knowledge for the peaceful exploration of space.

Not long after his departure from NASA, the Soviet news agency TASS announced that a mineral, newly discovered during an expedition in Mongolia's Gobi Desert, would be named Armstrongite, strong evidence of their respect for his achievements and efforts at space cooperation.

Disasters like the 1967 Apollo 1 fire were at least a great deal less likely to happen, and the extensive investigation of Apollo 13 he participated in was a worthwhile boost to program safety.

Like the Roman statesman Lucius Quinctius Cincinnatus, who, in 458 B.C., after rescuing the besieged consular armies on Mount Algidus, refused a proffered crown and returned to his farm, Armstrong was going to return to his roots as well, in Ohio. And, coincidentally, to the river town named for the great hero who, like Armstrong, eschewed the spoils of glory.

Neil's primary ambition on his forty-first birthday was to get on with his second career—teaching. As soon as he dropped a few hints that he wanted a professorship, offers of a position poured in, one even being a university presidency, which was precisely what he did not want; to use his celebrity to raise money. It would be worse than what he had been through in Washington.

Dr. Paul Herget, an early pioneer with the Vanguard space program and the Distinguished Service Professor of Astronomy at the University of Cincinnati as well as a trusted friend, urged him to consider an offer from his school as University Professor of Engineering, a broad interdisciplinary professorship. The professorship had a wide range, including a fundamental assignment in aerospace engineering and interdisciplinary work in geology, astronomy, physics, chemistry, psychology, biology, and medicine. Neil would work alongside Dr. Herget on astronomy projects and teach aircraft design, one of his lifelong passions, as well as develop a range of aeronautics projects.

While the job meant a sharp drop in salary from approximately $36,000 at NASA to $22,400, it freed him to accept lucrative consulting jobs, as well as seats on boards of directors, and occasional speeches for the then very steep fee of $3,500, which would have been impossible while he was at NASA. The extra income never made him rich, but it more than made up for the loss.

Once a contract was signed with the University of Cincinnati, Jan and Neil, along with Mark, then eight, and Rick, fourteen, began the search for a new home. The only place Jan truly longed for was Houston and the friends they had left behind, whom she missed terribly. But Neil had a dream of returning to the farm life he had left so many years ago, to gain privacy and solitude. An ideal property happened to be on the market, in Lebanon, Ohio, for $230,000, about thirty miles from the university. It was a 185-acre farm called Rivendell, guarded by thick copse of maple, walnut, and ash, with a huge nineteenth-century barn sporting a faded, hand-painted advertisement. There was a tall silo, several outbuildings, forty Hereford cows and their calves, and a starkly contrasting, ultra-modern glass-and-concrete house with a near–Frank Lloyd Wright design facing a man-made lake. It was a perfect retreat, both rustic and modern, a return to his far simpler past and yet forward-looking by design as well; even Jan came to love it.

The little town of Lebanon (population 10,500) was a sturdy community with roots two centuries deep, a good public school system, serviceable shopping, and a traditional Midwestern ethos of minding one's own business. It was a place where Armstrong and his family could pursue their interests in relative anonymity, safe and unmolested.

A decade later, addressing an Illinois farm bureau whose membership included his brother-in-law, Kenneth Shearon, Neil explained his disenchantment with big cities and what he had come to think of as big-city thinking. "I'm convinced that both the breadth and the details of our collective problems and progress are better understood in these heartland communities than they are in the big cities of the nation—particularly Washington. I was born on a farm, as were my father and his father before him, and they were wiped out more than once. It's not possible to farm without having an appreciation and understanding of risk."

It was a promising new beginning, but the first day at school was a crucible of fire, resembling a Hollywood premiere. Newsmen from around the world gathered on the sprawling campus north of Cincinnati, wielding boom mikes and cameras, blocking traffic with sound trucks; knots of curious students and faculty members gathered. The new professor walked quickly and purposefully past the shouting reporters, thin-lipped and determined, refusing to even acknowledge his tormentors, stepped into Rhodes Hall room 757 and pulled the door closed with a curt bang. Applied Aircraft Performance was in session.

"He was pretty nervous in his first class," David Burruss, a third-year engineering graduate student, one of the eighteen in the group, reported to the press fifty minutes later, "but that was only natural. When the class was over, the hall was still filled with reporters. I was the last one out. Professor Armstrong had his hand on the doorknob; he pushed us out as fast as possible and slammed the door shut again."

Once the rocky early days were over, and despite continued intrusions, including students standing on each other's shoulders to peep through his office window and occasional mob scenes from which he had to be extricated by security, Professor Armstrong turned out to be a popular, hands-on teacher. He devised special projects, including student-designed planes, and took favored students aloft in his own twin-engine Piper.

To his relief, students turned out to be "quite bright" despite dire warnings they were going to be desperately unprepared for college work and lacking vision or spark. "I think our students are quite bright.

The seniors I am teaching this year, I'd put against any, including my own senior class at Purdue." But he agreed that the verbal skills of many engineering students were woefully insufficient.

The new professor decorated his small Rhodes Hall office with reminders of his early career as a test pilot in the California desert rather than the space program, hanging color photographs of the X-15, a hang glider, the Dyna-Soar, and a homemade plane.

Watching the clamor accompanying Armstrong's first days at the university from a bemused distance was Dr. Henry J. Heimlich, who learned something about sudden fame from the buffeting he was to endure, a few years later, in wake of his introduction of the so-called Heimlich Maneuver, a simple innovative method to save choking victims, which rapidly became an international sensation and buzzword.

In the winter of 1972, when Armstrong joined the faculty, Heimlich was an associate clinical professor at the University of Cincinnati's College of Medicine, and Director of Surgery at Jewish Hospital in Cincinnati. He had been fascinated with the Apollo program and was particularly keen to learn how NASA scientists had dealt with keeping astronauts' spacesuits oxygenated and at a comfortable, constant temperature in the vacuum of space, where temperatures ranged from searing to frigid.

"It struck me that the space agency must have been very knowledgeable about oxygenating an individual, which had the potential for great medical applications," said Heimlich. "So I called to see Neil shortly after he settled in. We hit it off right away. The idea of mating the medical, surgical expertise with the high level of engineering Neil had worked on at NASA seemed a natural. One of my major areas of interest was in designing improved blood pumps for use in heart-lung machines and in artificial hearts and kidneys. The ones then available were all designed to duplicate the functioning of the human heart, which agitated the blood, damaging the fragile membrane of the red blood cells carrying hemoglobin. That flaw meant a patient's heart could be operated on for only a relatively short period of time, limiting the time allowed for corrective surgery.

"One day, shortly after our initial meeting, Neil walked into my office with a small package containing one of the few remaining Apollo moon packs. In it was the small pump they had devised to circulate water throughout a network of plastic tubes in a spacesuit. The Apollo program had ended—been scrapped—and apparently much of the equipment had been thrown away, lost, or damaged, so it was quite a find. As I examined the pump, I realized it was unique and quite brilliant in its simplicity."

The Apollo pump that so impressed Heimlich was designed with the same philosophy as the lunar landing module *Eagle* and all other equipment the astronauts' lives depended upon—with as few moving parts as possible. It was dual-chambered, with a rocking, electrically powered arm that raised and lowered a diaphragm in each chamber, emptying one and filling the other. In tests Heimlich and Armstrong commissioned using canine blood, the device exceeded their most optimistic expectations, damaging blood ten times less than conventional agitating pumps.

"What Neil had brought to us represented precisely the new concepts I was after: miniaturization, low energy consumption, and simplicity," Heimlich recalls.

Dr. Heimlich, Armstrong, and two other highly regarded scientists, Professor Dr. Edward A. Patrick, with a Ph.D. in electrical engineering as well as a medical degree, and University of Cincinnati special-projects vice president Dr. George Rieveschl, who discovered the first antihistamine for Parke-Davis Pharmaceuticals, decided to form an independently funded institute to study the possibilities they foresaw in the melding of space science and medicine. The result was the Institute of Engineering and Medicine, with Armstrong as director.

"When the project came to the attention of the president of the University of Cincinatti, George Harp, he signed on as well and we had our weekly meetings in the president's office from then on," says Heimlich.

The scope of the group's agenda and its portfolio were impressive—so impressive they stirred a wave of enmity among a large group of UC faculty members. Soon after the institute was formed, there was a tidal wave of protest from entrenched grant-dependent researchers.

"A half-dozen heads of engineering and medicine departments complained that the star power we had assembled would suck all the grant money away from them," said Dr. Heimlich. "They were outraged at the idea, and demanded it be stopped right away. We were all angry at the obvious self-serving motive behind their argument, but Neil very nearly walked out.

"'Look,' he said, 'we don't need this, I don't have any compunctions about walking away.'

"President Harp took a hard stand, saying 'Do you know how long it would take to bring these people together to work on such an important project at this university?' He shamed them into backing off. But we knew from the start we were not going to be terribly popular with the faculty."

Nevertheless, the small work group started immediately, with weekly lunch meetings that continued through six academic years.

"They were exciting meetings. We literally screamed with excitement; Neil would spring out of his seat to the blackboard to write something, then one of the others would add to it. The roof used to rock when we got together. The creativity and the way our ideas meshed was wonderful; the collaboration worked just as we had hoped, developing medical advances, combining technologies, and creating new ones. It was four men who got a lot out of each other intellectually, individually, and as a group."

One of the group's urgent concerns was heart-transplant technology. Early work in the field had shown some success transplanting human hearts, but in order for the recipient body to accept such a huge foreign intrusion, it was necessary to nearly destroy the immune system—with terrible consequences for the patient.

The institute studied and developed artificial hearts made of plastics and metals, as well as heart devices that could carry on the function of the heart from *outside* the body, using tubes no wider than the lead in a Number Two pencil to jet blood through the human system. Another breakthrough that worked splendidly was called the Heimlich Micro Track—also with a microthin oxygen tube with wings on the end that could be inserted through the nose directly into the lungs of a person with severely damaged trachea caused by cancer, black lung, emphysema, or other trauma.

"Patients we fitted with the device screamed with joy. Every breath had been a struggle for years; suddenly they could breath normally again. It is a highly efficient method of delivering oxygen. Previously as much as fifty percent was wasted; our method wasted virtually none, and the portable oxygen tank modeled after the Apollo device could fit in a large purse," recalled Heimlich.

During the years the men worked together, they also developed models for numerous artificial body parts, from tracheas to limbs, and explored innovative methods of oxygenating emphysema and cancer patients, allowing them to breathe better than ever before. Miniaturization was key to their work; just as the space program had reduced computers from room-sized to the size of a tabletop television, the institute sought to reduce the size and complexity of medical devices to reduce intrusiveness, and increase portability.

Armstrong also saw potential for the group's research to make deep-space travel and colonization practicable. In an essay published by *Saturday Review* magazine in August 1974, he proposed that travelers to distant planets, such as Saturn's largest moon, Titan, which has an atmosphere composed of methane, might consider surgical alteration. "If the oxygenator of the heart-lung machine could be miniaturized, it could be worn around the waist, surgically attached to the cardiovascular system, replacing both the lung and the need for breathing."

He pointed out that explorers of the giant planets Jupiter, Saturn, and Uranus would find their weight doubled due to the gravity the spheres exerted, making breathing or even moving about extremely difficult; only swimming would be unaffected by the increased gravity. "In a cabin filled with liquid, the body buoyancy would offset the burdensome weight, and the crew, equipped with their oxygenators and fluid-filled lungs, would move as freely as scuba divers on earth at a depth of fifteen feet."

"What we were doing was basic research," said Heimlich. "The ideas and techniques we developed contributed greatly over the years to medicine. But at the time we were ahead of the curve; new materials, particularly plastics that had yet to be developed, were essential to implementing many of our ideas. But in time that happened, and with some help from the blueprint laid out by our group, major strides were made in saving lives and improving the quality of life for people with severe cardiopulmonary problems."

Armstrong's colleagues and students at UC seemed to be trying during the ten years he taught there to peg him—without much success. Whenever they thought they had figured him out, he would in some way confound them.

Even Dr. Heimlich, who spent as much time with the former astronaut as anyone outside his family during the seventies, was often taken by surprise.

"The four of us, in our little group, went to Naples, Florida, for a few days to meet with the heads of a foundation considering offering funding for the Heimlich Micro Track. After a long day of work, Neil announced he was going for a swim in the Gulf of Mexico, just as the great ball of fiery sun was setting; a beautiful sight. I hadn't thought of

Neil as an athletic man; he occasionally played a game of golf with George Rieveschl, but that was about it as far as I knew, so I assumed he meant he was going to splash around in the surf."

To the doctor's amazement, Armstrong instead plunged into the pacific, azure gulf and swam toward the sun with strong, steady strokes, finally disappearing over the horizon.

"Neil was gone for over an hour; I was beginning to grow concerned, but he emerged from that long, long swim not even winded; it was quite a workout for a man in his mid-forties, particularly because his athletic side was totally unknown to those of us who thought we knew him quite well. Before we left Florida, he insisted on renting a swamp boat to take a ride deep into the Everglades; anything he hadn't done before he had a compulsion to experience."

Armstrong could also be something of an absent-minded professor. In one famous episode, running late for a meeting, Neil forgot to set the brake on his pickup truck and left the stick shift in neutral; minutes later, it rolled over a parking terrace and nearly flattened another professor's car. Less seriously, his pipe and tobacco pouch embossed in gold with the Apollo 11 mission emblem were lost and returned by campus security numerous times.

In February 1974, as the fifth anniversary of Apollo 11 approached, NASA's public-affairs people began cranking up the hype machine, preparing to remind the world once more of its crowning achievement.

Assistant administrator John Donnelly drew up a memo suggesting Neil be asked to take part in just three major events: the CBS *Walter Cronkite Space Special,* an ABC space special, and the dedication of a stained-glass window at Washington's National Cathedral with a space theme. Donnelly wrote, "You might remind Neil that I spoke to him several weeks ago about his involvement in the fifth Apollo 11 anniversary and that at that time he indicated he'd make himself available for certain special events. I assured him that we wouldn't ask him to do a month long dog-and-pony show, but would appreciate his cooperation in activities we thought offered good mileage."

Two weeks later, Neil responded that he liked the idea of the National Cathedral ceremony, would appear on Cronkite's show, but drew the line at appearing on an ABC show, purportedly devoted to the anniversary but billed *The Wide World of Entertainment.*

Certainly, he was reluctant each time a round-figure year spurred a new celebration, but for events that seemed appropriate Armstrong could be counted on to shoulder more than his fair share of the cere-monial burden.

"How long must it take before I cease to be known as a space-man?" he wondered to a UC public-relations officer briefing him on the most recent gaggle of requests for interviews. But it was impossible to deny that the reason he was so hectored by the public was its infatu-ation with him. Lloyd's Bank in London held a contest in the spring of 1976 asking sixteen- to eighteen-year-olds—who would have been just nine to eleven when *Eagle* landed—to name the American they wanted to meet most. Compared to such icons of the day as Robert Redford, Raquel Welch, Bob Dylan, Timothy Leary, and Jimmy Carter, Neil "stuck out a mile," according to a bank official.

Even on home turf at UC, colleagues spoke of treatment they wit-nessed when out in public with Neil that was totally beyond the pale; intrusions by strangers interrupting his meals with requests for auto-graphs, or sometimes approaching without a word and touching him, grabbing his hand, grabbing his shoulder, and even attempting to kiss him. On several occasions while dining at the Skyline Chili Parlor, near UC, when autograph seekers went over the line, he stood up, looking damaged, walked out of the restaurant despite having taken perhaps only a bite or two from his meal, and waited in his car reading until his friends finished their lunch.

Another galling irritant, having nothing to do the curse of fame, was the creeping intrusion of politics into campus life, which he deftly tried to avoid. Since joining the faculty he had been importuned to join the nascent union movement, which a large number of younger instructors saw as a way to continue the process of transforming academia they had begun as students in the sixties. Neil was as adamant about not joining as he was about refusing to speak about the reasons he didn't want to join. Even within family discussions, Neil was uncomfortable talking politics. In fact, when his mother, Viola, was asked about her son's opin-ions on politics during the Apollo 11 mission, she said, "I don't know; he's never talked about it."

For the whole of the decade he taught at UC, it was an issue that bubbled beneath the surface, sometimes boiling over in angry con-frontations at faculty gatherings. Though he refused to speak about it publicly or privately, friends believe it led to his gradual disillusion with teaching and rather abrupt departure on New Year's Day, 1980. While public espousal of causes seems to have been anathema to

Armstrong, he allowed a snippet of a lecture he had given to be published in *Reader's Digest* in June 1976. In typical *Digest* fashion, it was so truncated as to almost make no sense, but the gist of the article was that creativity needn't be stifled by reasonable government regulation. "The forest of restrictions that would have confounded our forefathers"—requiring manufacturers to conform to environmental standards, farmers to limit the use of pesticides, etc.—represented an "erosion of personal freedom" and "some decline in opportunity. Nevertheless, new challenges to our creativity always seem to arise: curing cancer, turning arid wastelands into fertile fields, extracting energy from wind and tide." The message was: All the new regulations that grated on the progeny of Midwestern frontier farmers made sense to a guy whose dad was a lifetime civil servant and whose dreams had been made real by a many-billion-dollar government outlay. It was the natural philosophical evolution of a moderate.

Despite the mantra that Neil was virtually "invisible," principally because he skipped events such as the first annual reunion of astronauts at Johnson Space Center in Houston during the late summer of 1978, and adamantly refused to participate in what would years later come to be known as Oprah-style self-confessional interviews, he was actually very engaged, both with his local community in southeast Ohio and in the world at large. Long involved with the Cincinnati Museum of Natural History, he served on its board of trustees and later accepted the post of board chairman. He worked to upgrade the planetarium; he cut the ribbon reopening the museum. He attended the twentieth anniversary of NASA at Cape Canaveral in the fall of that year, and at a reception hosted by President Jimmy Carter received the Congressional Space Medal along with Frank Borman, John Glenn, Alan Shephard, Charles Conrad, and, posthumously, Gus Grissom. Later, he even hosted a half-hour television show broadcast on five Ohio television stations to raise funds for United Way. During breaks from teaching he traveled all over the world, delivering lectures on the space program's history and future. All things considered, a lot of exposure for a hermit.

Neil's refusal to become a regular media talking head, reeling off half-baked opinions on myriad subjects, grated on some inside and outside the space program, who felt the first man on the moon owed it to NASA to spend the rest of his life in the limelight.

"I try to fulfill my obligations, but I simply don't comment on subjects where I'm not competent," Neil said by way of explanation. "People are a third-rank category of things to talk about. Someone once said, 'Great men talk about ideas; good men talk about things; and everyone else talks about other people.'"

Despite all the public appearances and cheerleading for the agency Armstrong did, his critics were still shrilly reproachful, even thirty-one years after the moon landing. Fellow astronaut Gordon Cooper, in his memoir, *Leap of Faith,* wrote: "I also feel strongly that the choice of Neil Armstrong to be the first American to set foot on the moon was greatly influenced by the fact he was a civilian pilot. . . . NASA later paid dearly for its selection. After his walk on the moon . . . Neil came home, sat for a news conference or two, then quit NASA and became a recluse rather than take part in NASA's grand plan to milk the event for all the public goodwill possible. In this regard, Armstrong was the opposite of John Glenn, who, come to think of it, would have made a *great* first man on the moon."

Chapter Nineteen

Armstrong has always maintained that the outsized attention paid to anniversaries of the moon landing was silly and meaningless. So on the ninth he penned a poem about the event as silly as the celebrations.

My Vacation by Neil Armstrong

Nine summers ago, I went for a visit,
To see if the moon was green cheese.
When we arrived, people on earth asked: "Is it."
We answered: "No cheese, no bees, no trees."

One of the most remarkable things about Neil Armstrong's career is the fact that he managed, for the most part, to escape even minor injury. He has long insisted the reason is a lifelong habit of careful study and determinedly risk-averse regimens: "I was a test pilot, not an adventurer." The one notable exception to the great personal safety record happened, not in space or even aboard a plane, but in his barn, and it was an excruciating nightmare of an accident that but for a typically composed response on his part would have cost a permanent lack of agility.

It was a crisp Friday morning, November 10, 1978; Neil was in a hurry to finish farm chores in the grand old barn and get to class at UC. He and his son Rick had been to auction to buy new heifers; the rest of the morning was devoted to preparing for the new arrivals. There were bales of hay and bags of feed still stacked in the back of the pickup; these he hurriedly tossed aside. He leaped from the pickup truck's bed, left arm held high for balance, as he had a thousand times, when he was suddenly snagged, like a stunned fish on a hook. A long gnarled and rusty nail, jutting from the barn door at a diabolically perfect angle, had speared his wedding ring so accurately it was as though it had been planned. As he helplessly arced toward the hay-strewn floor his arm snapped in the opposite direction, ring welded to the nail. For a moment of searing agony, the skin cleanly stripped away from the base of his finger all the way to the nail, followed by a nanosecond during which his entire weight hung by a flesh-bare ring finger; then, with a snap, blood vessels, nerves, and bone were jaggedly ripped away and Neil was free. The nail was finished with him; he fell in a heap on the muddy floor.

Blood spurted sickeningly, and the pain was like a vise; but he wasn't going anywhere without his finger. On his knees, desperately holding the gushing, mutilated hand higher than his heart, he searched in the riot of hay, manure, and dirt for his missing finger. Methodically he swept over the area, finally locating the severed finger that had been part of him for forty-eight years, plucked it up, and cradled it in his good palm, a feeling that must be like no other.

He staggered toward home, trailing blood, and called the local hospital, Bethesda North, explaining his situation succinctly, in clear, dull tones, as a pilot facing a tricky situation not in the rule book would do. Told to pack the finger in ice and stanch the bleeding, he complied precisely, then waited for an ambulance to reach the rural retreat. Some time later, an emergency medical services crew arrived and found the patient "composed and calm," with a wan, almost apologetic smile.

Dr. Robert Slagle, a plastic and reconstructive surgeon at Bethesda North Hospital in the Cincinnati suburbs, had been alerted to the former astronaut's condition and was waiting in the emergency room when he arrived. One look at the wound told him it was a job for Dr. Joseph E. Kutz and his skilled surgical team at Jewish Hospital in nearby Louisville, Kentucky. Kutz had been successfully replanting arms, legs, feet, hands, and scalps since 1965. Armstrong's wound was contained and cleansed, and he was given sufficient pain-blocking medication for the 115-mile trip from North Bethesda to Jewish Hospital.

In the thirteen years he had been reconnecting severed body parts, Dr. Kutz, then fifty years old, had seen many mangled limbs, but Neil's was particularly challenging. The majority of amputations are done with power saws, butcher's equipment, factory metal cutters—machines that at least make a clean, even cut. Neil's finger looked as though it had been lost to the maw of a beast; it was ripped, then raggedly torn off at the palm. "Prognosis was poor," recalled the surgeon. Kutz and his colleagues, Drs. Tom Woolfe and Tsmin Tasi, set to their difficult task Friday evening, first applying a regional pain blocker in the left arm, sedating him completely. Then, wearing magnifying glasses, they rejoined the bone. Beginning the extraordinarily delicate work of reconnecting tiny veins and nerves, the surgeons turned to a specially developed microscope. A nerve had to be removed from further up his arm, then spliced into the amputated finger and attached to the hand's intricate neurologic network. After three and a half hours of tedious surgery, the finger was reattached. Ostensibly, the surgery was a success, but it took five days before they would know for certain, and six to eight months to know if Neil would regain function in his ring finger. Kutz admitted that he had lost some reattached digits as late as six or seven days after an operation.

The following Thursday, Armstrong spoke to representatives of the world's press, who had quickly descended upon Louisville when news of the accident was made public. Dressed in a suit, his left arm swaddled in bandages, he explained what had happened, and held his left arm aloft with his right. In answer to a barage of questions, Neil insisted he did not appreciate the irony in almost losing a finger to a barn after returning from the moon, leaving little doubt that he found the idea rather trite. Dr. Katz said that he saw no reason why Neil shouldn't be able to begin wearing his wedding ring again. "I don't think so," the former astronaut responded quickly, eliciting nervous laughter. Despite suffering the "most severe" injury of his life, he felt "no substantial pain" and he was planning to return to work as soon as possible. The press conference concluded with an archetypal observation: "It wasn't a pleasant stay, but it was an interesting one."

By 1979, he had cut back to just one aerospace-engineering class per week and some research on "advanced configuration for aircraft." Instead, he was getting involved in business pursuits, including becoming a spokesman and research consultant for Chrysler, agreeing to appear in a $600,000 two-minute car advertisement set to run during the January 1979 Super Bowl XIII, as well as a two-page newspaper advertisement appearing in fifty newspapers. "My role will be as an outside voice in research and development and advertising." It was an announcement that perplexed and bemused both friends and the public.

Despite what most thought, however, Chrysler wasn't Neil's first commercial endorsement; it was his third. Armstrong's initial ad was in 1974, when his picture appeared in a full-page advertisement in the *Wall Street Journal* for General Time Corporation's Quartzmatic watch, extolling its accuracy. The quotes beneath his name said: "I knew that someday personal watches and clocks would use the same technology we used in Apollo. But I didn't realize it would happen so soon."

When advertising agents for the Dean Witter investment firm approached Neil's sister, June Armstrong, a registered nurse, to appear in an advertisement playing off the family name, he encouraged her to accept the easy money, seeing no harm in it. The ad was headlined WHAT IF YOUR NAME IS ARMSTRONG AND YOU'VE NEVER SET FOOT ON THE MOON? If there was any doubt left, the copy spelled it out, saying "Neil's sister, June, found a firm where you don't have to fly through the galaxies to be treated like a star."

In an alternately teasing and combative interview with *Cincinnati Post* reporter Tim Graham a few weeks later, Armstrong gave something of an explanation; it was a rare gesture. "I've worked in some commercial arrangements on and off, on kind of a modest basis. I've taken the position that, if the right situation came along, where I thought I could be of significant help and it would not jeopardize my honesty . . . One of the principal aspects for deciding to go with Chrysler is the engineering aspect. They have a long history of solid engineering, and that's the basis on which they approached me to represent their organization. And I have to be honest and say that it was kind of a challenge to help Chrysler get out of the hole. They lost a bundle of money last year, and I think it is very important to the country as a whole that we not be a one-automobile-company country."

The Chrysler campaign was set in motion when the fabled auto man Lee Iacocca, father of the hyper-successful Ford Mustang, quarreled with his boss, Henry Ford II, and ankled to the rapidly tanking Chrysler. His first edict was for the company's ad agency, Young & Rubicam, to produce a list of famous engineers who might be persuaded to endorse Chrysler's products. "The first name was Neil Armstrong's and they went no further," said Frank Wiley, Chrysler's head of public relations.

Chrysler publicist Bernard "Moon" Mullins added, "We wanted somebody who would add credibility, and his opinions are certainly well respected. Neil refused to do it based on Apollo 11; he wanted to make sure nobody would dress him up in a spacesuit."

When Armstrong was contacted by Iacocca in December 1978, it was a propitious moment. Neil and Jan's eldest son, Rick, was in college, and Mark would be there soon, a squeeze on any middle-class budget. The farm, which had been Neil's dream, was proving to be a burden financially; the fantasy that it would actually be a money-making proposition was just that—it was a money pit, and Jan had been bridling for some time. The fortune that was offered Neil, more than a million dollars by some accounts, would ease their lives, pay college tuition, and make retirement more comfortable. The prospect even encouraged Jan to gather brochures for the ocean voyage she had longed to take.

Neil had, in fact, been pleased with Chrysler's engineering for Apollo. Buick had been there first, but Chrysler made a major contribution and he had staked his life on it—successfully. So he saw no ethical quandary pitching for the troubled corporation. In addition, there was the fact he was going to be much more than a presenter, shilling, as Ricardo Montelban had done, "rich Corinthian leather." His ads were going to be about engineering, and, according to Frank Hoag, Chrysler's director of advertising, Armstrong would be "a partner, a member of Chrysler's research and development team, the top-level management-engineering group looking into future technologies."

The ad campaign, rolled out on the biggest television day of the year, Super Bowl Sunday, was certainly understated and restrained. Neil appeared, unannounced in a dark suit, admittedly portlier and with slightly receding hair, but relaxed (if a bit clench-jawed), and displayed the same boyish charm the world remembered. Surrounded by Chrysler's new line on a bare stage, he walked from car to car, then crossed his arms and said: "Long ago, I learned that all engineering is a matter of designing machines to solve problems. In the Apollo program, I acquired a respect for the ability of the Chrysler Corporation engineering to help solve the incredible problems of space travel. I'm convinced Chrysler engineering has solved many of the problems that concern all drivers. By pioneering the use of front-wheel drive in small, American-built cars, they've given them a new kind of control and handling. For bigger cars, they have engines and transmissions that are right for the times. Sport coupes have been given clean, aero-dynamic design that slices through the wind."

Terry Bradshaw, the other hero of the day, led the Pittsburgh Steelers to a stunning 35-to-31 victory over the Dallas Cowboys; Roger Staubach completed seventeen of thirty passes for four touchdowns. But the postgame buzz was about Armstrong, provoking top-rated *60 Minutes* to replay the ad, gratis, during a segment about the former astronaut's sudden emergence as a Chrysler spokesman: a tremendous bonus for the company that money couldn't have bought.

Back at Rivendell Farm, Chrysler's new line, plus experimental and developing models, arrived for Neil to drive, contemplate, and try to improve upon over the next several years. Eventually he worked on newly created computer models as well as, eventually, becoming a serious automotive engineer, with a good impact on the company's product.

But despite the efforts of Iacocca and Armstrong, the staggering industrial giant, which had once manufactured 25 percent of all auto-mobiles in the world and produced half a million trucks for the United States armed forces during World War II, was teetering on the brink of insolvency. The following year, 1980, showed a promising upswing, but Chrysler was forced to turn to the government, hat in hand, asking for a $1.5 billion bailout that a majority of Americans opposed, feeling the corporation's lack of foresight rightly spelled its doom. Chrysler had continued manufacturing gas-guzzling behemoths years after it was obvious that Japanese- and German-style compacts were the wave of the future. Nevertheless, President Jimmy Carter felt the economy, not to mention the country's self-esteem—hobbled at the beginning of the decade by the Vietnam quagmire, slammed by the oil shocks, and humiliated by the Iran hostage crisis as the seventies mercifully ended—couldn't stand the trauma of watching one of its signature industrial giants die. He pushed the loan-guarantee legislation through Congress.

The reaction in some quarters to Chrysler's dire straits and Neil's very public role in it was astonishment and withering scorn. The *Times* newspaper of Huntsville, Alabama, home of Marshall Space Center, where Saturn rockets were assembled, lashed out at the former astronaut's sudden reappearance on the world stage as a car salesman. "Neil Armstrong, the last American hero. Who would have thought he would have wound up making television commercials? His place in history was secure. So why, ten years later, does the now-portly figure of Neil Armstrong, dressed this time in a three-piece suit, come marching into my living room from the television screen? Did they offer him Fort Knox? Does he owe somebody a favor? Whatever the reason, there is something off-color when a genuine people's choice starts commercializing himself. When an institution sells himself to the highest bidder, I become narrow-minded and suspicious. Maybe the commander's agent can get him a spot as guest host on *Saturday Night Live*. They could probably get lots of laughs making fun of the space program's greatest moment."

A University of Cincinatti colleague told *Newsweek* he had upbraided Armstrong: "Heroes don't sell cars; what the hell is going on?"

In the opinions of some, he had become, not a man with a family to support, but an institution who should know better than to dust himself off and walk off the pedestal. Nevertheless, the campaign worked; Chrysler's retooled line built a head of steam, finally selling like never before. Just over two years later, Chairman Iacocca proudly paid back the $1.5 billion loan in full, seven years ahead of schedule. Armstrong made it clear he was proud of Chrysler and of the role he had played in turning its fortunes around.

Armstrong was spreading his wings, at age forty-eight, testing high-speed business jets for Harry Combs and accepting seats on the boards of a half-dozen big corporations, including Marathon Oil, United Airlines, Taft Broadcasting, and United Telephone. But flying was still clearly his passion. Since the mid-seventies, he had been associated with Combs's Gates Learjet company. By 1979—with many modifications and improvements, including an innovative new wing designed by fellow Purdue engineering student James Raisbeck, which slowed the hot jet on takeoff and landing, adding greatly to safety and control—he was ready to set some records for business flight. Taking off from Kill Devil Hills, North Carolina, in the shadow of the Wright Brothers' test field, he set five world records, including highest sustained altitude (51,000 feet) as well as one for fastest speed reaching that elevation.

Neil's brother Dean was in the auto business most of his life, heading up a General Motors transmission plant in Anderson, Illinois, in the late seventies. With the world reeling from energy shocks and Middle East chaos threatening America's supply of affordable oil, Dean believed that deep-well oil exploration was going to boom in promising fields and offshore locations all over the world that had been deemed too expensive to tap while cheap oil gushed from Arab spigots. The idea made sense to Neil as well; having finally severed his ties to the University of Cincinnati, he signed on as a partner in Caldwell International, Ltd., as Dean's partner, consultant, and overseas sales promoter.

Before leaving teaching and research posts at UC, Neil agreed to accept an honorary doctorate and to address the university's graduating class of 1980, which for the first time anywhere would include students who had earned a bachelor's degree in the subject of cable television. With the twenty-four-hour-a-day Music Television channel set to debut the next year, and a virtual explosion of other niche programming on the way, it was a prescient degree to hold.

In his university farewell speech before an audience of more than twenty thousand, Neil exhorted the new graduates to use their newly acquired knowledge to search for truth. "The simplest explanation is usually the best, but usually the most difficult to find." He urged them to learn the difference between fact and opinion and to continue the work and achievements of their parents' generation. And he asked the graduates to applaud their parents for sacrificing to send them through college. "They've come to applaud you, and I suggest, if you are so inclined, this would be a good opportunity for you to applaud them." They did, and then gave their former teacher a thunderous ovation.

The early fall of 1983, the twenty-fifth anniversary of NASA's founding, marked another milestone in America's annals of space exploration. Dutifully, Armstrong consented to narrate film clips on Bob Hope's NBC tribute to the space agency. It was yet another very public event that ironically stimulated news editors to dispatch reporters to Lebanon, Ohio, in search of the "moonwalker recluse." And, fittingly, quotes were found to back up the prepared headlines. "I see his office across the street, and I'll be damned if I ever see him," puzzled Mayor James LeFevers, as though Armstrong was the stealth citizen. "You won't find anyone in this town who knows Neil Armstrong personally."

Numerous other Lebanon neighbors offered contradictory accounts, including golf pro Dick James, who played nine holes of golf with Neil every Wednesday for a decade: "He really wants to live like a normal person. I tried to talk about the moon when he first got here, but you could tell he just didn't want to hear it. He'll talk all night about his kids and other things." And a neighbor, an Ohio state representative, talked about his charity work. But the headline, a falsehood attached to his legacy with Krazy Glue, would never come loose.

In truth, Neil continued to explore. Armstrong and Sir Edmund Hillary, the conqueror of Mount Everest, were about as well-traveled as any men on earth, but neither had planted their boots on the North Pole. So when an offer came from a Colorado adventure-travel agency to join twelve amateur explorers, who paid $10,000 apiece for the opportunity, both men eagerly agreed. For Hillary, making the trip was something of an explorer's triple crown, making him the only man to have stood at both the North and South Poles and at the summit of Mount Everest. His successive journeys represented a time-line of transportation technology; he had climbed Mount Everest on his feet, rode a farm tractor to the South Pole, and flew to the North Pole.

Admittedly, the eight-day plane journey was nothing that hadn't been done before many times, and Armstrong and Hillary were little more than passengers, chosen because their presence added cachet to the pricy trip. "I'll just relax and enjoy the view," said Sir Edmund of the "so-called adventure."

A Boeing 737 lifted the small party from Edmonton, Alberta, north to the Arctic Circle, where they landed on runways made of ice at Resolute Bay. The stinging blasts of cold impressed even Hillary, who thought the primitive quarters resembled a construction camp.

Next morning, the group set out on Twin Otters fitted with skis, small propeller-driven aircraft specially designed for frigid, mountainous, extreme climes. Bouncing on the powerful Arctic air currents that had the Otters hungrily biting frigid air for purchase, they flew into the sharp, eerie light that seemed to come from below, like light reflected through a Lucite table. The first leg of the route to the true North Pole, aided by sophisticated navigational guidance equipment to pinpoint the spot, took the group over the majestic mountains of Ellesmere Island to a fuel stop on Lake Hazen, north of Greenland.

The intrepid group clambered over ridges of tortured ice and up a steep snowy slope, where warm yellow light bathed crisp snow around a Jamesway, the Quonset hut–shaped structure used in Arctic and Antarctic exploration. Inside, it was possible to take a full breath without the biting sting of protest from insulted lungs.

Settling in for the night, Armstrong and Sir Edmund were able to huddle and "talk at some length . . . about opportunity and adventure," as Hillary remembered the evening. "I very much liked his relaxed personality, and when I rather naively asked him how he had been chosen to be the first man to stand on the moon, he answered, 'Luck! Just luck!' I had a definite feeling that it might have been a little bit more than that."

The meeting between the men, near-contemporaries in age, Sir Edmund being just eleven years older, has an interesting parallel in the time Neil spent with another man he admired, Charles Lindbergh. He was certainly never able to spend time with Lindbergh in his element—Lindbergh opened the era of transatlantic travel three years before Armstrong's birth—but Lindbergh was present at Cape Kennedy to breakfast with Neil as he prepared for his flight to the moon, lending a fine symmetry to the careers of three of the twentieth century's great explorers.

Armstrong's acquaintance with Lindbergh had led to the establishment of a memorial fund to benefit fellowships in conservation and science; now he joined Hillary in working to establish a Special Olympics in Nepal along with the organization's founder, Eunice Kennedy Shriver. The former astronaut was always aware that his signature or likeness on an object lent it an out-of-proportion value. Since that was so, whether he cared for the concept or not, he had zealously guarded the asset—in 1995 by successfully suing Hallmark Cards for issuing a "The Eagle Has Landed" Christmas-tree ornament—in hopes of using it for a good purpose. Sir Edmund's Special Olympics, which encourages athletics in children with physical disabilities, seemed a perfect use for the resource. The immediate hope for the project was to bring a group of Nepalese children around the world to Yale University, in New Haven, Connecticut, to participate in the international competition. The cost was high, $50,000 to $60,000, so the program would need extra help. Neil pitched in by signing moon-landing posters, which along with posters from celebrities including hockey legend Gordon Howe and actress Goldie Hawn quickly raised the money.

Early the following morning, the group woke to the whir of heat fans deicing their planes and prepared for the last leg of the journey.

Another Otter joined them, this one filled to capacity with forty-four-gallon drums of fuel. At the next stop, on a large slab of pack ice in the Arctic Ocean, the fuel was painstakingly hand-pumped into the Otters' engines.

Homing in closer to the pole, they stopped one last time for resupply on a large chunk of ice dotted with huts—a United States intelligence base monitoring the flow of Soviet submarines under the polar icecap.

Soon the pole was in sight, which sent a frisson of excitement through rookie and professional explorers alike. It is a unique place on the planet that has long fascinated pilots; even the most sophisticated navigational gyros have a very difficult time pinpointing a plane's location at the pole because longitude and latitude lines converge and all directions become south. Pilots only half jokingly refer to the phenomenon as the "plane flying up its own tail." To avoid suddenly tossing that particular spanner in the gyroscopic works, commercial planes flying over the pole, particularly flights from New York to Hong Kong, which come very close, carefully skirt the exact spot. Another anomaly was that looking out the right side of the plane was darkness. It was nighttime on that side of the world; on the other side, to the left, it was day.

"It was hard to believe," Hillary recalled in awe, "that the ice was only twelve feet thick and beneath that was fourteen hundred feet of ocean. Somebody produced a bottle of champagne and poured a little into glasses for Neil and me. Before we could even wet our lips, the champagne froze solid." The temperature was fifty degrees below zero Fahrenheit.

Chapter Twenty

In the mid-eighties there seemed a reason to spend a bit more time "in the barrel." Ronald Reagan was the first president in well over a decade to make serious proposals for new NASA funding and new space initiatives, including an ambitious plan to build a permanent manned space station, to consider a base on the moon, and to journey to Mars. More controversially, Reagan proposed a space-based missile-defense system that would react to the launch of an enemy ICBM anywhere in the world, launch in a split-second, and annihilate the intruder harmlessly high in the stratosphere. To relieve concerns of the Soviet Union that the defense system was intended to disable their offense while the U.S. launched an attack, Reagan promised to share the technology, insuring mutual safety. "It's not about war, it's about peace. It isn't about retaliation, it's about prevention," he said.

The idea was immediately mocked by an incredulous press as a harebrained "Star Wars" scheme, suggesting that the doddering old president had been bamboozled by his military-industrial complex friends or had spent too much time watching the George Lucas film.

Knowing a good deal about trajectory, guidance, and rendezvous, Armstrong was less skeptical about the possible efficacy of missile defense, but had concerns nevertheless. "I would hope that we don't have actual gunfights and fast draws in space. But I find no difficulty personally with the ethics of providing a shield when the other fellow has a sword. I think the military feels it's their obligation to use any technology possible, within the framework of international law, to preserve the sovereignty of their own nation."

Armstrong had been appointed by Reagan to serve on the National Commission on Space—a group of scientists, teachers, aerospace business executives, and other experts on the space program. The commission held public hearings in fifteen locations around the country during the fall of 1985, and reported the views of people from all walks of life on the question: What should be the nation's space priorities for the period ending fifty years hence, in 2035?

Exploration, like life, is replete with ironies, and the winter of 1985–86 presented a sterling example. Nineteen eighty-five ended as commission members prepared a glowing report entitled "Pioneering the Space Frontier: United States National Commission on Space," a blueprint to build a commercial "highway to space," anchored by a chain of stations dotting the sky like rest stops on an interstate, leading to self-sufficient "long-duration closed-ecosystem" colonies on the moon and Mars. Regular service would be provided by aerospace craft that would take off like conventional planes, fly to the outer reaches of the atmosphere, then use an auxiliary rocket engine to achieve orbital insertion. Dubbed the Scramjet, the prototype design engine inhaled and greatly compressed air, eliminating the need to carry many tons of liquid oxygen.

The ambitious outline sought nothing less than to free "humankind to move outward from Earth, as a species destined to expand to other worlds . . . to stimulate individual initiative and free enterprise in space . . . [to] create new wealth on the space frontier to benefit the entire human community, by combining the energy of the Sun with materials left in space during the formation of the Solar System."

Various proposed projects were estimated to cost about $25 billion a year by 2000, then rise to perhaps $40 billion by 2030, assuming 25 percent of the budget would be funded by allied nations. Economic benefit to the nation was envisioned as parallel to the "pulling through" technology that emerged from the World War II era. As jet propulsion, antibiotics, synthetic rubber, and computers had spurred America's high-growth industries during the sixties and seventies, space technology would benefit it during the twenty-first century.

The commission saw science as another huge beneficiary of its promising such leaps forward as thirty-day weather forecasts with 95 percent accuracy, earthquake predictions with twenty-four-hour and fifty-mile accuracy, gravitational waves man could surf to deep space, links between solar activity and our weather understood, and new semiconductors and fuels created in the perfect vacuum and zero-gravity atmosphere of space.

The ideas that were going to be put forth in the report came not just from the members of the board, but from thousands of people who attended the fifteen forums held around the country, from letters and users of the nascent e-mail technology, as well as from a mountain of responses to a tear-out questionnaire published in *Parade* magazine, the popular Sunday newspaper supplement.

On a blustery Friday in December 1985, Neil attended a party in a converted hangar at Dulles Airport outside Washington given by the Aero Club to celebrate the eighty-second anniversary of the Wright Brothers' first successful flight. Space-travel supporter Vice President George Bush and celluloid space hero William Shatner were in attendance, along with many government and industry leaders of the aerospace industry. Less than a hundred years after man's first tenuous baby steps toward space, a serious plan was about to be published by a presidential commission to colonize Mars, a planet fifty million miles distant. The only dark cloud on the horizon as champagne glasses clinked in the drafty hangar was an indictment against NASA administrator James Beggs charging him with defrauding the government, an embarrassment the agency would easily survive.

More than fifteen years after the launch of Apollo 11, the throngs that had jammed the Cape Canaveral area to witness the blastoff were long gone, replaced by a relative handful of locals and tourists who happened to be visiting the area. On January 28, 1986, an explosion in the sky over northern Florida sent shockwaves through the world, threatened to destroy NASA, the space program, and badly hurt confidence in manned spaceflight. Just seventy-three seconds after a picture-perfect launch into a clear blue sky on a chilly morning, onlookers stared in mute agony as *Challenger* Shuttle Flight 51-L exploded in a compact red fireball ten miles downrange, cleaving into two parts, briefly continuing its doomed trajectory, then slowing sickeningly and plunging into the sea.

A particular poignance to the tragedy was that among the seven crew members was the first private citizen to fly on a shuttle mission:

Christa McAuliffe, a fresh-faced New Hampshire schoolteacher and author of a winning "Teacher in Space" essay contest.

As the explosion was repeated endlessly on cable television, it became obvious that the shuttle disaster was viewed by the American public as far worse than a mere routine tragedy, like a commercial plane crash. NASA was a touchstone for the culture. Not only was it at the heart of the ubiquitous query, "If we can put a man on the moon, why can't we————?" It was also the salve for the nation's sixties traumas; it had restored Americans' faith in government competence and our "can-do" mythos. Its sudden failure, and the stink of corruption and slipshod disregard for the lives of seven noble American pioneers, was a national body blow.

Sensing this, the Reagan government quickly assembled a blue-ribbon panel to investigate the disaster, with vast investigative powers that would completely supersede NASA's authority.

The following day, President Regan addressed the stunned nation: "It's been almost a week since our nation and families stood together and watched *Challenger* slip beyond our grasp. The memories of that moment will be with us always, as will the memories of those brave Americans who were aboard. The death of the astronauts and the destruction of Space Shuttle *Challenger* will forever be a reminder of the risks involved with space exploration. As we move away from that terrible day, we must devote our energies to finding out what happened and how it can be prevented from happening again. The crew of the *Challenger* took the risks and paid the ultimate price because they believed in the space program. They were excited by the mystery of what is beyond the earth and [by] the limitless possibilities of space exploration. They knew the dangers they faced. Yet despite those dangers, they chose to go forward, not reluctantly, but with thumbs up."

Michael Collins expressed what other experts knew but hesitated to say publicly: The disaster had probably been inevitable. "The test pilot in me was not surprised when the *Challenger* blew up. I have been expecting something like this for twenty years, but knowing it's going to happen doesn't make the moment any less painful. On the contrary. I feel like I am part of a family that has lost seven children and will lose more. Anyone who has lived with rockets understands the awesome power produced by machinery churning away at very high temperatures, pressures, and velocities. A thin and fragile barrier separates combustion from explosion. Astronauts understand this very well. But I wonder if Christa or her family really grasped the seriousness of riding in the gigantic pile of machinery on Launch Pad 39. Ride one of the beasts and you get a different perspective."

The commission chairman was the well-respected former Nixon administration Secretary of State William Rogers, who had escaped even a suggestion of complicity in the Watergate scandals; the vice chairman was Armstrong. Already serving without compensation on the Space Commission, he dutifully accepted the second, far less pleasant unpaid commission, a job that inevitably pushed him onto center stage and spiked interest in his private life once again.

Armstrong told a press conference at the White House he was sure the investigation was going to be a tough job and not be the task any of the members would have chosen for themselves. But he admitted that "it's very difficult to turn the president down."

Expressing his usual concerns about taking an intemperate approach, Armstrong told reporters: "I suppose the biggest difficulty we'll have is to not jump to conclusions. We'll try very hard not to do that, and I will appreciate, to the extent that it's possible, that all of you support us in that effort."

Other members included Neil's old nemesis, General Chuck Yeager, who proved to be his curmudgeonly self, refusing to attend most public meetings, Dr. Sally Ride, the first woman in space as a shuttle mission specialist in 1983, and self-described "curious character" nuclear physicist Richard Feynman. It was an eclectic group with a great deal of knowledge and understanding of the space program as well as of bureaucracies.

The facts, as they emerged, were damning. At a meeting of the committee less than a month after the disaster, Chairman Rogers declared he was "appalled" at the initial information he was getting. Key facts about the safety of the launch had been deliberately withheld from top NASA officials and pressure apparently put on officials of Morton Thiokol, manufacturers of the solid-rocket boosters, to okay the launch despite deep safety concerns they harbored. It had been clear that launching in cold weather—colder than the weather at any previous launch—was likely to destroy the resilience of O-ring seals designed to keep hot exhaust gases from escaping the rocket joints and probably causing the catastrophic explosion.

The following June 9, when the 256-page report was issued, all those initial suspicions proved true. The single cause was the failure of the rocket joint, allowed to happen by a chain of systemic management lapses at NASA and miscommunication with the manufacturers.

Most troubling was the finding that NASA had become so sloppy, and so frenzied to keep up with its own schedule, that the safety rules and quality controls adopted during the Apollo program had been virtually disregarded. The commission concluded NASA successes during the previous decade had made the agency think itself "infallible," and the space shuttle was being serviced like a "space truck."

In the final draft of the extremely critical report was a plank recommending continued support for NASA, following extensive changes in the way it did business, but praise for the agency's past accomplishments, a sop to save the tone from relentless negativity and a signal there was still much to admire about the organization.

Richard Feynman, who had brilliantly demonstrated the O-ring problem during a committee hearing by simply dipping a model of the rubber ring in a glass of icewater and showing how loose the fit became, was dead-set against including any mitigating language. "I think this recommendation is inappropriate," Dr. Feynman said, and later expanded upon the point in a letter to the committee.

Armstrong was obviously sickened at what had become of the agency—his home for twenty-one years. And he was not in a mood to defend the indefensible. "Well, if somebody's not in favor of it, I think we shouldn't put it in," he said.

But the following Monday, Rogers overruled both men. "Dr. Feynman, I've read your letter, and I agree with everything it says. But you've been outvoted."

Nevertheless, confidence in the agency was hugely damaged, and it would take well over a year and a major shakeup in personnel before NASA was permitted to launch anything again.

One of NASA's initial reactions to the shuttle disaster was to announce that henceforth no one other than a professional astronaut would be allowed into space—which seemed an admission the space program was never going to be safe enough for anyone other than test pilots. Conversely, Buzz Aldrin was convinced the best hope for the future of space exploration lay in the private sector, with civilians of all stripes, including journalists, poets, teachers, businessmen, and tourists blasting off—particularly wealthy tourists who could make the whole thing financially possible. Most of the tickets would be very steep—a hundred thousand dollars or more—but some would be reserved for those who would write or teach about the experience, and others for winners of a lottery to stimulate the interest of the general public.

Space technology would have to change drastically to make tourism viable, such as a change to reusable single-stage liquid fuel rockets rather than solid-fuel boosters that fall into the sea and are never used again. Aldrin felt that using market-driven technology would eventually make space tourism not only practical but popular and available to the masses. Support from the elite club of men who have voyaged to the moon—there are twenty-two surviving members as of this writing—seemed a necessity to Buzz. Near the top of his list was Neil, who, over the years, he had seen or spoken to less and less, but was determined to visit in an attempt to enlist his support.

"In between speaking engagements, I went to Ohio and made a lunch date with Neil. We had never been close friends, but certainly the experiences we had shared made it worthwhile to get together. I have always thought it was regrettable that this group of people who carried out such a major event haven't had a close camaraderie. They seem to want to avoid each other." (In Michael Collins's words, the astronauts were little more than "amiable strangers.")

The two spent a leisurely lunch over salads at the Cincinattian Hotel and caught up on old times. Then Aldrin made his pitch for help convincing NASA to lend its support to his plans for space tourism.

"Neil immediately said there was no way he could get involved. I was surprised and asked why. He made it clear that he sat on the board of directors of Thiokol Corporation, the manufacturer of the solid booster rocket, and could in no way undermine that relationship by supporting alternative technologies. It was a great disappointment. But that business relationship was apparently that important to him."

Regardless of disagreements over technologies, Armstrong continued, as the twentieth anniversary of the moon landing approached, to support the U.S. space program and to take part in aviation record-making.

In early 1988 he set a speed record for circumnavigation of the globe aboard a luxurious United Airlines 747-SP as a passenger. Fueled by vintage Chateau Lalande-Borie, Laurent-Perrier champagne, smoked salmon, lobster, and filet mignon, Neil and ninety-nine others, who were donating $5,000 a piece to children's charities for the privilege, took off from Seattle, Washington, and flew around the world in thirty-six hours and fifty-four minutes at an average speed of 624 miles per hour, besting by 20 percent the 1984 mark of 512 miles per hour. It was a snail's pace compared to the ninety-minute orbits he had made on Gemini and Apollo flights, but "the service on Apollo 11 was pretty ratty," the former astronaut and United Airlines board of directors member pointed out, toasting the trip with a glass of champagne.

Later in the year, he made an appearance at a Sarah Vaughn concert, conducting a John Phillip Sousa march and narrating Aaron Copland's *Lincoln Portrait.*

All three Apollo 11 astronauts dedicated a portion of two months during the summer of 1989 to celebrations of the anniversary, and lobbying to boost the U.S. space program in Congress, where it was facing a harsh challenge.

Ceremonies began in Washington with speeches at NASA headquarters, followed by a trip to Paris and appearances at the Paris Air Show, where the astronauts opened the U.S. Pavilion at Le Bourget. Then back across the Atlantic for a visit to the Marshall Space Flight Center in Hunstville, Alabama, on to the Kennedy Space Center, west to flight-control headquarters in Houston, and back to Washington for endless television, radio, and print interviews.

Asked at one press conference if the moon journey had changed his life, Neil said, "I don't think I'm any different. I'm hemming and hawing in front of the cameras just like I did twenty years ago."

Even the Soviet Union participated in the twentieth celebration, allowing a tape of the moon-landing broadcast to appear on nationwide television for the first time in the course of a long documentary about the event. In 1969, Soviet state-controlled television aired a musical variety show during the moonwalk.

On July 21, the three men—approaching their sixtieth birthdays—lobbied Congress, which was engaged in a full-blown, heated debate over funding for NASA and the proposed space station. When the dust settled, attempts to slash funding by liberal Democrats had been turned back; $719 million was allocated for the space station and $12.3 billion for NASA, though that figure was one billion less than President George Bush had requested.

Chapter Twenty-one

In February 1990, Neil got the phone call everyone dreads; his father, Stephen, had died at the age of eighty-two. He and Viola had been living, comfortably, at the Dorothy Love Retirement Community in Sydney, Ohio, a few miles from Wapakoneta. Dean flew in from Kansas and June from Arizona to help Neil bury their father and comfort their mother. After sixty-one years of marriage, Viola was bereft. While it went unmentioned, it was hard not to think that she would soon follow.

Viola refused offers to leave her home and move in with her children, and spent the rest of the winter in the quarters where she and her husband had passed their last years together. When spring came to the Auglaize Valley in May, the marsh marigolds, bluebells, and wild geraniums blossomed, and Viola passed away. After the funeral, Neil found little reason to return to Wapakoneta.

During the months between the deaths of his parents, Neil's marriage of thirty-four years came apart. In divorce papers filed in Warren County, Ohio, over a period of years during the early nineties, Jan and Neil Armstrong agreed that the date they ceased to be a married couple was March 31, 1990, after which both would be responsible for their own expenses, neither would incur further expenses charged to the other, and both would pay their own legal fees.

During the grimmest period in early 1991, Neil was seized with sudden chest pains, later diagnosed as a minor heart attack, from which he fully recovered.

The painful breakup, and the disagreeable task of dividing an estate invested in retirement accounts, limited partnerships, and real estate took several years, with a separation agreement finally negotiated on New Year's Eve 1993. Spousal support was pegged at a relatively modest $6,000 per month and the couple's assets divided. Neil kept the farm, Jan another house the couple owned on Deer Valley Trail outside Lebanon. Jan was also awarded $2,239,200 in cash and securities. A final decree dissolving the marriage was issued on April 12, 1994. During the course of the divorce, Jan moved two thousand miles west to the ski resort of Park City, Utah—home of Robert Redford's Sundance film studios.

Following his heart scare, Armstrong embarked on a large project, a labor of love, taping thirty-nine hours of documentary footage telling the story of aviation. He narrated, flew many of the planes himself, rode as a passenger in others, and criss-crossed the country, doing interviews and visiting museums and government facilities. The series, which aired on the Arts & Entertainment Network and was syndicated around the world, was produced by Hollywood veteran Mark Tuttle, a writer on the seventies sitcom *Three's Company* and producer of the sixties comedy *The Beverly Hillbillies*.

The documentary started with an episode entitled "By the Seat of Their Pants," which extolled the early efforts of aviation pioneer Otto Lilienthal, whose work inspired and advanced the Wright Brothers' efforts, and of Louis Bleriot, the first man to fly across the English Channel, which he accomplished in a monoplane of his own design. Subsequent episodes sketched the emergence of the airborne warrior, commercial airline companies, the Flying Fortresses of World War II, and the introduction of the jet plane.

"Neil loved the project because it gave him an opportunity to fly all kinds of vintage planes, re-creations of obscure planes, famous warplanes like the Spitfire, and a number of experimental craft," said producer Tuttle.

Early in the series, Neil was able to fly a re-creation of one of the great disasters of aviation history, the GeeBee, a top-heavy plane that was dubbed "totally unforgiving" by General James Doolittle. All five of the originals crashed, killing their pilots, but Neil felt up to the challenge and successfully mastered the nasty little plane for the documentary.

Armstrong's own history is woven throughout the episodes, including a nostalgic visit to the pilots' locker room at Edwards Air Force Base, where he visited old friend Bill Dana to discuss the rocket planes they flew in the fifties. Explaining the evolution of computer technology likewise was a comfortable fit, considering he was a founder and head of Computing Technologies for Aviation of Charlottesville, Virginia, which produces software for the scheduling and maintaining of airplane fleets.

In his early sixties, the flyer took to the camera well, dressed in leather flight jackets, looking tanned and fit, his face etched with character, silver hair buffeted by the wind. The success of the television show encouraged him to take on the narrator's role in Tuttle's coverage of the 1997 First World Air Games in Turkey, an international Olympiad of flying, with competition in virtually every area of aviation, from hang gliding to jets.

The twenty-fifth anniversary of Apollo 11 rolled around with a cold inevitability Armstrong was likely loath to face, but dutifully did. He turned down interviews for cover stories in *Newsweek* and *U.S. News and World Report,* but accepted an invitation to the White House from President Bill Clinton that would be the largest gathering of astronauts in many years.

Reeling from the dual traumas of divorce and the death of both his parents, for Neil Wapakoneta would hardly have been the place to go in any case. But the town's boosters were planning an event so showy and commercial as to guarantee he wouldn't have attended in any event. Part mini-Woodstock, part Fourth of July parade, it was dubbed the MoonWalk Festival and was scheduled to last twenty days—a county fair featuring concerts by sixties bands Guess Who, a Canadian group known for the patently anti–United States anthem "American Woman," and the Mamas and Papas, who were by then most famous for dissipation and drug abuse. The grand finale on the night of July 20 was the Lima (Ohio) Symphony Orchestra playing during a fireworks display. Incredibly, Armstrong's demurral met with anger and resentment.

"Your hometown puts on a big festival celebrating the twenty-five-year anniversary of something you did, the least you can do is show up," Jeff Wells, then twenty-nine, told *The New York Times* petulantly.

Over the weekend, he did make a brief appearance in the area, at the Neil Armstrong Airport in New Knoxville, a few miles away, where he watched an airshow, visited relatives, and signed few autographs.

Later he played eighteen holes of golf with pal Jim Rogers, a fellow board member of the Cinergy Corporation. "During the course of the entire day, Neil never mentioned that it was the twenty-fifth anniversary of him walking on the moon," said Rogers. "He's an 'aw-shucks' kind of guy."

The White House ceremony on July 21 was more a reunion than a celebration of the moon landing, a gathering of ten of the twelve men who had walked on the moon, plus astronauts from the Mercury and Gemini programs, including Alan Shephard, whose fifteen-minute flight was the first for an American, and John Glenn, who, at age seventy-three, had one more space flight ahead of him, a shuttle ride in 1998.

Glenn shrugged off press characterizations of the gathering of gray eagles as "melancholy"—quite properly, given the burning ambition he still harbored, which at the time seemed remote in the extreme, and some would argue came true largely as a result of the convulsion of the American political system that was the Clinton impeachment. And of Glenn's steadfast loyalty to the embattled president, which earned him a seat on the shuttle despite his advanced age—ostensibly to study the effects of spaceflight on senior citizens.

Buzz Aldrin expressed his impatience and pique over the lack of progress since Apollo 11: "An eerie apathy now seems to afflict the very generations who were witnesses to and were inspired by those events. The past quarter-century has seen a withered capacity for wonder, and the growing delusion of retreat to a risk-free society."

Armstrong addressed his remarks to a group of grade-school students invited to the White House ceremony. "Wilbur Wright once noted that the only bird that could talk was the parrot, and he couldn't fly very well. So I'll be brief. There are great ideas undiscovered. There are places to go beyond belief."

When Neil started as a professor at the University of Cincinnati in 1970, news executives from the area's radio, TV, and print media were summoned to a downtown restaurant to hear an ultimatum: They were not to request interviews with the space hero who would be living in their midst, because none would be granted; they were to totally ignore his presence and not consider it legitimate news. Amazingly, the group agreed—with one exception. Lawrence H. Rogers, then head of Taft Broadcasting Corporation, owners of a chain of television and radio stations in the region, howled in protest. "The reason they gave was that Neil had no secretary and would be overwhelmed with requests. I raised my hand and said, 'That's the most preposterous thing I have ever heard.' I told them Armstrong was the most famous explorer since Christopher Columbus; it would have been criminal journalistically to not write about him and praise what he had accomplished."

"I had no idea what the reaction was going to be, but I felt I had to make my point. The next day Neil called me and said, 'Good for you—I like to see a man stand up for what he thinks is right. But I'm still not going to give any interviews.'

"We had a laugh and he invited me to his country club for a game of golf. We've been friends ever since. The business about him being jaded and reclusive is absurd. He doesn't like to be pestered by strangers, but who does? Neil is a gregarious, laugh-loving sport."

In the early nineties, after the Armstrongs' divorce, Rogers says Neil was quite bereft. "My impression was that Jan was the one who wanted out, not Neil; he was extremely upset and went through a very difficult period."

Rogers and his wife tried matchmaking, seating Neil next to Carol Knight, a friend and neighbor who had lost her husband a year earlier in an automobile accident.

"They are both dear friends and we very much hoped they would like each other, but you never know how people will get along. But it turned out better than we could have hoped. They hit it off right away and started dating. A while later they told us they were going out to California to meet each other's children. Carol had two grown children who were studying at Stanford University and Neil's son Mark is in the computer business nearby in the Silicon Valley. A few weeks later they told us they had gone down to Santa Barbara and gotten married."

The couple decided to keep Neil's farm, but to make their primary residence fifty-five-year-old Carol's large modern house in the affluent Indian Hills suburb of Cincinnati, across the street from the Rogerses.

"Neil and Carol share a love of travel. They are constantly jetting off to exotic places, and it's a great treat to have dinner with them when they return and hear their stories," said Rogers.

Over the course of years of friendship, Rogers learned Neil was diffident about discussing the moon landing—largely because, while there is nothing he can do about the world at large defining him as the moonwalker, he can choose friends who see him as a person above and beyond that long-ago deed. Nevertheless, Armstrong and that distant dead rock in the sky he once visited seemed to have a mystical bond.

"Neil and I were playing a round of golf a few years ago at a country club in Dayton, and he was having a lousy day. Every shot seemed to go wrong for him; he was quietly suffering a very frustrating afternoon.

"We got to the toughest hole on the course, a long par five, and it didn't look good; odds were his game was going to get even worse. Then a very peculiar thing happened. It was a crisp, cold afternoon in late October, and all of a sudden the moon rose in the eastern sky, straight ahead of us. It was a startling sight, a big orange harvest moon; it seemed close enough to touch. Neil went for a four-wood and hit one of the longest straightest drives any of us had seen in a very long time. Appropriately, he sunk an eagle. No one said a word about it; there was nothing to say."

Epilogue

"I am, and ever will be, a white-socks, pocket-protector nerdy engineer—born under the second law of thermodynamics, steeped in the steam tables, in love with free-flow dynamics, transformed by Laplace, and propelled by compressible flow," Neil Armstrong said, defining himself while speaking to a luncheon at the National Press Club in Washington, D.C., on February 29, 2000, during National Engineers Week.

Addressing an audience that was composed half of press and half of engineers, he said he was proud of his profession for helping to vastly improve the lot of the world's people during the past century; eradicating epidemics of tuberculosis, child labor, twelve-hour work days, and increasing life expectancy for the first time in a thousand years. But he warned that engineers don't deserve uncritical reverence for their deeds because "bridges fail, airplanes crash, radiation escapes, and automobiles are recalled." Armstrong pointed out, however, that these problems are rare and usually quickly analyzed to make them rarer still. The inadequacy of engineers, whom he admits are generally "a little too focused and a little too intense for some," is their inability to communicate that they are not insensitive technocrats, slavishly devoted to logic and uncaring about human values. Indeed, a list of the twenty greatest engineering achievements of the twentieth century, compiled by members of the National Academy of Engineers, bears out those concerns and exemplifies deeds accomplished by engineers that have greatly ameliorated suffering and improved society.

Number twenty on the list is plastics and other synthetics, followed by nuclear energy (particularly for its uses in medicine), fiber optics, and lasers that allow rapid copying, bar-code readers, and the transfer and storage of data. Next is petroleum, which powers our cars; number sixteen is medical improvements from pacemakers to prosthetics, then household appliances, imaging technologies for medical uses, weather forecasting, and the Internet.

Number twelve is spaceflight. "I believe that spaceflight was certainly one of, and perhaps the, greatest engineering achievement, but it was selected number twelve on the basis of its effect on the quality of life, and I do not disagree. While the impact of seeing our planet from afar has an overpowering effect on people around the earth, and provided technology for tens of thousands of new products, other nominees were judged to have a greater impact on worldwide living standards."

Number eleven was the interstate highway system—44,000 miles without a stoplight, "an engineer's dream."

The top ten started with air conditioning and refrigeration, followed by the telephone, computers, and agricultural technology. Number five was electronics, then water purification, and the runner-up was the airplane. The engineers rated as the most important invention, in its impact on humanity, electrification, without which few of the other nineteen marvels of the twentieth century would be possible. "If anything shines as an example of how engineering has changed the world . . . it is clearly the power we use in our homes and businesses."

As for walking on the moon, sometimes I wonder if that really happened. I can honestly say—and it's a great surprise to me—that I have never had a dream about being on the moon. It's a great disappointment to me.

—Neil Armstrong

I would hope that if my grandchildren and friends have memories of me it will be for the ledger of my daily work rather than one flamboyant hour.

—Kenyan aviator Beryl Markham

Index